BSA Competition History

Norman Vanhouse

Foulis

Haynes

ISBN 0 85429 479 1

A FOULIS Motorcycling Book

First published July 1986
© Norman Vanhouse

Published by:
Haynes Publishing Group
Sparkford, Nr. Yeovil, Somerset
BA22 7JJ, England

Haynes Publications Inc.
861 Lawrence Drive, Newbury Park,
California 91320, USA

British Library Cataloguing in Publication Data

Vanhouse, Norman
  BSA competition history.
  1. Motorcycle racing — History 2.B.S.A.
  motorcycle — History
  I. Title
  796.7'5   GV1060
  ISBN 0-85429-479-1

Library of Congress catalog card number
86-81146

Editor: Jeff Clew
Page layout: Mike King
Printed in England by J.H. Haynes & Co. Ltd.

Contents

	Preface and Dedication	4
	Acknowledgements	6
	Introduction	8
Chapter One	Sowing the seeds	12
Chapter Two	Between the wars	15
Chapter Three	Competition supremo	31
Chapter Four	Beginnings of the landslide	44
Chapter Five	The Middlesbrough Maestro	53
Chapter Six	The Irish wizard	73
Chapter Seven	Aces in the pack	94
Chapter Eight	Three-wheeled patriarch	102
Chapter Nine	European champion	113
Chapter Ten	Gold Stars supreme	128
Chapter Eleven	Star galaxy	145
Chapter Twelve	Trials riding supporting cast	180
Chapter Thirteen	Supporting role	198
Chapter Fourteen	Star all-rounders	212
Chapter Fifteen	The third man	230
Chapter Sixteen	From humble beginnings	249
Chapter Seventeen	World Champion	269
Chapter Eighteen	Family twins	292
Chapter Nineteen	The final years	308
	Epilogue	330
	Appendix	334
	Index	337

Preface & Dedication

WHEN FIRST approached on the subject of writing this BSA competitions history, the task appeared daunting in the extreme. My mind seemed full of vague and jumbled recollections and memories dimmed by time which threatened to defy logical presentation. Furthermore, having written a number of articles for the monthly motorcycle publications, I had learned by default that the last thing to be relied on is the human memory. I had discovered that it is possible for an idea to take root and over the years grow into an accepted fact.

When I began the absorbing and highly rewarding process of research, a routine including personal visits to many of the BSA riders featured in this book, I was relieved to discover that I was not alone. The infallible memory did not appear to exist. Brian Martin was so sure on one point about which I was somewhat dubious, he willingly wagered £1 on the outcome. His confidence was not rewarded.

The point I am labouring is that having worked for BSA from 1952 until 1973, and being well aware of the various developments and outline of the story, the details, facts and figures produced in this book are the result of careful research. The authenticity and validity can be readily checked by anybody with access to past copies of the weekly motorcycle magazines and newspapers.

Right from the outset, however, before one word was written, I was sure of the first and most vital need: to visit and interview Mr.A.E. 'Bert' Perrigo whose knowledge of BSA going back to 1926 would be greater than any known living person. Fortunately, as a near resident of Birmingham, I was able to visit him at short notice on a number of occasions until, suddenly and tragically, on 22nd February 1985 he collapsed and died from a heart attack. Bert Perrigo took with him a great deal of unrecorded BSA history and personal experiences of a lifetime devoted to the sport and industry of motorcycling.

Thankfully, he was spared long enough to give me a considerable insight of much that had transpired 'in the old days', thus providing a sound and accurate base for the story I relate. His sudden death at the age of 82, during the early period of my research, explains why he is referred to in the present tense.

I first met Bert Perrigo in 1946 when he still exuded that strange aura we sense when meeting famous people. During the following years, when we came into closer contact, I was better able to judge the shrewd qualities of the man who never failed to attract the loyal respect of all the famous riders who rode for BSA; indeed, if not the entire British industry, rivals or no.

Bert Perrigo seemed typical of the men who built up the British motorcycle industry, through thick and thin from a practical understanding of motorcycles. Moreover, he was the main pillar of BSA competitions success: indeed, he was the architect of that great landslide of victories which rolled forward, gathering momentum from 1946 with a world-wide impact.

For that reason alone, I consider it only fair and just that this book be dedicated to the memory of the one and only Bert Perrigo — the man who did not live to see completed that which he assisted me in starting.

Norman Vanhouse
Birmingham
October 1985

Acknowledgements

THE PREPARATION and writing of a book of this nature is largely dependent upon other people with an ability and willingness to assist where possible. Where some 30 to 40 years have elapsed since their personal involvement in the saga of BSA, it is inevitable that many have drifted far and wide, making location and contact difficult.

Nonetheless, many of the riders of whom I write have been visited personally — itself a rewarding experience — and others contacted by letter and telephone. Either way, each and every one has offered unstinted help and co-operation, giving their time and the loan of photographs from their personal collection for use in this publication. BSA stars of yesteryear who have contributed in this way together with personal recollections and scrapbook cuttings include Fred Rist, John Avery, Bill Nicholson, Harold Tozer, Geoff Duke, John Draper, David Tye, Basil Hall, Brian Martin, Terry Hill, Jeff Smith, Graham Beamish, Tom Ellis, George Pickering, Peter Rose, John Burton, Bob Heath, Roy Hanks and Chris Vincent.

If they represent what might be termed the cast of performers, there was likewise a production team; such as one-time Assistant Competitions Manager Ted Fithian, to whom I am particularly grateful for the provision of 15 years of national and international results which I found invaluable; one-time BSA Technical Writer Arthur Lupton, and BSA Director and General Manager Alistair Cave. Brian Martin too comes into this bracket as well as that of a 'performer.'

I must also thank Mike Tomkinson of Mead & Tomkinson, Hereford; Peter Howdle of *Motor Cycle News* and their invaluable photographic archives, the Auto Cycle Union of Rugby, that doyen of motorcycle sporting writers, Ralph Venables, and the life-long friend of the late Phil Nex, Peter Ryall. Above all I am deeply indebted to that towering colossus of motorcycle history, Bob Currie, Editor of *The*

Acknowledgements

Classic Motor Cycle, without whose forebearance — and extensive archives — this work would not have been completed with anywhere near the accuracy I believe has been achieved.

In addition there are the many BSA riders not referred to individually here who gladly loaned me photographs suitably annotated, doing so with alacrity and a genuine enthusiasm which reflects great credit on each and every one.

Finally, I am grateful to Jeff Clew, Executive Editorial Director of the Haynes Publishing Group, for the opportunity of attempting what I regard as putting straight the record and contributing to the restoration of the rightful credibility of a great British name.

Norman Vanhouse

Introduction

WHEN DISASTER strikes with sudden violence, all that has gone before seems obliterated by an unseen evil. Good previously achieved seems forgotten, pride often turning to humiliation as past accomplishments become lost in the shambles and debris. Such was the case when the once mighty Birmingham Small Arms company collapsed in 1971, forced by financial advisers to close down the Small Heath plant which had spawned BSA motorcycles for 61 years past.

The shock of this traumatic event reverberated around the world; and whilst the financial health of the company had been under strain for some time, nobody really believed that the up-dated plant at Armoury Road would be allowed to grind to a halt, bringing to an end one of the great names of British industry. Like some of the great institutions, the company had been regarded as a national asset and had played a major role in the defence of the realm.

The shock of the collapse was such that there was an instant clamour of voices seeking what went wrong; a probing of past events and affairs and the scrutiny of senior executives in an effort to root out the truth. It was, of course, grist to the mill. When the giant lay slain and prone, writers and journalists swarmed over the corpse with a rancid-like curiosity bordering on muckraking.

Such was the clamour and head-seeking that later generations can be forgiven for forming the impression that nothing had ever been right with BSA; that pride, achievement and glory had no place in the history of this famous company; that the name BSA, like that of the giant airship, is synonymous with failure. Understandable though that impression may be, it is a travesty of the truth. Within 20 years of making their first motorcycle in 1910, when the parent company was already nearly 50 years old, BSA had surged to the forefront as the world's number one producer of motorcycles, able to adopt as a slogan that 'one-in-four of all motorcycles on the road is a BSA'.

By the 1930s, with ever-increasing production volume and model types, BSA were able to proudly boast of being 'Leaders of the Industry', an undisputed claim. This solid progress was made, not by producing exotic machines of fancy specification but with a well-engineered range of conventional, value-for-money models aimed at a wide spectrum of potential customers. Their reliability and quality was promoted by teams of factory riders participating in competitive events; reliability and long-distance, one-day and six-day trials and, in later years, the glamorous and demanding sport of scrambles and motocross.

In the face of industrial unrest, unemployment and severe depression following in the wake of the 1914-1918 Great War, BSA prowess as motorcycle makers was rapid to the point where the general public — both customers and otherwise — came to regard the name of BSA as a household word and motorcycles bearing that illustrious piled-arms trade mark as robust and reliable machines. Yet, ironically, BSA only embarked on the business of making motorcycles — as they also did with bicycles, sidecars, three-wheelers and motorcars — with great reluctance. They were really craftsmen gunsmiths, first established in 1861 to produce rifles and shells for the British Government. But such was the pernicious and capricious policy of Whitehall over a period of 40 years, when contracts were turned on-and-off like a tap, that the directors were forced, with great reluctance, to adopt a policy of diversification, leading to the real growth of the company.

Having decided, at long last, to put their eggs into more than one basket and free the company from the straight jacket imposed by the British Government paymasters, the directors elected to take advantage of the new boom in safety bicycles, in full-flood at the turn of the century and, soon after, to stake a claim in the infant motor car industry. This was soon followed by the spectacular take-over of the Daimler Car Company in Coventry, then the biggest car maker in the British Isles. Production of motorcycles was logical and inevitable and in 1910, the first BSA motorcycle was introduced, a sturdy $3^{1}/_{2}$ hp side-valve single-cylinder model — comparable with those already on the market — a model well received by the specialist press.

From the moment the company diversified into bicycle and automobile engineering, it prospered at a rate hitherto not experienced. By the time the Great War broke out the financial strength of the company was such that it was able to meet the national need for arms during those years of conflict in a way which would not have been possible just ten years before. It is ironical to reflect that it was the threadbare finances of the company as gun makers that forced it into vehicle engineering and the prosperity which propagated growth into a major arms manufacturer during the Great War. This in turn created the production capacity, engineering know-how and financial stability which established BSA as a leader of the motorcycle industry during the twenties.

Notwithstanding the difficulties of that post-war market, BSA offered a wide range of popular models that was the most varied on the market. During those years several new models were introduced which, to this day, are recalled with respect and affection by those who knew and regarded them as the best of their type. There was the little 250cc side-valve 'round tank' model; the 770cc side-valve vee-twin and its big, beefy 986cc counterpart. In 1924 came the first overhead valve sporty 350 and in 1926, probably the most outstanding of all, the much-loved 493cc Sloper which remained in production for almost ten years. Unwittingly, by chance, it became the progenitor of the long line of BSA Star models. With the standard Sloper proving so popular it was decided to market a sports version with high-compression piston and similar internal aids to increase performance. Visually it looked identical to the standard model so to aid identification, a small red star was stuck on the timing cover. The 'Star' range was born. Then there followed the Blue Star, Empire Star, Silver Star and most fabled of all, the Gold Star.

It was this family of Star models in particular which established the reputation of BSA in competitions where the reward of success is good publicity. Today there are many ways of promoting products and with motorcycles as of old, the exploitation of competitive events is still one of the most convincing. Right from the beginning, British manufacturers exposed their machines to vigorous testing in the full gaze of the public, risking the adverse effects of failure with the rich rewards of success.

From the early days BSA avidly indulged in this form of 'promotion', employing at the factory, or retaining on contract, a long line of top-grade riders who reaped a great harvest of success; indeed, during the era of the Gold Star, they imposed a will and authority on certain areas of the sport which, at times, was almost total. In the combined area of trials, scrambles and motocross no other motorcycle manufacturer in post-Second World War years achieved such a monopoly of success. And neither was it thus confined, for road racing too provided yet another medium of success and publicity.

Whilst most of the prime successes were achieved by the official factory riders, to some extent their efforts were but the tip of the iceberg. By virtue of the availability of such highly competitive models as the Gold Star, private clubmen throughout the world — some paying their own way, others with the aid of local dealers or importers — contributed to the great tapestry-like picture of BSA sporting success. Whilst it would be near impossible to collate and relate the multitude of successes, this book is an attempt to present that BSA competitions history; in the process emphasizing the exploits and victories of the factory experts. In view of the vastness of the world stage, inevitably there will be a number of good riders who feel that their performance with BSA should have justified at least a mention. To such riders there can only be apologies and a plea for understanding.

During the exhilarating days following World War Two, when BSA were once more firmly established as motorcycle market leaders, a new trade slogan proclaimed that BSA provided the 'lion's share of the motorcycle business'. Few could argue that simultaneously, going from success to success, they scooped also the lion's share of competitions success.

This then is a story of shrewd endeavour; of great achievement and sustained glory. A story of the undoubted success of a once great British company spurned by fate and history.

Chapter One

Sowing the Seeds

INITIALLY, AS motorcycle makers, BSA were slow starters, even cautious; the latter commercial trait no doubt fostered by their frustrating and costly experience as gun and armaments manufacturers dependent upon the fickle policies of the British Government. By the time the principles of diversification were being applied thick and fast, the company was almost 50 years old before the first BSA motorcycle was introduced. By then, in 1910, other British makers had been producing motorcycles for several years and, significantly, the Isle of Man TT was already in its fourth year. Long-distance reliability trials were already established as an ideal means of promoting both reliability and publicity.

Introduced at the 1910 Olympia Show, the new $3^{1}/_{2}$ hp, single-speed BSA was well received; indeed in describing the model, *Motor Cycling* stated that 'what astonishes us is that such an excellent example of the touring motor bicycle should have been evolved by a concern practically at the first attempt.' But of course BSA had already acquired a reputation for superb quality with their bicycles and bicycle fittings. Clearly it was policy from the outset to achieve the same standard with the new motorcycles and this was spelled out by the company chairman, Sir Hallewell Rogers, who stated: 'Our policy in connection with the motor bicycle is the same as with our other manufactures, namely to produce only the best and spare no expense in embodying improvements and perfecting the machines, rather than attempt to cheapen the cost with a view to reducing the selling price.'

Nonetheless, with a retail price of £50, the new $3^{1}/_{2}$ hp BSA was very competitive with comparable types, despite the accent on quality. It was the marketing policy which produced instant commercial success, for the first year's production in 1911 could have been sold several times over like that of the following two years. Despite such initial success,

The industrial empire of BSA at Armoury Road, founded in 1861, the fountain-head of the competitions legend. Looking north to Small Heath beyond, the famous kidney-shaped test track with its 1 in 4 test hill is clearly visible in the foreground.

from the long-term view, the need to demonstrate the attributes of their products was recognised by the BSA directors, no doubt influenced by and envious of the success of rival companies such as Matchless, Rex and Triumph who were already enhancing the reputations of their machines by participation in sporting events and the Isle of Man TT in particular. So BSA took their first tentative steps into the harsh world of open competition in 1913, modestly and cautiously, by entering their head tester, Ken Holden, in the Easter Monday meeting at Brooklands track, already well established and patronized by the experienced racers of the day. When the unknown Ken Holden won the first race easily at 60.75 mph on what seemed to be a more-or-less standard $3^1/2$ hp BSA, everybody was somewhat surprised, including the press reporters, but none more so than Frank Butler (Rudge) who finished second and Harry Collier, of the Matchless company, who finished third.

Thus encouraged, BSA then set their sights on the prestigious Isle of Man TT races in the June of that year with no less than seven entries. The race was a two-stage affair spread over two days, interrupted by two rest days. By the end of the second stage only one BSA rider had survived. He was Irishman R. Carey who finished 17th with a speed of 41.89 mph, the race being won by H.O. Wood who averaged 48.27 mph with his rapid Scott.

13

BSA: Competition History

Disappointed but undaunted, four BSAs were entered in the French Grand Prix just one month later, with Englishmen Archie Fenn and Jack Woodhouse plus two local French riders in the saddles. Archie Fenn finished third and also recorded the fastest time of 60.27 mph through a measured timed stretch of the course. One of the French riders finished sixth.

Concluding their tentative and moderately successful racing efforts for 1913, BSA went back to Brooklands with their $3^1/_2$ hp model fitted to a sidecar. With works tester Ken Holden once again in the saddle, it broke the five-mile sidecar track record with a speed of 50.56 mph.

Apart from road and track racing, BSA also embraced six-day events for the first time in 1913 when all-rounder Archie Fenn, competing in the Scottish Six Days in July (the same month as the French Grand Prix) won a gold medal. One month later the energetic Fenn won another gold medal, this time in the ACU Six Days Trial staged in the Lake District of Cumberland and Westmoreland with its fearsome gradients. Five other BSA-mounted riders also completed the ACU Six Days, including 'Pa' Applebee and Maurice Breese, who won bronze medals.

It had been a modest enough beginning but sufficiently rewarding to ensure future involvement on an increased scale. For the 1914 TT races no less than nine machines were specially prepared several months in advance, incorporating modifications as a direct result of the lessons learned throughout 1913. Of the eight BSA entries (with Ken Holden nominated as a reserve) three were officially entered by the works. Of these R. Carey finished 22nd, F.A. Maylott finished 42nd, and R.M. Lewis retired. The highest placed BSA rider was, however, Dan Young in 12th place. It was not a startling result but comfort was gained by having six of the eight starters complete the course.

Over in Ireland, a BSA team comprising W.J. Woods, C. Jones and Jackie Chambers won the team prize in the 500 mile End-to-End Trial but, with the international atmosphere getting distinctly ominous, time was running out with the attention of the BSA directors being focused on other and much more important matters. Before the military storm clouds finally erupted over Europe on 4th August 1914, one of the last events to be staged was the MCC three-day event in the Peak District of Derbyshire. The Solo Cup was won by G.P. Howe on a 557cc BSA.

Whilst BSA continued to manufacture military bicycles and motorcycles during the war years that followed, their main contribution was in their former role as armaments manufacturers, and as such the company had grown beyond all recognition by November 1918. It was to put them in a commanding position as motorcycle manufacturers thereafter, with a production capacity unsurpassed before or since.

Chapter Two

Between the Wars

FROM THE vantage point of the 1980s, the panorama of BSA competitions activity spanning a period of 58 years can be closely studied and put into perspective. As a result, the brief and modest excursion into the early years of motorcycle competitions before the First World War can be seen as little more than a sowing of seeds on relatively barren soil, producing little or no harvest, followed by four fallow years.

When the world regained its sanity, beginning the long, slow process of restoring normality — with some like BSA starting from where they had left off four years before — there followed a period of twenty years of rapid development and progress in motorcycle design and its allied sport. To those involved as the second decade neared its end, it seemed an ultimate had been reached. In the Isle of Man TT lap speeds of over 90 mph had been achieved; and it was no longer enough to have a reliable motorcycle capable of going from check to check in trials, riding against the hands of the clock. Rider's skill had become the yardstick. To test this as riding skills developed, increasingly severe conditions were imposed, leading in turn to the development of specialized machines in the relentless quest for the success which would bring the desired publicity.

By the end of the 1930s, when once again world conflict brought such things to a jarring halt, the pattern of motorcycle sport had been firmly established, with a foundation on which it is based to this very day. In the process it had spawned an elite of factory riders who, despite the claim of riding for the fun of it, were dedicated professionals in every sense of the word. Most British factories of note had their teams of expert riders, sharing the spoils of victory when it came their way, all the more valued by virtue of the intensity of the competition posed by the opposition factories.

During the inter-wars span of 20 years BSA fielded a long line of 15

Right from the early days BSA were successful in Australia, both as a means of transport and in sport. Here B.Schwer is pictured after winning the 15-Mile All Powers event on a 1924 2³/4 hp model (BSA's first production ohv model) at Penrith, New South Wales.

such professionals who stamped their authority with commensurate regularity. It was a concentrated effort aimed at sporting trials and long-distance events, at the expense of road racing, directly as a result of the fiasco of their 1921 Senior TT involvement. The details of this sad chapter have been recounted time and again, concerning the failure of all fourteen models taken to the Isle of Man to support the official works entry of six riders. Despite this, the real truth has never come out, and in this day and age it is no longer of any consequence. What does matter is the profound effect it had on BSA competitions policy from that moment on, for the then board of directors, suffering from shock and fright, vowed never to race again. Instead, they decided to devote time and

16

money to participation in trials, six-days events and ACU-Observed Tests. The Senior TT of 1921 thus proved to be a significant milestone in BSA history, and a pointer to greater things in other branches of motorcycle endurance events.

Having joined BSA in 1920 with the brief to establish an autonomous competitions department, Harry Perrey, fresh from army service, found himself the spearhead of increased interest in trials, long-distance events and promotions aimed at creating a new image of reliable durability. A sidecar specialist himself, he soon set the pattern of post-war success in trials; and even when riding solo he was no mean performer — as witness the BSA assault on Mount Snowdon in 1924. On that occasion he, together with George McLean, George Savage and Harold Briggs, successfully reached the summit, with Perrey himself on a 350 ohv model completing the climb in 24 minutes 6 seconds as compared with the 58 minutes of Harold Briggs who had climbed by a different route.

The BSA team for the 1929 Scottish Six Days. L to R: Peter Chamberlain, Bert Perrigo and John Humphries, the two former gaining silver cups, the latter a gold medal. Peter Chamberlain, writer, journalist and in later years, ACU official, was reputed to be related to the political Chamberlain family of Birmingham. Photo: The Classic Motor Cycle.

The British Trophy Team for the 1931 International Six Days Trial based at Merano, Italy. L to R: George Rowley (AJS), Harry Perrey (Ariel s/c) and Bert Perrigo (BSA). Perrey retired on the first day but both Rowley and Perrigo won gold medals. Note the braced Webb racing-pattern front forks on the Perrey outfit – and Marjorie Cottle in background.

Nonetheless, Harry Perrey's reign at Small Heath was comparatively brief, for he transferred his loyalties to Ariel in 1926 and, later still, to Triumph at Coventry.

It would be misleading however, to give the impression that it was the 1921 TT episode which turned the then directors gaze towards trials and endurance events for such competitions had been contested from the outset. It was the contrast in success which reinforced their resolve in favour of the latter activity. For example, in that year's Scottish Six Days Trial, all five BSA works entries gained gold medals; indeed, the year previously they had won the manufacturers' team prize. In 1922 it was a repeat performance with another five golds, Harry Perrey himself sharing the honours. The team prize had been achieved also in 1919 when Harry Edwards, Len Sealey and Fred Turvey had won gold medals in the ACU Six Days, the latter making best individual performance in the same event twelve months later. It is not surprising that the directors felt it was with such events their future lay.

The departure of competitions manager Harry Perrey in 1926 made way for Birmingham garage owner Phil Cranmore to take over Perrey's 350 trials outfit and promptly win the Colmore Cup Trial (a trial he had won the year before with a Zenith). Over the next few years he went on to win many more major awards, including the sidecar premier in the Scottish Six Days Trial of 1930. Although not directly employed by the factory, it seems that Cranmore also acted as competitions manager in an advisory capacity.

Later that year another member of the trials riding team left Small Heath to join the Douglas Company at Bristol; and it was this move which had a profound effect on the future events of the company, for it made way for a newcomer. That newcomer was one A.E. Perrigo, formerly of Connaught, who had begun to establish a reputation as both a solo and sidecar competitor in trials but who in later years blossomed as a solo expert. As the years went by, Bert Perrigo was to acquire respect and influence within the company like few others before or since; he staked his claim to posterity by his sensational win in the first-ever

British riders being presented to the Duke of Saxe-Coburg Gotha at the 1934 International Six Days Trial at Garmisch Partenkirchen, in Germany. L to R: Jack Williams, Bert Perrigo and Allan Jefferies. The Duke was reputed to be related to British Royalty. British official Major Watling is on the Duke's left.

BSA: Competition History

British Experts Trial of 1929. His win was an appropriate way of setting the seal on the 1920s; a decade associated with such names as Jack Humphries, John Lloyd, Nancy and Betty Debenham, Cyril and Muriel Lord, Bertie Bird, Howard Uzzell, Phil Cranmore, Jack Amott and Jack Parker, all of whom enhanced the name of BSA in open competitions. Jack Parker, who went on to become one of England's greatest speedway riders, joined the BSA payroll on the same day as Bert Perrigo and they remained firm friends from then on. It was Jack Parker who won the Colmore Cup Trial in 1928 with the works BSA 350 sidecar outfit. There can be little doubt, had not speedway attracted the talents of the young Parker at that stage, he would have become one of the great trials riders of the era.

Jack Amott, who had finished tenth in the Junior TT of 1926, left Small Heath in 1928 for Rudge of Coventry, for whom he finished eleventh in the Senior TT of that year. In 1936 he elected to return to BSA, to make a fine contribution not only as a rider but as a talented development engineer in the quest for more performance. A former TT rider and chief tester for Velocette, Fred Povey, whose best placing in the TT was ninth in the Junior of 1926, also joined the BSA squad in the early 1930s to make a great name as a trials rider with notable wins on BSA.

The growth in popularity of motorcycling during those inter-war years led to a mushrooming of clubs and sporting events such that classification and segregation became necessary. Thus emerged the closed-to-club event with entries limited to members of the organizing club; events of open-to-centre status with entries open to all members of clubs affiliated to that centre; regional-restricted permit events with entries available to a consortium of centres; and, most prestigious and competitive of all, those with a national permit open to all riders in the British Isles in possession of a current ACU competitions licence.

It was the latter 'open' events the British industry supported and utilized for the purpose of publicity. It was practicable for factory teams to contest only a limited number of events so through the medium of the then-named Manufacturers Union (today renamed The Motor Cycle Association) a number of 'opens' were selected, mainly on a geographical basis, for official trade support. It was also further agreed that all success advertising would be limited to these trade-supported events. The agreed system ensured that all factory experts would be competing against each other in the one event rather than going off to compete for easy victory in some obscure event against private clubmen.

Thus was born the trade-supported open trial and scramble. Organizing clubs with events bestowed with trade support basked in the glamour and prestige of having once a year a whole coterie of factory

The Royal Tank Corps team of (L to R) Fred Rist, R.Gillam and J.T.Dalby, who won the Motor Cycling *Trophy in the 1938 International Six Days Trial in Wales with factory-loaned 1939-type M24 Gold Stars. Riding in his first-ever competitive event, Fred Rist won the only gold medal gained by the team.*

experts patronize their event and area, with its resulting publicity. Such competition riders' skills grew apace with machine development, with event-organizers meeting the challenge with stiffer courses. They now included ever-steeper gradients, more vicious rocks, deeper ruts and quagmires of glutinous mud — sometimes with all three hazards encompassed in one long meandering hill or lane, broken down into observed sub-sections without neutral ground between.

It was these severe conditions which produced a generation of expert riders equal in skill and ability to any before or since. Men such as the lofty Len Heath with his plonking Ariel, the Yorkshire humourist Allan Jefferies with his Triumph, the brilliant Norton all-rounders Vic Brittain and Jack Williams, the versatile George Rowley and his AJS, the Royal Enfield trio of Jack Booker, George Holdsworth and Charlie Rogers, northerner Bill Tiffen Jun. with his lone Velocette, and so on. Facing this array of competitive opposition and carrying the BSA flag were Bert Perrigo and Fred Povey, reinforced from 1936 by Jack Amott who, in 1938, proved the true potential of the new 250cc Empire Star   21

Regular soldier Fred Rist riding the factory 350cc B25 on Breakheart in the 1939 Cotswold Cups Trial in which he, Paddy Doyle and Jackie Wood of the Royal Tank Corps won the team award against factory opposition. Photo: The Classic Motor Cycle.

model by winning the premier award in the Cotswold Cups Trial. These front-line riders were assisted by works-supported men of the ilk of J.J. StJohn and Mike Riley; the latter to such good effect that he made best 350cc performance in the 1935 Scottish Six Days Trial with a loss of only six marks – four more than winner Bob McGregor (500 Rudge). To prove it was no fluke, Mile Riley repeated his Scottish success two years later with a win of the 500 Class Cup.

Marjorie Cottle, one of the most famous of the lady riders of that era, enhanced her reputation with her 250 BSA by winning, among other trophies, the best lady rider performance in the Scottish Six Days no less than four years in succession, from 1932 to 1935. But it was Harold Flook, the sidecar expert, who won more for BSA during the 1930s than any other rider, winning two sidecar premier awards in the Scottish Six Days (1934 and 1936) and the British Experts sidecar title an incredible five times in a row from 1932 to 1936.

A youthful Harold Tozer circa 1938 outside the Tozer garage in Selly Oak, Birmingham, with DOA 664, the outfit he used initially post-war. The competition number plates suggest the picture was taken prior to departure for the International Six Days Trial in Wales. Note the BSA Scout car parked on the right.

Flook's name will live for ever in the legend of the Scottish, for the first rocky right-hander on that long, meandering hill called Mamore, rising from the majestic shores of Loch Leven, is named after him; it was here in 1938 that his outfit, passengered by his brother, crabbed out of control to hurtle over the side and plunge a sheer 200 feet to total destruction. Whilst his brother was hurled from the chair as it went out of control, Harold Flook only just managed to extricate himself as the outfit went over the side. Used for the first time since 1933, the hill was promptly by-passed for the rest of the sidecar entry.

Harold Flook's sidecar wins in the British Experts of 1933 and '34 were particularly welcome, for fellow works rider Fred Povey did likewise in the solo class, thus making it a BSA 'double' two years in succession.

In 1937, with the name of BSA firmly established in the world of sporting and long-distance events such as the Scottish and International Six Days — events far removed from road racing but which, nonetheless, produced a fine harvest of good publicity — came a small 23

Start of the BSA ACU-Observed Test of March 1939 from ACU Headquarters Pall Mall, London. The M23 Silver Star solo rider is Jack Amott and his opposite number in the saddle of the M21 sidecar outfit is Bill Johnson, with ACU observer E.B.Ware as passenger. Starting them off, on the extreme left, is ACU secretary, Sam Huggett. Photo: The Classic Motor Cycle.

At the finish of the 100-mile high speed test at Brooklands which concluded the 1939 ACU-Observed test, with Harold Tozer at the helm of the sidecar outfit and Roy Evans in the saddle of the Silver Star. The latter averaged 73.5 mph compared with the 48.5 mph of the combination with passenger. Photo: The Classic Motor Cycle.

news item like a bolt from the blue. On June 30th, at a mid-week meeting at Brooklands race track, one-time TT winner Walter Handley won an outer-circuit race at 102.27 mph with a fastest lap at 107.57 mph. The news item was unusual on two counts. Firstly, Handley had retired from active racing, and secondly, he was riding a BSA. It was a 500cc ohv single-port Empire Star running on alcohol fuel, a model re-designed by the talented Val Page before he moved back to Triumph at Coventry. Whilst it was a BSA factory entry, it could not be construed as a reversal of the firm's non-racing policy. Today it would be termed a promotion; a demonstration to prove the potential of a model as well-engineered as any comparable model on the market. The Ariel Red Hunter model in particular was proving a very potent value-for-money, short circuit

The Royal Tank Corps team of Paddy Doyle (left) Fred Rist (centre) and Jackie Wood with reserve Joe Acheson (left rear) on the 1938-registered Gold Stars used for practice prior to the 1939 International Six Days Trial in Austria. Picture taken at the BSA factory, with Bert Perrigo.

racer. Surely it was not beyond the ability of the Small Heath engineers to better it? Only five years before a 350cc Blue Star with sidecar had taken the Double 12-Hour Class B/s record at Brooklands, covering no less than 1,029 miles, 491 yards at the average speed of 42.88 mph — an outfit owned and ridden by Brooklands devotee Jim Hall, assisted by P.Brewster, E.A.Dussek and M.Couper who shared the riding.

Whatever the motive, those at Small Heath who had sponsored the Brooklands venture on that auspicious day in June 1937 were well

The British Army team of (L to R) Jackie Wood, Paddy Doyle and Fred Rist with reserve Joe Acheson at Southampton in August 1939, en route for the ill-fated International Six Days Trial in Austria. They are mounted on their new 1939-registered Gold Stars.

rewarded by the faultless performance of Wal Handley, for his success paved the way for the obvious and logical development — the introduction of an out-and-out sports 500 of high performance. Designated the M24 and launched for 1938, the new model was based on the Empire Star. It had an aluminium alloy cylinder barrel and cylinder head incorporating a built-in pushrod tunnel, the barrel being fitted with an austenitic steel liner and the cylinder head having its valve seats screwed in (though later shrunk in). Every M24 engine was claimed to be individually built and brake tested. In the interests of weight-saving, the gearbox shell was cast in Elektron. With a long line of forebears blessed with a Star nomenclature there was a tradition to be observed and the Handley Brooklands success was enhanced by the BMCRC-awarded Gold Star — an automatic award to all those who lapped the Surrey circuit in excess of 100 mph. In consequence it provided the inspiration for the adopted name. Thus was born the BSA Gold Star, the greatest and most versatile standard production motorcycle ever made by the British industry. From the moment the new Gold Star went into production it found instant favour with private clubmen, mainly for short-circuit racing, both at home and overseas in Australia. Without a shadow of doubt, the most significant result pre-war was the fifth place achieved by Roy Evans of Oswestry in the 1938 Ulster Grand Prix, a top-grade international road race and at that time the fastest road circuit in the world. It is true that Roy Evans' speed of 79.86 mph was some 14 mph slower than the winning BMW of Jock West's at 93.98 mph, but the

Fred Rist (101) at the control at the top of the Grossglockner Pass, included in the ISDT of 1939. BMW rider (100) is Hess Fleichman — 'the finest gentleman and sport I have ever met' according to Fred Rist. The picture was taken on August 25th — just 9 days before the declaration of war with Germany. Photo: The Classic Motor Cycle.

supercharged racing twin was then in its ascendancy. Stanley Woods and Dave Whitworth on works 500 Velocettes were respectively second and third, with J.Mead fourth on an ohc Norton. It is also true that both Freddie Frith and Harold Daniell on works Nortons retired, but nonetheless, the Gold Star was the first ohv single to finish, over 3 mph quicker than the next ohv single, the 500 Rudge of Jock McCredie who finished sixth. That result was clearly indicative of things to come.

Despite the arrival of the new 500 Gold Star for use in competitions, 1938 proved a relatively lean year for BSA with few major results. Fred Povey had left BSA to open his motorcycle shop in Shirley, Birmingham. He had ridden a 350 AJS in the previous year's Scottish Six Days, only to change to Ariel for 1938 and promptly win the Highland classic. Harold Flook had returned to the Norton combination   27

With World War Two just eleven days old, this BSA press advert tells the whole BSA story of that last pre-war International before Hitler's hordes enslaved Europe.

he had deserted back in 1932 and Harold Tozer, who succeeded him in the saddle of the BSA chair outfit, had yet to find his winning form. Bert Perrigo, although in South Africa for several months during the year, had retired from one-day national trials but was still taking part in six-day events.

In the Scottish Six Days the only award of any note was won by the young Birmingham GPO worker Freddie Perks who, having first competed in Scotland in 1936 as a member of the winning CSMA club team when he rode a 250 BSA solo, turned up with a hefty 500 BSA and sidecar to win a silver cup with a loss of 19 marks. Perks went even better in the following year's Scottish when, with a 350 BSA outfit, he won the best 350 sidecar award.

Marjorie Cottle had changed to a 250 Triumph. For the International Six Days Trial, held that year once again in Wales, her place on a 250 BSA being taken by Miriam Anning. During the war years Miriam was to represent BSA in a sales capacity in her West Country home territory. The BSA factory team for the Welsh ISDT consisted of Jack Amott, Jack Ashworth and Reg Spokes of Northampton who, between them, experienced a very bleak time without winning a single gold medal. Jack Amott and Reg Spokes were reduced to silver standard whilst Jack Ashworth won only a bronze. The Gold Star-mounted team of the Royal Tank Corps comprising J.T.Dalby, R.Gillam and F.M.Rist did rather better, the last winning a gold medal; the first of several ISDT golds he was destined to win in later years.

The BSA success pattern for 1939 was not unlike that of the previous year, though the season started well enough with two sidecar premier awards in the two early classics of the season, the Colmore and Victory. Harold Tozer took best sidecar in the former — one of his earliest BSA successes — and the versatile Freddie Perks won the sidecar premier in the latter. In the Victory, supporting the Perks success, Jack Amott collected the best 250 Cup and, together with Bert Perrigo (out of retirement to strengthen the BSA team) and Fred Rist helped to win the manufacturers team award. A.C. Doyle was the best Army rider who, with J.L.Wood and Fred Rist, won the best Army team award; Perrigo and Rist won first class awards.

Soon after the Victory Cup Trial the Royal Tank Corps trio of Rist, Doyle and Wood won the team award in the Cotswold Cups Trial in which 'Paddy' Doyle also won the 350 Cup. These Royal Tank Corps regular soldiers were getting very competitive in the company of the factory experts, a significant development of the mechanized elements of the regular British Army at a time when the storm clouds of war were gathering fast over Europe.

In the Scottish Six Days in May the Royal Tank Corps trio collected yet another best army team award with a loss of 59 marks. Fred Rist being their best performer. Jack Amott on the 250 model won a silver cup and, as previously noted, Fred Perks was best 350 sidecar. He lost 53 marks compared with the 29 dropped by sidecar winner Fred Whittle and his big Panther outfit.

29

BSA: Competition History

Viewed in restrospect, it seems that neither 1938 nor 1939 was BSA's best year in motorcycle sport — despite the birth of the Gold Star. Without doubt that can be attributed to the bellicose noises emanating ever more loudly from the continent of Europe, distracting the attention of the BSA directors and diverting their thoughts and energies into far more important things of national interest.

If ground had been lost to their competitors in the world of motorcycle sport, it was to be six years before the situation could be retrieved.

Chapter Three

Competition Supremo

BSA POST-WAR motorcycle history and the prolific growth of competitions activity was an extension of the company's wartime growth and achievement as a major arms and munitions producer of gigantic proportions; a story in itself (one told by Donovan Ward in his book entitled '*The Other Battle*' published in 1946). Whilst that story is outside the scope of this book, it is sufficient to recall that at the peak of the war effort the Small Heath administration controlled 67 widely-dispersed factories employing 28,000 people, equipped with 25,000 machine tools. It was an industrial conglomeration with multiple lines of communication looking like the arms of a giant octopus from which flowed no less than five thousand million munitions components. This vast and diverse volume of material and finished products was a staggering achievement by a team of senior management headed by the autocratic James Leek, managing director of both BSA Guns Ltd and BSA Cycles Ltd.

Managers from both the Small Heath and Redditch factories, previously employed in the production of peacetime merchandise like bicycles and motorcycles, were directed into new engineering roles as a part of the new wartime team. They were motivated by the single-minded need to give Winston Churchill not only the tools with which to finish the job but, more importantly, the tools with which to begin. One such manager was pre-war trials star Bert Perrigo, who had first joined the company in 1926 as a trials rider, to replace George McLean who had left to join Douglas at Bristol. By 1932 he had been appointed competitions manager and over the years he became increasingly involved with development work by virtue of being closely related to competitions activities. To broaden his horizons and to temper his riding and engineering experience with commerce, he was appointed BSA sales representative for the West Country of England in 1937 (in   31

Bert Perrigo with the 1937 350cc B25 Empire Star, with which he won both the Colmore Cup and Victory Cup trials of that year. Note the riding coat and waders, worn by all works riders of that era.

succession to George Savage who had assaulted Mount Snowdon with Harry Perrey's team in 1924 and had been appointed BSA car sales manager).

Bert Perrigo's role as a salesman was short-lived, however, for in 1938 he was taken ill and subsequently spent six months recuperating in South Africa. Not that he was left in peace for his fame had preceded him. On arrival, he was swept off his feet with VIP treatment, made guest of honour at various official functions, interviewed and persuaded to give talks all over the Union. Whilst his six-month's stay proved a treasured experience, it was hardly the relaxed break intended.

Nonetheless, he returned to England, sun-tanned and fit and keen to resume his working role with the company which, by then, was already heeding the alarming noises from Germany. From then on he was employed on special projects such as liaising with Government departments, police forces and in-the-field training of British Army teams for the International Six Days Trial. In addition, he became responsible for the planning and managing of the BSA ACU-Certified tests of 1938 and 1939, the former resulting in the award of the prestigious Maudes Trophy to the company for the first time. His standing with the company grew with the years.

Winner Bert Perrigo lustily footing in the 1937 Colmore Cup Trial, an event blessed with rare winter sunshine. Photo: The Classic Motor Cycle.   33

Nevertheless Bert Perrigo, like so many more of his generation, had come up the hard way, his prospects blighted by the recession which crippled many small engineering firms in the wake of the First World War. It was to one small, old-established family firm that Bert was apprenticed in die-sinking and toolmaking when he finished school toward the end of the War. It was when this business was forced to close its doors for good that fate steered him in the direction of Connaught and for the first time he became involved with motorcycles — by circumstance rather than by desire. It was with Connaught that he first tried his skills at trials riding, both as a solo competitor and with sidecar. Indeed, in the very first Victory Cup Trial in which he competed, that of 1926, he won a silver medal with a Connaught sidecar outfit. By then he had established himself as a man to be watched in the field of reliability trials and when the Bordesley Engineering Company — makers of the Connaught — went the way of so many of that era, it was Howard Uzzell of BSA who recommended the young Perrigo as the replacement for the departing George McLean. Thus in 1926 Bert Perrigo joined the Small Heath payroll on which he was destined to remain for the next 42 years until his retirement in 1968.

Bert Perrigo sets out from the Sale Yard at Shipston-on-Stour for the 1946 Colmore Cup Trial, the first post-war trade-supported national trial — and Perrigo's last. Photo: The Classic Motor Cycle.

A close-up picture of Bert Perrigo at the start of the 1946 Colmore Cup Trial on 'BSA 350', the first post-war 350 B32. Note the B29/B30-type cylinder head. Photo: The Classic Motor Cycle.

During his first full year with BSA in 1927, Bert Perrigo won an enormous number of trophies both solo and with a sidecar outfit. His successes continued throughout 1928 and 1929, to reach the ultimate when he won the newly-established British Experts Trial in 1929 — an event for which only the élite qualify to this very day. Perrigo's Experts victory of 1929 was probably unique in that he had qualified for the event with a sidecar outfit — to compete and win with a solo. It was a Blue Riband victory he was to repeat just two years later.

During the following years he was to win many of the established classics such as the Colmore Cup, Victory Cup and West of England — some more than once — plus a host of capacity class cups. Not surprisingly, during his peak years he was selected to represent Great Britain no less than six times in the International Six Days Trial, either in the Vase or Trophy teams, winning a gold medal on every occasion. One such International vividly recalled by Bert was the one staged in

35

Experts all. 1929 and 1931 British Experts winner Bert Perrigo admires the 1951 ACU Trials Drivers' Star won that year by Bill Nicholson (astride the B34 Gold Star). Centre is Tom Ellis who won the 1951 British Experts and left, Harold Tozer who won the ACU Sidecar Star (jointly with Arthur Humphries) in 1951. Picture taken in the sumptuous BSA showrooms at Small Heath.

Italy in 1932 when the British Trophy Team comprising George Rowley (AJS), Bert Perrigo (BSA) and Peter Bradley (Sunbeam s/c) arrived at the concluding speed test with a clean sheet and level-pegging with the Italian trio. This meant 'racing' for the International Trophy.

36

Riding a prototype 500cc Blue Star the one-hour speed test proved a very dicey affair with the course lashed with driving rain throughout; so much so that it ran down the petrol tank top and into the downdraught carburettor, to wet the plug points. Bert lost valuable time in stopping to change the plug and when he restarted he rode furiously in an effort to regain lost time and forge ahead of the Italians. Such was his progress that he even overhauled team mate George Rowley, the real road racer of the team, in the process unashamedly foot-trailing on the bends, speedway fashion, to control the slides — an unheard of technique in road racing; for road racing it surely was. His efforts were not in vain — the British trio had beaten the Italians on their home ground. A hard-won and well-deserved British team victory, one of many in the days when British riders reigned supreme.

Many years later Graham Walker, that great rider and authority on matters motorcycling, eulogized a similar ISDT Perrigo epic he had witnessed whilst at another European-based event where Perrigo again represented Great Britain. On this occasion Bert had the misfortune to puncture his front tyre during a very tight check. With no time in hand to replace the tube on the spot, he pressed on to the next time check at speeds of up to 70 mph over rough, rutted tracks, with the front tyre flat, to reach the check on time. Graham Walker claimed it was one of the most courageous and inspired pieces of riding he had ever seen.

Bert Perrigo spoon-feeds his runners in the field! Picture taken in Sweden with left, Bill Nicholson (getting like treatment from Harold Tozer), Basil Hall, John Avery and right, John Draper, only slightly amused. The models are Gold Stars with plunger-type rear suspension.

BSA: Competition History

By the 1930s national trials had become very competitive, with professional factory teams going from event to event in the trials season, not unlike their road racing counterparts in the Continental Circus. Bert recalls that the trade riders' drill or routine was to arrive at the event (always a Saturday fixture) on the Friday in time to practise on as many of the actual sections as possible, then to return to the hotel booked for the occasion. After a meal a spot of steady drinking took place, the object of the drinking session being, Bert recalls with wry humour, "to make sure we all started next morning with the same headache." Bert continued by saying "Those who had shown good form during practice but resisted such blandishments during the evening were subjected to a subtle course of psychology — not that we called it that in those days. By the time we had finished with them, their nervous state was such that a common headache was much better."

Good friends socially, deadly rivals on parade, they never hesitated to take advantage where they could. With the girder front forks of the period it was relatively easy to alter the fork trail to suit the event from a selection of links of varying lengths taken with them, although it has been known for riders to rush back to their factories in the Midlands

'That's the way to do it' Bert Perrigo seems to be saying on his return from Oslo with the legendary Maudes Trophy party in October 1952 with from L to R: Norman Vanhouse (author of this book), Mary Barker, Brian Martin, Mrs. 'Cherry' Perrigo, Bert Perrigo, Fred Rist, Mr. Rist Senior and Charlie Barker. The party was met at Newcastle by Fred Rist's father and the Barkers.

One of the many proud moments in the life of Bert Perrigo, with Brian Martin (left), Fred Rist (centre) and Norman Vanhouse displaying the coveted Maudes Trophy won by BSA in 1952. Picture taken outside the main entrance of the BSA office block.

after practice sessions in such local classics as the Colmore and Victory Trials to carry out certain modifications. In the main, however, factory riders had little choice but to make do with the machine built with standard production components, with most variations aimed at satisfying their personal fads and fancies. Whilst it is true that girder   39 forks with longer blades have been used to secure greater ground clearance, the bikes of those days had much more in common with the standard production counterpart than the pure-bred specials of today.

1937 proved to be Bert Perrigo's last full season with the factory team, one as good as, if not better, than any of the previous ten years. After winning the Lister Trial in Yorkshire — under the nose of local hero Allan Jefferies — he proceeded to win both the Colmore Cup and the Victory Cup Trials of high prestige. He then tied with Allan Jefferies for the premier award in the Wye Valley Traders Cup before going to Scotland for the Scottish Six Days where he had the bitter-sweet experience of losing the premier award to Jack Williams and his Norton by one mark. Second best performance seemed poor consolation with so little in it.

In the ISDT of 1937, again in Wales, Bert won yet another gold medal as a member of the BSA team, as did Jack Ashworth, but the third member of the team, sidecar specialist Harold Tozer, came unstuck on the first day. It was soon after the International that Bert Perrigo took up the position as BSA sales representative in the West Country, to be followed by his illness and convalescence in South Africa in 1938 and thence his increasing preoccupation with matters related to both the British Army and the company's escalating armaments production activities.

Bert Perrigo was much respected among the higher echelon of the British motorcycle industry. Here, at a social function, he is seen with left, Ernie Humphries of OK Supreme, Gilbert Smith, managing director of Norton Motors, and Rem Fowler, winner of the twin-cylinder class of the first TT in 1907.

In 1953 Bert Perrigo moved from BSA to Ariel as sales manager. In this picture Harold Tozer presents Perrigo with a leaving present on behalf of the riders. Left to right standing: Bernal Osborne, Motor Cycling *journalist, Jeff Smith, Bill Nicholson, Arthur Crawford, George Pickering, Ted Fithian and Tom Ellis. Back row: Norman Vanhouse, David Tye and John Draper with seated L to R: Mrs. May Harris, Mrs. Perrigo and BSA sales manager George Savage.*

Over the years the competitions department had operated closely with the experimental department and as such Perrigo's work had not been confined within narrow limits, bringing him into contact with the development of prototypes as they came along, year after year, as well as with quality control and investigation. When war eventually came — just as James Leek had forecast on his return from his visit to the Leipzig Trade Fair of 1935 — Bert Perrigo's wide-ranging experience and shrewd mind were brought to bear on the many engineering and production problems with which the company had to deal in the mammoth task undertaken on behalf of the United Kingdom. Armed with Government authority, his varied duties included scouring the Midlands for suitable factories to be taken over for the expanding production of the desperately-needed Browning machine guns for the aircraft of the Royal Air Force. With the military version of the 500cc

41

side-valve M20 in production throughout the war, produced at Small
Heath at a rate of 600 per week, there was still motorcycle-related work
nonetheless. He also worked on the BSA-Daimler Scout Reconnaissance
Car — a BSA-designed vehicle utilizing a Daimler engine and produced
at the Daimler Coventry factory.

Another motorcycle-related function undertaken by Bert Perrigo
during the war years was that of a civilian riding instructor seconded to
the Army authorities, like other pre-war factory experts whose job was to
visit Officer Corps Training Units (OCTU) to demonstrate to
commissioned ranks the correct methods of riding a motorcycle under all
types of conditions.

Dennis Hardwicke, the Motor Cycling *journalist who succeeded Bert
Perrigo as BSA competitions manager in October 1953.*

This latter duty could be described as little more than pleasant light
relief in contrast to the years of unremitting factory grind endured by
both management and the army of shopfloor workers. If it had left them
exhausted and weary it would have been understandable; instead, a
growing sense of pride dispelled any feeling of war-weariness. As
enthusiasm grew with the prospects of victory, James Leek began to
assemble his team of managers with whom it was planned to seek new

commercial objectives, to re-establish BSA as leaders of the motorcycle industry.

This new team, brimful of confidence, included Bert Perrigo, restored to his pre-war role as competitions manager. Having scaled the Everest-like peaks of wartime production the management team sparkled with enthusiasm, and none more so than the pragmatic Bert Perrigo with his down-to-earth outlook, a man who called a spade a spade, never afraid to speak his mind.

Having been given the task of establishing and implementing the post-war competitions policy, it was this very attitude which led to the foundation and growth of the greatest dynasty of trials and scramble riders ever known. 'Uncle Bert's' men, in their hey-day, travelled far and wide, at home and overseas, with an insatiable thirst for the spoils of victory.

Chapter Four

Beginnings of the Landslide

MANY THINGS lack a sharp black and white definition, rendering demarcation lines difficult to perceive. The end of hostilities in 1945 and the dawn of the peacetime era was no exception, with no clear-cut line defining one set of conditions from the other though most people did feel a great sense of uplift and relief. Nonetheless shortages and rationing, including that of petrol, remained a feature of daily lives for several years after, with only a low-grade of 72 octane rating being available in normal cases against a basic ration. It was 1953 before branded, premium grade petrol, was once again restored.

Although the Ministry of Fuel and Power relented in due course and allocated a supplementary petrol ration to facilitate the running of trade-supported, national open trials (in the interests of boosting export business), for a time all motorcycle sport had to make do on the basic ration, thus limiting the mileage of all sporting trials.

Whilst Bert Perrigo faced up to the fact that he and his pre-war contemporaries could not be expected to go on riding for ever (he himself having started over 20 years previously), with prospective new and younger riders still awaiting release from the armed forces it was a case of planning short-term with known options. Nonetheless, some of the pre-war factory experts still felt capable of giving a good account of themselves despite the six-year lay-off and, in fact, some did. This was admirably demonstrated in November 1945, just three months after the Japanese surrender, when the BSA works team of Bert Perrigo, Jack Amott and Jack Blackwell carried off the premier award in the Stroud Team Trial. Just one month later, in December, Jack Blackwell won the premier award in the Mitchell Memorial Trial in South Wales. He beat Bert Perrigo on the special test, both having tied with a loss of three marks, with Perrigo winning the 350 Cup on the new prototype 350cc B32 fitted with telescopic front forks.

Fred Rist astride his first post-war works B32 on which he won the 1946 Colmore Cup Trial and put up best solo performance in the Victory Cup Trial soon after. The B32 is fitted with a standard iron cylinder barrel and head.

Jack Blackwell was no newcomer to BSA, having ridden a works model pre-war as one of several riders recruited by Bert Perrigo in a policy of backing good riders in various parts of the country. Hitherto, most BSA works riders had been based in the Midlands and mostly employed by the factory, with the result that apart from national open events, their influence was largely confined to the Midlands area. Bert felt that the talent was too concentrated and that supporting good riders in other centres would be beneficial. Accordingly, during the 1930s, he 45 recruited such riders as Mike Riley in the South East — the hotbed of AMC activity — and one R.T.Viney whose younger brother was to achieve immortality in the Scottish Six Days Trial after the war. Then there was Jack Ashworth of Preston, who won several class cups in national opens and was drafted into the works team for the 1938 ISDT, as was Reg Spokes of Northampton, who had won a gold in the 1937 ISDT and who also enjoyed similar works support. Other such riders enjoying works support included J.J.StJohn and Joe Heath of Farnham, Surrey, brother of Len Heath, the Ariel ace.

Born in Bournemouth in 1915, freshly demobbed from the army, and then working as a civilian fighting vehicle tester at the MOD, FVRDE complex at Chobham, Surrey, Jack Blackwell became the first post-war BSA exponent to win a national open trial with his Mitchell success of December 1945; a success he was to repeat just two months later in the national Kickham Trial of February 1946. This early success of Jack Blackwell tended to confirm what Bert Perrigo had suspected; that a new generation of riders would soon be calling the tune. Within two months, the message crystallized with near startling clarity.

The Colmore Cup Trial of 1946, organized yet again by Sunbac (Sutton Coldfield & North Birmingham Auto Club) as it had been since 1911, could be described in several ways. Certainly it was a landmark for it marked the full resumption of a sport rudely interrupted in 1939. It was also a symbolic crossroads where two generations of riders came together for the first time: the recognized, established pre-war experts, and the unknown newcomers whose riding ability had developed by various means during the war years but who had been denied the opportunity of putting it to the test in open competition.

Perhaps above all the Colmore could be described as a diabolical event resulting from dreadful weather conditions and lack of organizational skill, the latter blunted by lack of experience since 1939 where club officials with previous experience had forgotten certain fundamental lessons and principles. The chaos was such that it was 3 am on the Sunday morning before the results were announced to those still on their feet in the normally quiet market town of Shipston-on-Stour. During the day, hordes of riders had persisted in their dire struggle against the odds imposed by the organizers and the elements, to battle on, desperate and exhausted, until well after dark. It was hardly the auspicious start many had dreamed of for years, with the majority of the 180 entrants struggling up 'unclimbable sections in blinding rain' as one press report put it, and with 'competitors trying to reach sections well after dark' as the report went on.

Nonetheless, it was a memorable occasion, the entry list reading like a Who's Who of the motorcycling world with such names as ten-times

February 28, 1946.   MOTOR CYCLING   Advts. 3

VICTORY TRIAL

won
CRANFORD BOWL

Best Solo Performance — F. M. Rist, B.S.A. 350 O.H.V.

WATSONIAN CUP — TEAM PRIZE

F. M. Rist   J. Blackwell   W. Nicholson
(Middlesboro')   (Surrey)   (Belfast)

Kickham Memorial Trial, Feb. 9

KICKHAM TROPHY
J. Blackwell, B.S.A. 350 O.H.V.

350 CUP
Runner-up — F. J. Keevil, B.S.A. 350 O.H.V.

WILTSHIRE CUP
H. Tozer, B.S.A. 500 c.c. Sidecar.

Manufacturers Team Prize
J. Blackwell, F. M. Rist, F. Povey.

Colmore Cup Trial, Feb. 2

COLMORE CUP
F. M. Rist, B.S.A. 350 O.H.V.

CRANMORE TROPHY
Runner-up — W. Nicholson, B.S.A. 350 O.H.V.

WATSON SHIELD
Best Sidecar — F. Perks, B.S.A.

BAYLISS CUP
A. Hollinson, B.S.A. 350 O.H.V.

PREMIER CUP

Best 250 — J. H. Amott
(Birmingham)

CHEKKO CUP

Best 500 Sidecar — H. Tozer
(Birmingham)

and

7 FIRST-CLASS AWARDS

(Provisional Results)

LEAVE IT TO YOUR BSA

The powerful press advertisement proclaiming the list of awards won by BSA in the Victory Cup Trial and the Colmore and Kickham Trials which had gone before.

47

TT winner Stanley Woods, current TT lap-record holder Harold Daniell, the great all-rounder Bob Foster and Eddie Bessant, at that period dubbed the Uncrowned King of Bagshot. One must not forget the lady of pre-war Brooklands days either, Theresa Wallach, who, together with Ruby Slade and Molly Briggs, represented the fair sex. There were also, of course, all the pre-war experts of the trials world. A true gathering of the clans.

Equally memorable was the BSA line-up of top-grade riders headed by Bert Perrigo himself, backed-up by fellow works riders Jack Amott, Phil Hewitt and the 1938 Scottish Six Days winner, Fred Povey, the last having returned to the BSA camp after his pre-war flirtation with AJS and Ariel. There was also Jack Blackwell, fresh from his Mitchell victory of two months before, plus Fred Rist, another pre-war regular soldier who had made an impact in civilian trials before the war. From across the Irish Sea came a BSA-mounted contingent of talent rarely equalled since for, in addition to Stanley Woods, there were Artie Bell, Edmund Gill, Terry Hill and, most significant of all, a then unknown character of stocky build by the name of William Nicholson who, within months, was to become the hottest property in the field of trials and scrambles.

Other BSA riders included Cliff Holden from Bury, Lancashire who was to prove equally effective in both trials and scrambles during the months ahead, Bill Walker and Reg Slinn, both employed in the Small Heath experimental department — the latter a one-time passenger to Harold Tozer — and in the sidecar entry, additional to Harold Tozer, Freddie Perks, who had won the sidecar premier in the last pre-war Victory Cup Trial. Another BSA sidecar driver was Bill Howard who, whilst a successful chair competitor in his own right with many awards to his credit, becomes even more famous in retrospect by employing the services of a very youthful Brian Martin as his passenger.

When at last announced during the early hours of Sunday morning, the results were impressive to the point of being sensational: BSA had pulled-off the 'double', winning both the solo and sidecar premier awards. In so doing they set in motion a pattern of consistent wins rarely achieved before. Fred Rist, not long demobilized from years of overseas service, had won the prestigious Colmore Cup, and CSMA clubman Freddie Perks had again beaten the official works sidecar entry, as he had done before in 1939, to win the sidecar premier award. His loss of 41 marks was one solitary mark down on the winning solo performance of Freddie Rist and a substantial 27 marks less than the next best BSA sidecar outfit of Bill Howard, who won a first class award. Harold Tozer, who had made best sidecar performance in the last pre-war Colmore, had a disastrous day and did not figure in the awards list. It was a lapse he was to redeem many times over during the years ahead.

The same dominant BSA advertising message on the front cover of Motor Cycling, *reminding all that BSA had won 12 trophies in the first three classic trials of 1946.*

Another profound performance was that by Bill Nicholson from Ulster, who finished runner-up on his privately-owned 350 BSA. He was best also of the Irish contingent, with Stanley Woods only a further three marks adrift. Fellow Irish road-racers Artie Bell and Edmund Gill won first class awards, as did Jack Blackwell, Phil Hewitt, Fred Povey and private clubman Arthur Merrett from Oxford.

The evergreen Bert Perrigo was riding the recently-announced 350 B32, with the personalized registration number of BSA 350, fitted with an alloy cylinder head and barrel. He made the most of his early number but missed the premier award by the slim margin of six marks. In so doing, he won the best Sunbac member award and also the club team award together with Vic Brittain (Norton) and George Rowley (AJS) who represented the organizing Sunbac club.

Not a bad swan-song by any standard; and even if no such thought crossed Perrigo's mind as he rode from the Sale Yard start point in Shipston-on-Stour that morning, it had taken root during the event, to become crystal-clear by the time the awards were announced. As a rider he was no longer needed. The day's events had shown several potential winners for the future. His role from now on would be one of administration and planning, to build on the firm foundations already laid.

With the firm hand of Bert Perrigo at the helm, the competitions department at Small Heath gradually developed its individual identity, with all clerical matters handled by the capable May Harris. She had joined BSA during the war years as directed labour, only to stay on for many years with a loyalty that was a characteristic of BSA employees in those days. When Bert Perrigo became involved with other problems such as chasing steel supplies up and down the country, it became necessary to appoint an assistant to help things along and in this capacity he appointed John Boynton, a blond-haired ex-Army captain with an attitude of infectious enthusiasm for his job and the sport of motorcycling. He became the first man to ride a BSA in the 1946 Manx Grand Prix, the first race in the Isle of Man after the war, and, whilst failing to finish, he led that tidal wave of BSA success which followed soon after. Before emigrating to South Africa in 1947 (where he died at an early age) Johnny Boynton tried his hand with a 500 BSA trials outfit, taking part in that year's Colmore Cup and D.K.Mansell Trophy Trials. When he left BSA for his new life in South Africa, his place as assistant competitions manager was taken by Ted Fithian, already employed in another section of the great factory, and it was a job he was to do for the next seven years before he too left the company for pastures new. When Ted left, his position was never re-filled.

At that time the competitions shop itself, backing onto the old canal

By the end of the 1946 season the company was able to advertise that over 50% of the classic trials of that year had been won by BSA — a veritable landslide in comparison to others.

This shot of Fred Rist riding to his victory in the 1946 Lancashire Grand National goes a little way towards portraying the mudbath horror which faced all riders in that Northern classic during post-war years — an event for 'men only'.

which ran alongside the factory on one side as did the London railway line on the other, was in the charge of Phil Hewitt who himself had a place in the official works trials and scramble team until he too left the company and country in search of the sun. Arthur Crawford, already working in the competitions shop, was placed in charge on the departure of Hewitt and it was a position he filled for many years to come. It is Arthur Crawford with his dry Brummie humour — and repertoire of rich expletives — whom most of the riders featured in the following pages recall with affection. He was regarded as a lovable character, typical of the many who made up that great BSA empire with its multitude of production noises and smells.

Chapter Five

The Middlesbrough Maestro

FRED RIST'S victory in that first post-war Colmore Cup Trial of 1946 must have surprised most people for, despite his meteoric rise to fame in 1939, he had not been one of the select factory experts in the accepted sense. He had been a regular serving soldier — a sergeant in the 2nd Battalion Royal Tank Corps. Those not familiar with his pre-war record could have been forgiven had they judged his Colmore win as a flash-in-the-pan. Any such doubts were dispelled for good just a couple or so weeks later when he made best solo performance of the day in the old-established Victory Cup Trial, staged by the Birmingham MCC among the old local muddy sections which abounded in those days just south of the city in the Warwickshire and Worcestershire countryside.

That really established his true potential as a rider of great ability and during the course of that very competitive year he went on to win two more national trials (the Reliance and Northern Experts), three 350 Class Cups (in the Cotswold Cups, Mitchell and Travers Trophy) and, most prestigious of all, outright victory in the most traumatic scramble ever devised in the United Kingdom; the devastating Lancashire Grand National. Normally run across the remorseless bogs of Holcombe Moor high above Bury, in 1946 it was switched to a similar inhospitable, rain-swept and misty terrain at Close Barn Farm on Ashworth Moor, between Bury and Rochdale.

That Fred Rist regards that early victory as one he treasures more than most can be fully appreciated by those who have suffered this one-time Lancashire horror. Apart from an entry list that contained the names of everybody who was somebody in the sport of scrambling, there was also the bleak, desolate moorland to conquer. With a winning time of 1 hr 9 mins 54 secs, Fred was almost four minutes ahead of runner-up Jack Williams of Cheltenham who, in turn, was nearly a minute ahead of that great all-rounder Bob Foster. BSA-mounted Cliff Clegg was fourth   53 and in fifth place, a full seven-and-a-half minutes astern of Fred Rist, was that great little Irishman, Bill Nicholson, who went on to dominate the sport for a year or two. The wide time gap between the leading finishers is indicative of the severity of the event, as does the running time of well over the hour devalue the top scramble events of this day and age.

Those early successes of Fred Rist during 1946 were merely the fulfilment of the great promise he had shown whilst serving as a regular soldier in his first full season of motorcycle sport during 1938/39. Indeed, it encourages speculation as to what he would have achieved in the sport had not war brought it all to an end. Although he had first ridden a motorcycle in 1923 at the early age of seven (with a small open-frame Ladies two-stroke Royal Enfield) on his father's poultry farm near Stokesly, in the Cleveland area of Yorkshire, he did not enter his first motorcycle competition until 1938. Then he was a member of an official British Army team mounted on works-supplied BSA Gold Stars in the International Six Days Trial, held that year in Wales. It was an experience akin to being thrown in at the deep end. As a member of the 2nd Battalion Royal Tank Corps team with Sergeant J.T. Dalby and Corporal R. Gillam, who won the *Motor Cycling* Trophy for the best performance by an Army team, Fred Rist was the only member of the team to win a gold medal. Moreover, he was the only BSA-mounted rider that year to do so.

To put his performance into perspective, it is necessary to recall that of the 200 starters that year only 82 survived the week, with a mere 34 qualifying for gold medals — 21 of which went to foreign competitors leaving but a miserly 13 for British riders. It was further testimony to the training he had received from the master, Bert Perrigo, in those very same Welsh mountains. Having joined the regular Army in 1934 and completed his tank training at Bovington in Dorset, he was posted to the 2nd Battalion Royal Tank Corps, then based at Farnborough in 1938 at a time when the Army was taking a keener interest in motorcycles and competitive events as a basis of training.

Soon after, it came up on Battalion Daily Orders that volunteers to train for motorcycle trials were being sought and after four years with tanks Fred decided a change was as good as a rest. In the face of the old soldiers' golden rule of never volunteering, he put pen to paper.

Having volunteered, Fred Rist then underwent a series of training events which led to his eventual selection for the team representing the Royal Tank Corps in the ISDT of 1938 and, later in 1939. Thus became established the RTC trio of 'Paddy' Doyle, Jackie Wood and himself, the most successful British Army team ever. Even before the 1938 ISDT had taken place, Bert Perrigo had recognised the natural ability of Fred

Fred Rist on the pre-war B25 winning his first civilian trial — the West London Trophy Trial — as a serving soldier in his first season of competitions in 1939.

Rist in particular, and had arranged the loan of a factory B25 350 trials model to facilitate his entry in civilian national trials. It was with this model that he travelled north to his native Yorkshire, with his ISDT success to his credit, to tackle the notorious Scott Trial, the most severe of its type in the British Isles. Only recently had he completed the Two-Day Inter-Command Army Championship Trial with a standard WD 16H Norton.

That 21st Scott Trial of 1938, won by Len Heath for the third time within a period of six years, was as tough as ever, for of the 80 entries only 20 managed to finish. Yet Fred Rist, not having ridden in a competitive event of any sort until two months previously, competed with the cream of trials riding experts to make the second best performance on observation and third best performance overall, winning no less than three trophies in the process. It was a remarkable performance, notwithstanding his rear chain coming off three times during the event. Within two weeks of his Scott Trial success, Fred Rist had finished eighth in the British Experts Trial — the most prestigious 55 event of all. To be beaten by a mere seven factory experts was astonishing for a serving soldier. His first civilian trial premier award came the very next day when he won the West London Trophy Trial, the first of several similar civilian trials wins over the next few months. But he really established his reputation on 22nd April 1939 by winning the Travers Trophy Trial — a trade-supported national event in which all the factory teams competed. Fellow Royal Tank Corps riders 'Paddy' Doyle and Jackie Wood, also BSA B25 mounted, had been performing well in both army and national trials; indeed, in the Cotswold Cups Trial, Paddy Doyle had won the 350 Cup and the three of them — Rist, Doyle and Wood — had won the one-make team award, beating all the factory teams.

In the meantime it had been decided by the Director of Military Training that the British Army would contest the Scottish Six Days Trial with four teams mounted on standard issue WD machines of BSA, Norton, Triumph and Matchless manufacture. In the case of BSA this meant using the low ground clearance side-valve M20 model, to be made in large numbers during the war years which followed. To use them in an event like the Scottish must have been a daunting prospect, but nonetheless, with Rist, Doyle and Wood to ride them, an attempt was

Fred Rist with the 350 B32 leading Roger Wise with his 500 5-stud JAP at an Astwood Bank grasstrack meeting near Redditch in 1946.

made to render the M20s more suitable for the Highland rockery by fitting a 21 inch front wheel with a 3 inch section tyre to increase ground clearance and a smaller engine sprocket to reduce the overall gear ratios.

This BSA M20 team proved easily the best of the Army Teams: indeed, when reporting events from notorious Mamore, *The Motor Cycle* journalist wrote, " . . . Easily the most impressive climbs were made by the BSA Army Team. They arrived when the hill was in bad condition and proceeded to make three perfect climbs. The riders were F.M.Rist, A.C.Doyle and J.L.Wood. The crowd clapped long after they

The British ISDT Vase 'B' team of Fred Rist (350 BSA) left, Jack Blackwell (500 Norton) centre and Bert Gaymer (500 Triumph) at San Remo, Italy, in 1948, the first such post-war event supported by Great Britain.

57

were out of earshot . . . " Praise indeed. With a loss of 59 marks Fred Rist won a silver cup, with Paddy Doyle on 67 marks winning a silver plaque as did Jackie Wood with a loss of 79 marks. No other Army rider got anywhere near those Royal Tank Corps experts. Ray Scovell on one of the 16H Nortons was nearest, with a loss of 87 marks.

By the summer of that year, the main preoccupation of those involved was the International Six Days Trial, to be staged in the mountains of Austria. It was based at the music-festival town of Salzburg and due to start on 21st August, at a time when the brown-shirted officials of the Nazi movement were revelling in the euphoria of jingoistic nationalism. To win the prestigious Huhnlein Trophy for their homeland would be a point of honour. The British Army was determined to make that task as difficult as possible. With Lieut. Col. C.V. Bennett responsible for all planning and arrangements,

Riding in the successful British Trophy team for the 1950 ISDT in Wales, Fred Rist with the 500cc B34 Gold Star negotiates a water splash on the mountain road between Tregaron and Abergwesyn. Rist went on to win his fourth ISDT gold medal.

Fred Rist on the 650 Golden Flash he used when captain of the British Trophy team for the 1951 ISDT at Varese, Italy. The light alloy petrol tank in the picture was replaced by a standard steel tank for the event, which produced Rist's fifth gold medal.

assisted by the British motorcycle industry, the British Army had entered three teams of factory-prepared BSA, Norton and Matchless models. It almost goes without saying that the three Gold Star models prepared by BSA were to be ridden by Fred Rist, 'Paddy' Doyle and Jackie Wood, with QMS Joe Acheson as reserve rider.

What happened during that International of 1939 is now one of the legends of motorcycling, for by the fourth day, the political situation had deteriorated to the point where the British contingent of competitors was advised to leave immediately for the Swiss frontier. By then the Army Norton and Matchless teams had been decimated. Only Rist, Doyle and Wood on the BSA Gold Stars remained unpenalized. However, without official instructions to leave for Switzerland as received by the civilian riders, the British Army party stayed on and the BSA team set out and completed the Friday's run — still unpenalized. That night they too packed their bags and hurried to the Swiss border and safety. But for that turn of events, Bert Perrigo is convinced that the BSA trio would have won the Huhnlein Trophy for the British Army. They got back to England on 30th August — just four days before war was declared.

Before civilian trials closed down for 'the duration', the British Experts Trial was run in December, as usual from Rodborough

A 1950 shot of Fred Rist demonstrating his famous sand racing cornering technique at Pendine Sands in Pembrokeshire, this time with the iron engine 350cc B32 running on 'dope'.

Common near Stroud. Fred Rist was ninth best solo, but fellow soldier Paddy Doyle did even better by making fourth best solo performance.

In the short space of twelve months, Fred Rist as a serving soldier had established himself as a rider of outstanding ability equal to the best of the factory experts. There can be no doubt that had the war not intervened, he would have gained many more successes over the years. It was not surprising that his first post-war trial — the Colmore Cup of 1946 — should produce that outstanding win. After over five years overseas service during the war years, he got back to England in July 1945 to be demobilized in September and settle in his home town of Middlesborough. It was to be twelve months before he moved to the Midlands and BSA, initially with the staff of the competitions department. During that first summer of 1946, having established himself as one of Britain's leading trials riders, he 'amused' himself with some grasstrack racing. To race a BSA 350cc B32 against the established five-stud JAP-engined specials was pure joy; not unlike putting the cat among the pigeons.

During the seasons which followed he even took the 350cc B32 to a race meeting at Oliver's Mount, Scarborough. He won a race there too — though with due modesty Fred points out it was a handicap event in

One of the spectacles of motorcycle sport! Fred Rist drifting the 140 mph, 650 BSA A10 twin running on 'dope' at Pendine Sands on August Monday 1950. Note how the front tyre is almost forced off the rim.

A smile of satisfaction! Another Fred Rist picture, taken between races at Pendine Sands.

which he enjoyed a generous allowance. However, he was never seriously attracted to road racing. He had grown up on the mud and rocks of the countryside and the soft, sandy tracks of moors and commonland. It was with nostalgic thoughts of his old Bagshot Heath training days with the Army, with its deep-rutted, sandy tracks demanding its own special technique, that his thoughts turned to sand racing. Whilst not a part of his brief as a works rider, it was an aspect of the sport to which he was attracted, so when an opportunity arose to try his hand at it, he went along to his first meeting with just the 350 B32 tuned on alcohol fuel.

From this very first meeting, his record of success was sensational, winning almost every class he entered. For example, at the Welsh Speed Championship held at Pendine in 1948, he won the 1000cc One-Mile Sprint; the 350cc Six-Mile Race; the 600cc Thirty-Mile Race and was placed second in the 1000cc Ten-Mile Race. It wasn't long before he was racing in addition to the 350 B32 a 500 B34 (both with iron engines) and a 650cc A10 Golden Flash twin also on alcohol, with a maximum speed of 140 mph. It is said by those who remember that to have seen Fred Rist sliding that mighty A10 on dope was one of the rare spectacles of life.

Fred Rist refueling between races at Redcar in his native Yorkshire where he was very much the local hero.

It can be claimed that he added a new dimension to sand racing, deploying a style and technique which was electrifying to behold. Instead of shedding speed for the turn at the marker flag by going down through the gearbox and taking the tight turn of established practice, he would leave his braking much later, then lay the bike right down on its footrest, inducing a high-speed, wide-radius power slide, spewing-up plumes of flying wet sand to leave the opposition struggling in his wake like part-time amateurs. His fame soon spread far and wide to north of the Border where the hard-riding Scots who dominated the sport on the sands of St. Andrew doubted whether reality could match the legend. After all, he was only using a humble pushrod engine. He shouldn't be too difficult to beat.

So with his fame preceding him, Fred Rist undertook the long journey north with his stable of BSA sand racers, to contest the old-established Scottish Speed Championships held on the sands of St. Andrews. He not only upheld but enhanced his reputation by winning every race in which he rode, with the sole exception of the 250 class in which he was beaten into second place. It was a similar story at the

63

BSA: Competition History

Easter Pendine meeting of 1949 when the Press reported that: ". . . F.M. Rist swept the board in the racing classes . . ." Such headlines were commonplace at that period and it was an area of the sport in which he indulged until the mid-1950s by which time he had opened his own motorcycle business in Neath among the people of the Welsh Valleys. It was they who had thrilled to his exploits at Pendine and who, to this day, talk of Fred Rist as though he was one of them.

Additional to his sand racing successes, Fred Rist still contested the important national trials and scrambles, his main function as a BSA works rider. He scored two early wins in the 1947 season, the first being when he crossed the Irish Sea to beat the Irish at their own game — including Bill Nicholson — by winning the Hurst Cup, a time and observation event, like the Scott Trial. Soon after he was victor in both the 250cc Junior and Unlimited Race in the Hants Grand National, run on a two-mile course at Avon Castle, near Ringwood, on Good Friday. According to the press report, the 250 Junior Race was 'completely monopolized by Rist and his 'Flying 250 BSA' who finished a good three-quarters of a lap ahead of Les Archer (250 Velocette). Having seen-off Eddie Bessant (500 Matchless) in the early laps of the unlimited heat, Fred lost several places when mud blocked the petrol filler cap vent hole of his 350 B32 and he was lucky to qualify for the final. In this he made no mistake, winning from Jack Stocker (Ariel) and Ray Scovell (BSA) who was third.

The 'Flying 250 BSA' referred to in that press report, and raced so successfully by Rist during that period, had a quite interesting pedigree. Basically, it was a pre-war B21 built by Jack Amott and ridden by him in trials in 1939 and again in 1946 before he retired from the sport. During 1946 Rist converted it for scrambling, and used it many times thereafter. Indeed, in June he was second with it in the Senior Race of the Cotswold Scramble, headed only by Bill Nicholson. A high-compression piston was later fitted for use with alcohol fuel so that the little 250 could be raced on the sands at Wallasey and Pendine. In that trim the engine would run happily up to 8,000 rpm, never giving trouble. It remained virtually untouched by spanners from one year's end to the next. At Wallasey on one occasion it won the Gold Cup — against the 500cc opposition. At Bank Holiday Pendine meetings Fred would race it on the beach in the morning and afternoon, then change the wheels and engine sprocket, to go scrambling with it during the evening on a course near Carmarthen. "It seemed to thrive on hard work," Fred Rist recalled, "and was a great credit to those who made it."

In the first trade-supported scramble of 1947 — the Sunbeam Point-to-Point at Liphook with its Le Mans-type dead-engine start — Rist was second to Bill Nicholson in the Junior race. Then in the month

The Mayor and Mayoress of Wallasey presenting Fred Rist with the Daily Despatch *Gold Cup Challenge Trophy after his win in the 50-Mile Race at one of the Wallasey meetings of 1950. Photo: Thomson Withy Grove Ltd.*

of June, once more with the 'Flying 250', he won the 250 class of the Cotswold Scramble with its mud, grassy cambers and steep hillocks. One month later he was a member of the victorious British 'A' team with Bill Nicholson and Bob Ray (Ariel), winning the first-ever Motocross des Nations, held that year on a sandy course in Holland. Soon after he was off to Sweden together with Jack Blackwell and Ray Scovell (both BSA) where he won the Swedish Motocross Grand Prix.

At the conclusion of the season, once more doing battle with the energy-sapping bogs of Holcombe Moor, he had to concede victory to Bill Nicholson in the Lancashire Grand National. Nonetheless, a second place in an event of that nature is only achieved by the élite. With fourteen of the first twenty finishers BSA-mounted, it was a flood-tide victory for the Small Heath factory.

Although Bill Nicholson again dominated the arduous Scott Trial in the November, as he had done the year before, Fred Rist made fourth-best performance. As those who have had personal experience of the Scott will know, this can be classed as a gilt-edged performance.

Fred Rist's best scramble ride in 1948 was his victory in the 350 Junior race of the Cotswold Scramble — with Bill Nicholson winning 65 the 250 class — but in national trials he had to be content with class cups in the Kickham, Victory and Hurst Cup trials. His best Scottish Six Days Trial ride came in the 1949 event when he made fifth best performance to win the Jimmy Beck Memorial Trophy with a loss of 33 marks.

Nothwithstanding the wide spectrum of success achieved by Rist in sand racing, scrambling, trials and grass track racing, his name will always be synonymous with what can be regarded as the most demanding and prestigious type of event of all: the glamorous International Six Days Trial — once dominated by some of the greatest riders ever produced within the British Isles. Fred Rist, with his safe and calculated style of riding, coupled with a shrewd intelligence, was the very epitome of responsibility and discipline; two attributes which, as much as riding skill, go to make up the ideal six-days team man. He never left anything to chance with his machines. Even when they were built for him at a time when he was employed in the factory at Small Heath as a free-ranging quality investigator, he would work overtime in order to strip the bike to the bare frame in order to rebuild it himself. Not that he lacked confidence in those around him. It was a case of accepting full responsibility himself. There would be no other to blame.

George Wilson of The Motor Cycle *examines the mighty 'dope' 650 BSA before trying it at Pendine Sands in 1949. On the right is the famous 'Flying 250' with behind it a rare shot of American Tommy McDermott of Daytona Beach fame.*

He was rewarded with an impeccable International Six Days record, never having incurred a single penalty point in all those he contested and apart from the ill-fated event of 1939 when forced to withdraw whilst still unpenalized, he won a gold medal in every one. Furthermore, he represented Great Britain in one of the national teams, in four of the five post-war events. Curiously enough, in the 1948 event staged at San Remo, Italy, using a 350cc B32, he was nominated for the British Vase 'B' team only, notwithstanding his pre-war record and experience. However, with both the International Trophy and International Vase

Fred Rist demonstrates his neat, unflurried riding style, in the national Southern Trial of circa 1950.

secured by British teams in the dusty conditions of Italy, the ACU team selection had been justified.

For the 1949 event, staged among the mountains of Wales in extremely dry and dusty conditions, and on this occasion using the bigger 500cc B34, Fred Rist was promoted to the British Trophy Team together with Bob Ray (500 Ariel), Jim Alves (500 Triumph), Hugh Viney (500 AJS) and Charlie Rogers (350 Enfield). As in Italy the year before, the British Trophy Team gave another faultless performance to win the Trophy without loss of marks. The British Vase 'A' team likewise lost no marks, but the Vase went to the Czechoslovakian team with their speedy CZ lightweights as a result of the speed test at Eppynt, after they too had lost no marks during the week. Despite the dusty conditions, the event was not severe and this resulted in a near-record of gold medals awarded — twenty-three of which were won by BSA riders.

As a result of the 1949 British Trophy victory, the event was once again staged in the United Kingdom, with Wales again the selected venue. For this event Fred Rist was appointed captain of the British Trophy Team, with Jack Stocker (350 Enfield) replacing Charlie Rogers (who had retired from the sport) as the only change in the previous year's successful team. This time the climatic conditions were the exact opposite to those that prevailed in 1949, with torrential rain lashing the countryside on most days, causing severe flooding at the river crossings that needed to be forded. The mountain passes and stony tracks now became muddy and riddled with spine-jarring cross-gullies, making them severe and demanding in relation to the tight time allowance. The British Trophy Team led by Fred Rist, and the British Vase 'A' Team, left the Continental opposition floundering, with the Austrian Trophy Team runner-up in the former contest with no less than 1224 marks lost. Italy, who were third, lost a massive 2582 marks. The Holland 'A' Team' were second to Great Britain in the Vase contest with a loss of 300 marks. Britain's Vase 'B' Team was fourth having lost 600 marks during the eventful week.

Like the event way back in 1938, it proved a disastrous week for the majority, with only 81 of the 213 starters surviving of which only 38 won gold medals. From this total a mere four went to foreign competitors, surely a measure of British supremacy in those days.

For 1951, with the Six Days based at Varese, Italy, the ACU had pinned its faith on the victorious Trophy team of 1950 without change, again with Fred Rist as team captain, though on this occasion riding the

Opposite: A superb shot of Fred Rist on 'BSA 350' negotiating a rocky track near Falls Hill on the third day of the 1949 Scottish Six Days. Photo: The Classic Motor Cycle.

bigger 650cc A10 Twin. It was a repeat performance by the British Trophy Team who, without loss of marks, achieved victory for the fourth year in succession. Whereas in 1950 only three manufacturers' teams gained team awards — all British teams — in 1951 no less than seven manufacturers won team awards including a BSA team from Holland ridden by J. Flinterman, P. Knijnenburg and J. Roest.

An unfamiliar shot of Fred Rist riding Bill Nicholson's 500 B34 ('BSA 500') in the 1952 Scottish Six Days. Nicholson was a non-starter. Photo: Ray Biddle.

From then on, Fred Rist turned his back on both national and international events in favour of devoting his time and energies to the motorcycle business he was planning to open in Neath during 1952. This was a project he tackled with his customary enthusiasm until suddenly he was asked to take part in one of the boldest enterprises ever planned by BSA — one which Fred Rist with his experience, expertise and intelligence was ideally suited to lead. If anything demanded inspired leadership it was this BSA project in which three 500cc A7 Star Twin models — selected at random from standard factory stock — were to be submitted to the jurisdiction of the ACU for a Certified and Observed Test. The test involved a 3500-mile trip across Europe and up to Oslo in Norway, together with participation in the International Six Days Trial, that year based at Bad Aussee (included in the second day's run of the ill-fated event of 1939) situated high up among the lakes and mountains south-east of Salzburg.

Fred Rist, one-time regular soldier and gifted raconteur, was one of the great riders and characters to grace motorcycle sport in the immediate post-World War Two years.

Having agreed to delay the opening of his new business in Neath, Fred put his heart and soul into what was to become one of the great motorcycling epics. That year the ISDT proved to be one of the toughest ever, such that it eliminated every British team with the sole exception of that team of Star Twins ridden by Fred Rist, Brian Martin and the author of this book. Between them, they lost not a single mark, notwithstanding the standard specification of the models they rode. For   71 the British Trophy and Vase teams the event was an unmitigated disaster which put into perspective all the more, the incredible performance of those legendary Star Twins. That BSA won the Maudes Trophy for that glowing achievement goes without saying. That the Maudes Trophy has never again been won by a British manufacturer gives food for thought.

That whole enterprise can be looked upon as Fred Rist's last performance, completed in his usual elegant style. Unlike his two team mates, he never fell off once. At the conclusion of that epic 5,000 miles, not a scratch or blemish gave any indication of what had been accomplished.

A natural extrovert — though modest with it — ebullient, gregarious and a gifted raconteur, Fred Rist, one-time regular soldier, devoted his whole competition career to BSA. In so doing, he emerged as one of the brightest and most colourful segments in the great BSA competitions mosaic.

Chapter Six

The Irish Wizard

WITH BSA's five solo premier awards won in succession during the immediate post-war period, it is possible that the other manufacturers felt somewhat out in the cold. Nevertheless, even BSA would know that it could not go on for ever; that it was only a question of time. The break came with the Cotswold Cups Trial in early March 1946 when Jim Alves — first time out as a Triumph works rider — shattered the trials world by winning the premier award with a 350cc vertical twin. He went on to consolidate both the Triumph Twin and himself as leading contenders by winning two more national trials that season; the Mitchell in April and West of England in October.

Royal Enfield also broke their duck by winning the Alan Trophy Trial in September, then, a little later, the John Douglas Trial in November. Ariel of Selly Oak also had two victories with ex-Army riding instructor Bob Ray winning the Travers Trophy Trial in September and the highly-prestigious British Experts in December. Norton, Matchless and AJS, however, had a poor year, with one win in the Bemrose for the former and one win in the Clayton Trophy (a non-trade supported national) for Matchless and a solitary win for AJS in the Southern Experts. Without a doubt it was BSA's year and they made capital out of it with full-page press advertisements in big, bold type.

It was a similar success story in the Irish Republic where in March that year Artie Bell — destined to win the 1948 Senior TT on a works Norton — won the old-established Patland Cup Trial with his 350cc BSA. At the end of the season BSA adverts were proclaiming *Over 50% of the 1946 Classic Trials won by BSA*. They were merely stating fact.

1946 also saw the re-birth of national scrambles with two receiving trade support; the Cotswold Scramble in June and the Lancashire Grand National in November — both producing BSA victories. They enhanced still further the envied list of success, the famous Cotswold event proving the launching pad for a long sequence of impressive wins by Bill Nicholson, to establish him as a rider without par. In this his first ever scramble, he used his own 350 BSA fitted with McCandless swinging-arm rear suspension, riding with an effortless style which became his hall-mark. He won both the Junior and Senior races looking, according to press reporters, deceptively slow in comparison to most riders who were clearly working hard at the same job. In winning the 350 Junior Race he had to beat pre-war expert Jack Williams (Norton) who eventually finished second. Ray Scovell (BSA) was third and Phil Hewitt (BSA) was second in the 250 Lightweight Race. Fred Rist, on the little 'Flying 250', was second to Nicholson in the Senior Race despite being slowed by a flat rear tyre during the last few laps.

Another old-established classic re-introduced on 23rd November 1946 was the notorious Scott Trial, a unique event decided on time and observation wherein the fastest finisher establishes 'standard' time against which all other finishers are penalized and to be deemed a finisher a rider must do so within two hours of Standard Time. Unquestionably it is one of the most demanding events of its type in the world, so it was only fitting and appropriate that such an event be added to the list of BSA successes for that year.

In winning, Bill Nicholson achieved the rare double of making both fastest time (Standard Time) and best performance on observation, to win the Alfred A. Scott Memorial Trophy. In addition, the BSA team of Nicholson. Fred Rist and Terry Hill won the manufacturers' team award. Terry Hill from Belfast was Best Newcomer and Rex Young (BSA) made fourth best performance (tying with Allan Jefferies).

Rounding off the season in the British experts Trial, Fred Rist lost the premier award to Bob Ray (Ariel) by four marks, with Nicholson, hindered by tyre trouble, in sixth place. There was a degree of compensation when Fred Rist won the Northern Experts with fellow BSA competitor A.C. Partridge winning the sidecar title.

If the list of successes for 1946 was impressive then that for the following 1947 season could almost be described as stunning. Of the fifteen trade-supported national trials held during the season, BSA won no less than nine, leaving the remaining six to be shared by AJS (three wins), Triumph (two wins) and Matchless (one win). Norton, Ariel and Royal Enfield never broke the duck. In the non-trade-supported nationals, Norton did manage to win one, as did Royal Enfield, with Triumph adding three more wins, AJS a further two, and BSA two more.

But that was not all, for on top of that impressive list of wins, BSA also won nine best trade team awards and six sidecar premier awards,

This picture of Bill Nicholson winning the 1948 Mitchell Trial in South Wales personifies the neat, aggressive and classical style which characterized the most successful British trials rider of that period. Photo: The Classic Motor Cycle.

A pensive-looking Bill Nicholson at the start of the 1949 Colmore Cup Trial from Shipston-on-Stour, Warwickshire, with 'BSA 350' instead of the more customary 'BSA 500'.

with no less than 18 class cups. As for the three classic scrambles — the Sunbeam Point-to-Point, the Cotswold Scramble and the Lancashire Grand National — all trade-supported, it was a pure BSA benefit with the incredible Bill Nicholson winning the lot. He won both the Junior and Senior races of the two former events and was outright winner of the one-race Grand National on Holcombe Moor. As icing on the cake, Fred Rist followed Nicholson home in the Sunbeam Junior Race, with Phil Hewitt winning the 250 class. Setting the seal on another BSA day they won the team award in both events. The Bill Nicholson double victory in the Cotswold Scramble in June was backed-up by Ted Ogden finishing second in the Senior race, Fred Rist winning the 250 class.

Profound as was the BSA achievement for 1947, even more so was the individual performance of Bill Nicholson, that short, stocky, irascible character from Ulster. From his first appearance on the British mainland in the Colmore Cup Trial of 1946, he had stamped his authority in both trials and scrambles like few before. Apart from the Colmore Cup Trial of 1947 every other trade-supported national trial victory of BSA that year had been accomplished by the irrepressible Irishman. Although the two principal events in the calendar — the Scottish Six Days and the British Experts — eluded him, his domination was virtually complete.

Bill Nicholson 'gunning' the BSA up a typical Cotswold leafmould-surfaced gradient in the 1949 Colmore Cup Trial. Photo: Ray Biddle.

Nicholson's riding style was that of the born artist, natural and gifted, and of the perfectionist where every move is co-ordinated, elegant and precise, like that of a ballet dancer. In trials there was never the need for him to dally at observed sections with the hope of improved conditions imposed by time or the passage of other riders — a tactic destined to blight trials in later years. One quick look seemed sufficient for him to determine tactics before he kicked his B34 into life to tackle the observed section in the neat, positive style which was his hallmark.

If possible, his riding style in scrambles was even more impressive; neat, polished and poetical, completely devoid of untidy aggression yet masterful and dominant. He was the supreme trials and scramble artist of the period and there are many who believe that his style has never since been equalled. Endearing yet unpredictable, the enigmatic Bill Nicholson was not attracted to motorcycles until relatively late in life in his native Ulster where, for a period, he was employed in the preparation of racing cars. Born in 1917, it was not until 1939 that his interest in two 77 wheels was aroused sufficiently to purchase a brand new 350 Triumph Tiger 80.

Hardly had he got started in the sport when war came and with it the loss of the Tiger 80. It was commandeered by the Army authorities. Then in 1941, working for Chambers of Belfast, the BSA distributors for Northern Ireland, he was able to purchase one of the rare military-type 350cc ohv BSA models turned down by the British War Department — the lightweight B30 model with hairpin-valve springs. It was with this model that he began his meteoric riding career, winning the 1942 Patland Cup Trial in the Irish Republic, his first big win.

Bill Nicholson astride the A7 Twin he tried in the early events of 1948 and with which he won the Hurst Cup time-and-observation national in Northern Ireland. He is pictured with Arthur Crawford of the BSA competitions shop.

By 1945 he was working for Artie Bell and it was this move more than any which influenced the future course of events, bringing him into contact with that coterie of blue-blooded Irish enthusiasts like Terry Hill, Cromie and Rex McCandless and Ernie Lyons who, between them, more than upheld and perpetuated the already great reputation of Irish riders. In such infectious and talented company it is not surprising that Bill Nicholson soon developed a taste and appetite for speed events. In

78

June 1945, in a grasstrack meeting at Dunmerry organized by the Ulster MCC, he was beaten only by Ernie Lyons and Artie Bell to finish in front of the McCandless brothers and Terry Hill. One month later, at a road race meeting run by the Ards MCC at Bangor Castle, he was second to Ernie Lyons, when Rex McCandless, riding his first Triumph-engined special, finished third. At the same meeting twelve months later, in winning the class 'D' event on his 350 BSA, Nicholson equalled the lap record set by Ernie Lyons with his 500 Triumph the year before.

The 1952 Bemrose Trophy Trial held on March 29 — the coldest March day for 81 years — was won by Bill Nicholson on his B34 Gold Star. Here he is seen entering a watersplash used in the Derbyshire course.

At the beginning of the 1946 season, in which he was destined to rocket to stardom as a BSA works rider, he won the Rusk Memorial Trial (organized by the Ards MCC in memory of their countryman Walter Rusk). After his very successful début in English trials with his second best performance in the Colmore Cup Trial (beaten only by Fred Rist) it was back home to Belfast before returning to England for the Cotswold Scramble in June. It was this latter event which established him as a brilliant and peerless rider with a neat, feet-up style, which defied adequate description.

Thereafter the motorcycle press frequently eulogised his superiority in almost lyrical prose, such as after the Isle of Man Grand National Scramble of TT week 1947 when *The Motor Cycle* reporter wrote: 'Effortlessly, stylishly, safely, the unapproachable Nicholson (500 BSA with McCandless suspension) was a whole lap ahead of the second man before six laps had been covered, eventually winning by more than seven minutes.' It was that element of superiority which so often made his victories outstanding; the means rather than the end which put him in a class of his own. In the 1946 Scott Trial, for example, Bill Nicholson not only made best performance on observation but also made fastest time, being *twenty minutes* ahead of the next fastest, Bob Ray (Ariel), himself not noted for hanging about. Organized by the Middlesbrough & Stockton Clubs amongst the Cleveland Hills of North Yorkshire, the event started from Swainby and traversed a 25-mile course of wild virgin moorland littered with gullies, streams, rocks, mud, water holes, bogs, bracken, heather and precipitous gradients — a mixture of sheer horror which had to be covered twice.

Notwithstanding his talents in the saddle, Nicholson was also a very able engineer. During September of 1946 he had accepted an invitation to join the staff of the BSA competitions department where, over the years, and with the backing of the factory facilities, he was able to pursue a programme of development with the objective of making the B32 and B34 trials and scramble machines more competitive. His previous involvement in Belfast with the McCandless brothers and Ernie Lyons in their private pursuit of making a better motorcycle rolling chassis had given Nicholson definite ideas in this direction.

Bert Perrigo recalled that during Nichoslon's eight years at Small Heath he was given a free rein within the guidelines of company policy which enabled him to make a useful contribution to frame design with improved damping systems on both telescopic front forks and rear suspension damper units. The all-welded trials frame with duplex front down tubes running in one loop, from steering head to rear wheel, was a product of the Nicholson fertile brain. Considerably lighter than the existing lugged frame, the Gold Star engine/gearbox unit mounted in an

Bill Nicholson on his way to winning his one and only International Six Days gold medal in the 1950 event held in Wales. This picture, taken during the one-hour speed test, gives some idea of the rain-lashed conditions prevailing at Eppynt at the time.

alloy sub-frame could be removed in minutes as a sub-assembly. Bill Nicholson used his one-off prototype throughout the 1951 season, when he won the first of his ACU Trials Stars and by 1953 the frame had been adopted for the production trials model and the rest of the works team.

The Nicholson influence was also apparent in the new swinging-arm frame first used on the works scramble models during the 1952 season and on the production Gold Star models used in the International Six Days Trial of 1952.

Although using a 350 B32 up to and including the 1947 Colmore Cup Trial in which he won the 350 Cup, thereafter he always rode a 500cc B34 model blessed with the distinctive (too distinctive, some would argue!) personalized number of 'BSA 500'. Despite his shattering dominance with the 500cc single in 1947, Bill was curious to know more about the potential of the twin-cylinder engine under trials conditions, a curiosity no doubt engendered by the success of Jim Alves with the Triumph twin. Nicholson thus converted a rigid-frame A7 twin, substituting lightweight 'C' group forks and a 21 inch front wheel with a   81

Bill Nicholson (left) outside the BSA competitions shop in 1953 with two namesakes: Staff Sergeant Alick Nicholson who won a special first class award in the Scottish Six Days with (right) American Nick Nicholson who won the 1951 Catalina Grand Prix with his Gold Star.

$5^{1}/_{2}$ inch diameter front brake, for the standard heavyweight components. With alloy mudguards, a two-into-one exhaust system, and a larger rear wheel sprocket giving ratios of 5.4, 7.9, 12.7 and 17.1, the complete machine was alleged to be lighter than the B34 single then in use.

Other than trying the model on local muddy sections, he first used the twin in serious competition during the all-important Colmore Cup Trial of 1948 when, rather ironically, the premier award was won by Jim Alves on a Triumph twin without loss of marks. Nicholson won the 'closed' award as best Sunbac member with a loss of two marks. A pretty good start by any standard. In the Kickham Trial which followed — won by Hugh Viney (AJS) — Nicholson won the Unlimited Cup. Just one week later, in his favourite Hurst Cup Trial in Northern Ireland (another time and observation event), he won the premier award. Despite this early success, after the next two nationals — the Victory Cup and Bemrose Trophy — in which he won a first class award in each, it seems that Bill Nicholson knew in his heart that he could be better on the traditional big single.

In the Cotswold Cups Trial he reverted to a B34 and proved the point by winning the premier award without loss of marks, in doing so making dashing clean climbs of such hills as Henwood where the exhaust note of the BSA on 'full chat' reverberated among the trees, thrilling even those at the foot of the curving hill who were unable to witness the spectacle of the climb. Although victory in the Scottish Six Days eluded him as it had the year before, during the season three more trade-support nationals were scooped-up by Nicholson and the B34 (the Travers, Mitchell Memorial and West of England) and the 500 Cup in the Southern Trial.

Clearly the characteristics of the twin-cylinder engine were not suited to the Nicholson technique or temperament. Unlike Jim Alves, who had to persevere with his twin, like it or not, Bill had the big B34 single to fall back on when his curiosity had been satisfied. It has been alleged that the main purpose of the Nicholson-A7 twin exercise was to obtain data relative to the use of Star Twins in the ACU-Observed test of 1952. 'Nonsense'! said Bert Perrigo with feeling when the point was put to him. 'When Bill played with the trials A7 we had not even thought of the ACU test'. Perrigo also added that when Bill Nicholson forsook the B34 in favour of the A7, the choice was his own, freely taken.

After Nicholson's West of England victory, he had to settle for the 500 Cup in the Southern Trial — an event won by arch rival Hugh Viney (AJS) on 16th October — then suddenly it was near disaster. Practising locally on Gay Hill, a section where there was usually the need to skirt deep bog-holes by brushing close to the bushes and trees bordering the lane, a sharp thorn pierced his eye, causing temporary blindness in that eye. As a result he missed both the John Douglas Trial and the awesome Lancashire Grand National, yet despite the injury impairing his sight for at least six months he could not resist competing in the Scott Trial which he had dominated for the two previous years. However, with the event as tough as ever, he had to pull out at the conclusion of the first lap, which he completed in some distress. That unfortunate incident robbed him of the chance to win the Scott Trial six times in succession, for thereafter he won again in 1949, 1950 and 1951.

Even in 1952, when he lost a footrest very early in the 'race' and also suffered a flat tyre, he still finished runner-up to winner John Draper (that year Norton mounted). Like the Hurst Cup Trial of Northern

The Nicholson scramble style which elevated him above all others for a period, winning every trade-supported national scramble in 1947. He 84 *rarely, if ever, used his feet. Photo:* Ray Biddle.

Bill Nicholson winning the 1950 Italian Motocross Grand Prix on a B34 Gold Star with plunger-type rear suspension. Note also the exposed primary chain covered only by a guard.

Ireland, where time as well as observation are of equal importance, the Scott Trial was a happy Nicholson hunting ground. It was the type of event in which he was supreme, demanding, as it does to this very day, skill, split-second judgement, courage and great stamina, all of them attributes possessed in full by the great Bill Nicholson.

So whilst he did not dominate the 1948 trials season as he had the year before — his pattern of wins was disrupted by the A7 Twin experiment then his eye injury — he still headed the opposition with five premier award wins from the total of fifteen trade-supported nationals. In comparison, his main rival, Hugh Viney, won four, and Jim Alves three. Taking into account non-trade-supported nationals, Hugh Viney's score went up to six wins, with AJS the top-scoring factory with seven wins. Nicholson, Viney and Jim Alves dominated the season with 14 wins between them. Eight other riders secured one win each from the rest of the nationals.

As in 1947 all the BSA national trial victories of 1948 had been achieved by that remarkable Irishman.

Having started the 1948 scramble season with another characteristic double win in the Sunbeam Point-to-Point Junior and Senior events, it came as rather a surprise when he failed to finish in the Senior Race of 85 the Cotswold Scramble. After a race-long duel with Basil Hall, he was forced to retire with gearbox trouble. With Fred Rist winning the Junior Race, however, it was still a good day for BSA. In addition to winning the team award, Bill Nicholson, first time out on a 250 model, made amends by winning the 250 Lightweight Race.

On reflection it seems that despite Bill Nicholson's ascendancy in British scrambles — with few doubting that he was the finest British rider in the sport during that era — he was nowhere near as effective on the European Continent. In the first Motocross des Nations in 1947, for example, he had to concede victory to Auguste 'Man Mountain' Mingels of Belgium with his Triumph, a fiery performer who later rode Matchless before changing to his locally-produced FN. In the same international classic of 1948 he was beaten by Nick Jansen of Belgium who, like his countrymen Marcel Cox and Andre Milhoux, was BSA mounted — the trio winning the team prize for BSA. One of Nicholson's rare Continental motocross victories came with the Italian Motocross Grand Prix of 1950 when he finished ahead of M. Meunier (Sarolea) of Belgium and fellow-countryman Nick Jansen, by then Sarolea mounted.

In British events, however, whilst no longer dominating as before, he was still in contention; still the man to beat. In 1949 he again did the double in the Cotswold Scramble, winning both Senior and Junior Races. Earlier in the 1949 season though, with the young John Draper winning the Junior Race of the Sunbeam Point-to-Point, Bill had to concede victory in the Senior Race to Basil Hall, then Matchless mounted. But yet another team award went to the Small Heath team. At Shrubland Park in a new trade-supported event near Ipswich in deepest Suffolk, Bill Nicholson won the Senior race (with another team award for BSA) despite a tremendous effort by Basil Hall who had to settle for second place in extremely dusty conditions. It seemed that whilst Bill Nicholson was riding as brilliantly as ever, his high standard was being emulated by a new breed of post-war scramble exponents who began to dispute his authority and share the glory. It was a similar situation in national trials where he did not quite measure up to his remarkable level of 1947. Nonetheless he won four national trials in 1949 — the Victory, the Hurst Cup, the inevitable Scott Trial and the Cambrian. Again the Scottish Six Days eluded him, despite having taken the lead during the week together with team mate Draper.

1950 was significant as the year in which the ACU first introduced the Star contest with the result based on the season's events — a series later renamed the British Championships that applied to all classes of motorcycle sport. For 1950 a rider's ten best results from the season's 25 national trials were taken into consideration, with the result that Jim Alves with his Triumph went into the history books as the first solo

Another shot of Bill Nicholson taken after winning an international motocross at Malmo, Sweden in 1951.

winner of the ACU Trials Drivers' Star with a total of 76 points. It is of interest to note that in claiming the title, Alves had won only two nationals during the season (the West of England and Perce Simon) for whereas in 1948 the season had been dominated by three riders (Nicholson, Viney and Alves) no less than 15 riders shared the national wins for 1950. Like Jim Alves, Hugh Viney won only two (the John Douglas and St. Davids) but both Rex Young (Norton) and Artie Ratcliffe (Matchless) won three each.

Bill Nicholson also won three nationals during the season — the Southern Trial, the Scott (yet again) and the British Experts; the latter being BSA's first solo victory since that of Fred Povey in 1934. Based on victories only, the honours for 1950 were shared by Rex Young, Artie Ratcliffe and Bill Nicholson.

All Bill's victories in 1950 came very late in the season and it seems that he maintained this form for the early events of 1951 with three quick victories in the Victory Cup, the Hurst Cup and the Kickham trials. His form could have been attributed to his new prototype with the lighter frame, or simply a renewed determination to win the 1951 ACU Star. Either way, he maintained that form for the remainder of the season to   87

Plastered from head to foot with liquid mud, Bill Nicholson forges ahead in the atrocious conditions often encountered in British scrambles. Circa 1950/51, location not known.

win three more trials — the Red Rose, the Scott and the Perce Simon — and for good measure the Southern Experts. During the season he had won no less than seven nationals, plus five 500 Class Cups to claim the ACU Star convincingly with a total of 90 points out of the possible 100. Joint runners-up were Rex Young and Jim Alves on 78 points. It was very much a Bill Nicholson season.

It was a very similar pattern for 1952, with Nicholson again winning the solo ACU Star, the first rider to win it more than once. He did so by gaining premier award wins in five nationals; taking the 500 Class Cup in four, and being runner-up in the Scott Trial. With a total of 85 points his Star win was almost as convincing as that of the previous year though in this instance runner-up Gordon Jackson was only four marks astern.

John Draper, David Tye, Tom Ellis and Brian Martin also finished inside the top ten.

The Nicholson era of scramble dominance lasted just five years. During the later 1940s it seemed he was capable of going on for ever. Short and stocky, he was as strong as an ox and at most events where fellow riders had come off and bent handlebars, it was Nicholson who was prevailed upon to straighten them out with nothing more than the strength of his well-proportioned arms. Apart from his victory in the Italian motocross Grand Prix in 1950, his only British scramble win with the 500 B34 was in the Senior Race of the Cotswold Scramble. He was second in the 350 Junior Race at Shrubland Park and second in the Experts Grand National at Rollswood Farm. But he did have three additional wins which seemed almost out of character when he won the Ultra-Lightweight Race at the Cotswold Scramble, Shrubland Park and the Experts Grand National — with a little 123cc BSA Bantam, the first time the factory had entered their lightweight utility in national scrambles. At the end of the season, Nicholson also tried the Bantam in the non-trade-supported Manville Trial when he won a first class award. He did not feature at all in the trade-supported national scrambles of 1951, but in 1952 he was runner-up to Geoff Ward (AJS) in the Experts Grand National.

Bill Nicholson's relative failure to shine in either the Scottish Six Days Trial or the ISDT is one of the strange paradoxes of the sport, and not easily explained, for ability was there in abundance. It supports the view that skill in itself is not enough. Temperament and attitude have a bearing, probably more so with long-duration events than with those of short duration. Whilst his best ride in Scotland was a sixth place in 1947 it can hardly be termed a failure, yet relative to his dominance in the other nationals that season, Bill himself would class it thus. In view of his form that season he clearly started in the Scottish as red-hot favourite and completed the opening day without loss of marks. But he was not alone for seven other riders did likewise, including two other BSA riders — fellow works rider Phil Hewitt and privateer Tom Miryless.

From the second day, the story was quite different for with a loss of six marks, Hugh Viney (AJS) emerged as the new leader. Whilst all the other competitors — including Nicholson — increased their losses daily, Viney pegged his at six, to score the first of his history-making hat-trick of wins. With a total of 36 marks, Bill Nicholson had to settle for a 'humble' special first class award having lost the 500 Cup to Bob Ray (Ariel).

For 1948 Bill made a disastrous start by dropping no less than 13 on the first day. Even the immaculate and phlegmatic Viney dropped five that day, leaving only Jim Alves (Triumph) and Tom Ellis (Royal

BSA: Competition History

Enfield) unpenalized. By the end of the week, however, by which time Viney's winning score had gone up to 27, Bill had conceded 44 marks — to again lose the 500 Cup to Bob Ray (Ariel), taking home another one-pint pewter tankard awarded to those to win special first class awards.

In 1949 it looked like being a case of third time lucky for by the end of the third day the little Irishman was in the lead with a loss of eight

The BSA double victors of the 1950 British Experts Trial with (left) Bill Nicholson holding the Skefko Gold Cup and (right) Harold Tozer and passenger Jack Wilkes with the Palmer Trophy. BSA works manager Tom Whittington congratulates Tozer, whilst sales manager George Savage does likewise with Jack Wilkes.

marks, which he shared with fellow BSA teamster John Draper. Hugh Viney was in a lowly fifth place, with a loss of 15 marks. Then on the Thursday disaster struck. It had been raining hard all night long, and as riders got away from Fort William, heading for the rough Mandally Road to Tomdoun, it was still teeming down.

At Kinlochhourn, after a 17-mile stretch of atrocious going to be covered in 39 minutes, a long queue of riders waited to tackle the ten-section hill which wound its way up the slippery mountainside, adding to the wet misery of all concerned, riders and officials alike. After Kinlochhourn, where only Viney and Jack Blackwell (Norton) cleaned all ten sections, there followed twenty miles of remote moorland devoid of any form of residence or shelter, to the lunch check at Glenelg. In between, after winding down the innumerable hairpin bends of Corron Hill, spread the vast flooded expanse of the Arnisdale River, which had to be forded by competitors. Before long, the far bank of the swirling brown river was like the aftermath of a battlefield, dotted with stranded riders working desperately to restore life to their drowned and salvaged bikes.

Some were successful, others were not. The latter included favourite Jim Alves, whose Triumph twin had sucked in water and bent the con-rods to put him out of the trial. Those with drowned motors who got going included both the leaders of the day before, Nicholson and Draper, the former getting mobile without too much trouble but poor Draper was stuck for half-an-hour before he induced life to the electrics once again. The river crossing played havoc with most competitors, changing the face of the trial. It cost Nicholson twelve marks on time and Draper a massive 34. As if by magic the incomparable Hugh Viney conquered the river and reached Glenelg unpenalized, to put him in a lead he never relinquished for the remainder of the week.

Fred Rist finished fifth overall with a loss of 33 marks and Bill Nicholson seventh, with a final tally of 34. Draper slumped to 21st with a final total of 70 marks lost. The Scottish solo premier award continued to elude BSA.

Another average ride in the Scottish of 1950 earned Nicholson nothing more rewarding than a special first class award and though entered for the events of both 1951 and 1952 he rode in neither. For 1953 he was not even entered (replaced by new boy Jeff Smith) but for the 1954 event he reappeared on the Scottish scene, this time on an unfamiliar 348cc B32 model. During the first three days he rode like the maestro of old and by the Wednesday was in sixth place — but before the day's run had ended, his luck had run out. On the way to Camashurich he collided with Bill Tiffen, the Velocette veteran, who had the misfortune to break his wrist. The incident also severely damaged 91

Nicholson's front forks, and at the conclusion of the day's run the officials took the unprecedented step of granting him one hour in which to repair them. Although he did his best, it proved of no avail for during Thursday the damaged forks seized up, putting paid to Bill's efforts. It proved to be Nicholson's swan-song in the Scottish.

If Nicholson's experience in the Highland classic was not the most rewarding of his career, neither was that of the ISDT. Although he had not taken part in the 1948 event in Italy, he was selected by the ACU to represent Great Britain in the British Vase 'B' team for 1949 on the strength of his overall ability. At the conclusion of that very dusty,

With competitions manager Bert Perrigo and sales director Stan Digby, Bill Nicholson displays his second successive ACU Trials Drivers' Star won in 1952. He rode the all-welded, duplex downtube frame model fitted with a Gold Star engine.

though relatively easy week, the British Trophy team was victorious, and though the British Vase 'A' team also remained unpenalized during the week, they lost the Vase contest to the Czechoslovakia CZ team on the results of the speed test at Eppynt. For the British Vase 'B' team, however, it was catastrophe, with Ted Breffit (Norton) out on the first day after a collision with Dutch Vase 'B' team member H. Veer (Jawa), who also retired. Then Bill Nicholson collided with a tree on the second day, which forced his retirement.

In the 1950 event, again held in Wales under devastating conditions, it seems Bill set out to redeem his reputation by winning his one and only ISDT gold medal after a faultless performance. Of the 61 competitors mounted on BSAs who set out on the first day, only nine won gold medals, such was its severity.

After his successful years of 1951 and 1952 with two ACU Trials' Stars to his credit, Bill's premier awards and class cups in national trials became fewer with the passing of time. In 1953 he won the popular Lamborelle Trial in Belgium and in 1954 the St. Davids Trial in Wales. Then, right at the end of 1954, marking the end of his employment at BSA, he pulled-off the British Experts solo title yet again. That Experts victory was a fitting climax, though he did have the occasional ride during the next year or two. He won the 500 Cup in the Shropshire Traders Cup of 1955 and in 1956 he could not resist one more go at his beloved Scott Trial wherein, riding a 50cc B32, he qualified for a first class award with a loss of 235 marks.

From then on he devoted his energies to sports car racing — to enhance even more the legend of his name. During his eight years as a BSA works rider he had achieved in excess of fifty premier awards in top-grade trade-supported national trials where competition was always at its greatest, during a period when it was at its toughest. Big-hearted, forever helpful, yet provocative and opinionated, no-one could deny — least of all his contemporaries — that Bill Nicholson was a superb and gifted rider who furthered the interests of BSA during those years of 1947 and 1948 in particular, more than all his fellow team riders put together.

In modern parlance, that great little Irishman was BSA's first Superstar.

Chapter Seven

Aces in the Pack

BY THE January of 1951, the BSA advertising department, headed by the pipe-smoking Noel Brealey, was in full cry with press advertising featuring the wins of those they termed the 'Five Aces in the Pack'. Full-page advertisements claimed that in 23 events during 1950 the 'five aces' had won between them 22 best solo awards, 7 best sidecars, 9 team prizes and 13 class awards. Whilst only card sharpers are capable of producing more than four aces in any one pack of cards, the BSA advertising gimmick was powerful stuff, emphasizing the collective strength of the works riders and their prolific success.

However, in this instance it seems that the BSA advertisement copy writers got carried away, indulging in a spasm of fantasy, for the figures claimed do not stand up to close scrutiny. Even with the assistance of two non-works riders (Bob Chidgey who won the Bemrose and W.G. 'Nipper' Parsons who won the Beggars Roost) BSA won only eight solo premier awards in national trials that year. Curiously, the sidecars wins are understated, for Harold Tozer actually made best sidecar performance in nine nationals, not seven.

A moot point indeed, for without doubt the five riders featured — Fred Rist, Bill Nicholson, John Draper, Harold Tozer and Basil Hall — were brilliant aces in the BSA pack who could be relied on to win most of the tricks without pretension. The make-up of the works team during that rewarding period changed to some extent by the end of the 1940s. Jack Blackwell was riding for Norton in 1947 and Phil Hewitt had departed from the UK for a new life in Australia (to return within months to take up a position with Douglas of Bristol).

Fred Povey retired quietly at the end of the 1946 season and pre-war development engineer and works rider Jack Amott, saturnine and reserved by nature, did the same thing during 1947 to devote the balance of his time with BSA developing the Gold Star. During 1946 he had won

THE MOTOR CYCLE, 11 JANUARY 1951

The striking BSA press advertisement of early 1951 proclaiming the BSA 'pack of aces' and detailing the very considerable catalogue of success achieved by them in 1950 when they were sweeping all before them.

the 250 Cup in the Victory, West of England and Southern Trials and he bowed-out with the 250 Cup in the Colmore of March 1947. As already noted, Jack worked for Rudge from 1928 until 1936 during which period he rode in the TT, having first ridden in the Junior of 1926 when he   95 finished 10th on a Montgomery. Despite his riding skills he devoted most of his time to development and by the time he returned to Small Heath he knew a great deal about cam design; indeed it seemed his main obsession. When riding in national trials with the 250 Empire Star BSA — on which he won the solo premier award in the Cotswold Cups of 1938 — he always carried a set of spare cams in his riding coat pocket, which he would fit at the bottom of any steep hill which he felt called for more power than he was getting from the 'soft' cams. Professionalism in motorcycle sport is as old as the hills.

Basil Hall — described by Ralph Venables as scrambling's greatest gentleman — secured many wins at home and abroad, riding BSA Gold Stars from 1950 to 1954.

Whilst the development of the Gold Star from its original 1938 specification can be attributed to a number of engineers, there are those who claim that it was Jack Amott who did more than most to put the Gold Star on its illustrious throne. He disappeared from the world of motorcycles when he left BSA to join the Austin Motor Company at Longbridge, Birmingham. However, before that came about, it was to Jack Amott in the engine test department that a young man who had just joined the BSA payroll was directed as an assistant. The young man's name was Geoff Duke. It was August 1947 and he had just been demobilized from the Army as a sergeant in the Royal Signals.

Sergeant G.E. Duke was first noted by the motorcycle press in the Ilkley Grand National when he rode a BSA WD M20 side-valve model which, with the help of Bert Perrigo, had the benefit of more ground clearance and lower gearing. He used the M20 in about six events, including the Scott Trial of 1946.

Never did the Gold Star look prettier than in 1949, here adorned with three of BSA's greatest aces — John Draper (left), Fred Rist (centre) and Bill Nicholson (right), positioned in front of the BSA main entrance.

Today, Geoff Duke recalls that when his Army demobilization date was approaching at a time when he was a member of the Royal Signals White Helmets Display Team, he wrote to Bert Perrigo about the prospects of a job in the BSA factory. When the reply was in the affirmative and the day of release came, Geoff invested his Army gratuity in a brand new B32 350 BSA; the perfectly standard over-the-counter catalogue model, and it was this on which he competed for the rest of that season. Turning his back on his home town of St. Helens, Geoffrey Duke, now in mufti, headed for the industrial Midlands, not unlike Dick Whittington, to seek his fame and fortune. In doing just that — becoming one of the greatest road racers of all time — he had never fogotten the help he had from BSA and Bert Perrigo in particular. 'I will always appreciate the help Bert Perrigo gave me as an unknown in those days,' he recalls. 'It was Bert's help which put my feet on the bottom rung of the ladder,' he added.

BSA aces in the pack surrounded by L to R: Bert Perrigo, Stan Digby, George Savage, Alf Child of the Rich Child Corporation (BSA importers for the East Coast of the USA) and Tommy McDermott, who rode brilliantly in British scrambles in the summer of 1949.

In the short space of three or four months, on the standard production B32, Geoff Duke won the Cheshire Centre Championship; the 350 Cup in the national Clayton Trophy Trial (only one mark down on winner Charlie Mein), tied with Rex Young as runner-up to Bill Nicholson in the infamous Scott Trial of 1947, tied with Hugh Viney for the premier award in the John Douglas Trial — losing by $1/5$th second on the special test to settle for the 350 Cup; and finished ninth in the British Experts. In addition, he was seventh in the Lancashire Grand National.

Auspicious as that brief spell was, and as much as he liked trials riding, it was not what Geoff Duke really wanted. He had set his heart on road racing and after a brief meeting with AMC at Woolwich, he made an appointment to see Gilbert Smith of Norton Motors (even here Bert Perrigo was the go-between) with the result which is now a part of motorcycle history.

On the 31st December 1947, Duke's five-month stay at Armoury Road came to an end, but not before leaving Jack Amott's shop to join

Bill Nicholson, Fred Rist and Arthur Crawford in the competitions department. In January he moved over to Bracebridge Street on the other side of the town where he was to ride Nortons in both trials and racing. But by 1952 he was back with a 350 B32 in the Kickham Trial and in 1954 he once again rode in the Scottish Six Days, winning a first class award with a BSA B32.

With the departure of both Phil Hewitt and Geoff Duke, a new name was added to the list of BSA works riders; a new ace in the 'pack'. It was that of John Draper, who joined the works line-up in time to ride in the 1948 Kickham Trial as a fully-fledged works runner. Then in 1950, with the beginnings of the most dramatic decade in the competitions history of BSA, Basil Hall — the first of the new post-war breed of scramble specialists — joined and strengthened the impressive BSA line-up.

A feature of those immediate post-war years in the British motorcycle industrial setting of the Midlands was the number of overseas riders— both competing types and otherwise — who left their homelands for periods ranging from months to years, taking jobs in the various motorcycle factories. This gave them the opportunity to taste and revel in the British and European world of motorcycling which, to many, — Australians in particular — had represented their Mecca since boyhood. BSA and Norton, more than most, were almost cosmopolitan. In this bracket fell one Tommy McDermott who hailed from the United States of America. Sponsored by Alf Child, president of the Rich Child Corporation — East Coast BSA importers and distributors — McDermott was included in the payroll of BSA during 1949, when he joined Bill Nicholson and Arthur Crawford in the competitions shop to quickly prove more than adept at the British sport of scrambling. In the Cotswold Scramble in June that year one of the motorcycle weeklies reported: 'The highlight of the 350 Junior Race was undoubtedly the fine riding of T. McDermott, an American over here to see how we do things. If he stays much longer he will be showing us! At the end of the first lap he was leading by a considerable distance. Although he increased his lead on lap two, on lap three both Nicholson and Alves got past him. But when Alves had trouble and slipped back to sixth place, McDermott moved back into second place behind Nicholson.' Completing a BSA one-two-three-four was Fred Rist who was third, and W.H. Millburn who was fourth.

He repeated the performance at Shrubland Park when only Basil Hall denied him victory in the Junior Race of that trade-supported classic. In September he tried his hand in the International Six Days Trial in Wales, where he won a gold medal, almost certainly the first American to do so post-war. But then a study of his record would have

99

revealed him as a rider of no mean ability, for earlier that year he had finished sixth on a works-prepared prototype 500 Gold Star in the Daytona 200-Mile Experts classic — in those days held on a course embracing a long stretch of the famous beach with a parallel section of surfaced highway. On his return home, he did even better in the 1950 Daytona event by finishing third, again on a Gold Star. Four years later, in 1954, he was third once more when BSA filled the first five places, with a sixth BSA in eighth place. In the 1956 200-Mile Expert Race he was fourth, one of four BSA riders chasing home winner John Gibon on the big Harley who won at 94.21 mph. There can be no doubt that had that quiet and unassuming young American stayed to contest the British scamble season of 1950, quite a few feathers would have been ruffled.

More familiar in riding gear and helmets, this line-up of BSA aces look a little self-conscious in their natty suiting with L to R: Basil Hall, Harold Tozer, John Avery, Bert Perrigo, Bill Nicholson and John Draper. Taken in Sweden in 1951 'baggy' trousers must have been 'in' at that time!

By 1950 both the 350 B32 and 500 B34 models were proving very popular with the average private clubman, with an increasing number featured in the entry list of every national and open-to-centre event. At the 1949 North v South Scramble for example, held on the old grass circuit at Brands Hatch, no fewer than ten riders in the field of 25 were BSA mounted, that being easily the most dominant make.

The official works riders, still using B34 engines with alloy cylinder head and barrel, were by then relying upon the BSA plunger rear suspension frame, including Bill Nicholson who hitherto, had used the McCandless conversion. To improve its behaviour when subjected to the rigours of scrambling, the standard springing was aided by a simple system of oil damping. It was never intended to be other than a stop-gap measure because Nicholson was already campaigning for the superior swinging-arm system.

Although the solo title in the British Experts Trial, like the solo premier award in the Scottish Six Days, continued to elude the pack of BSA aces as the forties came to an end, it had been four years of considerable achievement, excelling that of all others in the business. It was but the beginning; no more than the rumbles preceding the storm created by the launch of the swinging-arm Gold Star which was destined to achieve world-wide success on an unprecedented scale.

Chapter Eight

Three-Wheeled Patriarch

OF ALL the aces featured by BSA in the press advertisements of 1951, there was one name above all that stood out for consistency, like an anchor man, the solid pillar of the team. It was the name of the phlegmatic and corpulent Harold Tozer of droll wit who, with his regular passenger Jack Wilkes, established a near-monopoly in the sidecar class of trials during his peak years.

In his seven-year reign as the leading chair expert he achieved a total of wins probably matched only by Harold Flook before him and Ron Langston since. In 1947 he beat the entire solo entry to win the Colmore Cup itself.

Unfortunately, the record books do not indicate his true greatness when measured by wins in the ACU Trials Drivers' Star contest for this series was not established until 1950 when, true to form, Tozer won the title with nearly double the marks scored by his nearest rival, Arthur Humphries. When studying the results of that period, it becomes crystal clear that had the championship been established in 1946 at the outset of post-war events, Harold Tozer would have won the title six years in succession (though, through the vagaries of the adopted formula, the title in 1951 was shared with Arthur Humphries). Nonetheless, Tozer did win the British Experts sidecar title no less than five times, including a hat-trick of wins from 1946 to 1948.

But it wasn't roses all the way. With the old pre-war outfit DOA 664, first registered in late 1936, fitted with a 1939 M24 Gold Star engine and updated by the fitting of telescopic front forks, it was months before Harold Tozer found his true form in that first post-war season of 1946. The first six trade-supported events did not produce a single sidecar premier award. The Colmore sidecar award went to Freddie Perks — a BSA win nonetheless — and the Kickham to the forceful one-legged, one-time racer Harold Taylor (Ariel), who also took the

Passengered by Maurice Wright, Harold Tozer mounts the wall at the top of 'Mount Pleasant' in the Kickham Trial of 1946. Later, he struck a long sequence of dominating wins in British national trials. Photo: The Classic Motor Cycle.

sidecar premier in the Beggar's Roost West Country national at Easter (and later also the Southern Experts at the end of the season). Dennis Mansell, the jovial and rotund Norton director, won the Victory Cup itself, plus the sidecar premier in the Bemrose and Mitchell Trials, with Bill Hayward winning the Cotswold Cups with his sidecar-wheel drive Baughan outfit. The old master Harold Flook won the Travers. All this without Tozer getting a look-in. If he felt despair he didn't show it.

Then suddenly, in August, amid the hills and dales of Derbyshire, he won the Clayton Trophy Trial, a non trade-supported national event, highly popular with trade riders and private clubmen alike. That was his first post-war success and it was like opening the floodgates. Although Dennis Mansell won the Reliance Trial in October, with fellow Norton-driver Harold Flook winning the John Douglas in November, Tozer won the rest in quick succession: the Red Rose, the Alan Trophy, West of England and the Southern. Then, in early December, the most prestigious of all, the British Experts. So, after seven months without a   103 win, he finished the 1946 season with no less than six national sidecar premier awards in comparison with the four wins of Dennis Mansell, the three of Harold Taylor, two of Harold Flook and the solitary wins of Freddie Perks in the Colmore and A. Partridge (BSA) in the Northern Experts. BSA crews had won 50% of the sidecar premier awards in the sixteen major events of the season.

Harold Tozer, passengered by Jack Wilkes, on his way to his sensational outright win of the Colmore Cup Trial of 1947, beating the entire solo entry with no marks lost. The section here is Kineton and Tozer is using his pre-war outfit 'DOA 664'.

By 1946, however, Harold Tozer was no newcomer to three-wheels. He had campaigned sidecar outfits from the early 1930s in trials, grasstrack and road racing, having entered his first grasstrack race meeting at Chipping Norton in Oxfordshire on 26th July 1931 when only 17 years of age. By the time he was 20, he had graduated to road racing, to become both a star and lap-record holder at Donington Park where he battled with the greats of the day — such as the likes of Harold Taylor, Bill Marsh, Len Taylor and Kim Collett. Then his luck ran out. At the race meeting held in conjunction with the ACU National Rally which converged on Donington Park on 8th July 1934, the rear bottom fork-link spindle broke while he was scrapping for the lead with Bill Rose in the second sidecar race and approaching the Hairpin on lap five. The frame cradle dug into the track surface, causing the outfit to somersault.

Although the accident looked horrendous, Harold recalled that

With typical pouting expression and almost displacing passenger Jack Wilkes in the chair, Harold Tozer storms Mamore in the Scottish Six Days circa 1947/48. He won the sidecar premier award in both 1948 and 1950. Photo: The Classic Motor Cycle.

relatively speaking, the injuries to himself and his passenger were of a minor nature, so much so that they were back racing before the season was out. However, just two months previously, he had gone to Scotland for the first time to compete in the Scottish Six Days with his 596cc Norton trials outfit where, with a loss of 53 marks, he collected a silver cup. He was also noticed by the press when *Motor Cycling's* reporter observed that: 'Although still very young, Tozer is already a star at Donington and may one day be so in trials.' How right that reporter was.

Soon after the Scottish, Nortons loaned him a 350cc ohc works outfit and it was with this that he won the national Southern Trial. In the meantime, not entirely happy with his racing form since the accident, he decided to concentrate on trials only and soon after accepted an offer to ride for Ariel. It was with the Selly Oak product that he won the sidecar premier award in the 1937 Victory Cup Trial. It was that win which impressed Bert Perrigo at a time when he lost the services of Harold Flook. With the need to find a replacement, Harold Tozer was approached. Harold recalls that when he decided to accept the BSA offer, it made him feel pretty mean, and to make matters worse, Tom

Davies of Ariel made no attempt at disguising his displeasure. 'After all' Harold recalled, 'The BSA offer was so much better. Ariel only supplied the outfit whereas BSA agreed to pay all expenses as well.'

His first ride with the unfamiliar BSA outfit was in the Scottish Six Days of 1937 where Harold Flook, again Norton-mounted, proved the victor with a loss of 24 marks. Harold Tozer won a silver cup with a loss of 39. There is no doubt that he had a tough job on his hands for the sidecar class of national trials throughout the 1930s was completely dominated by three men; Harold Flook, Dennis Mansell and Stuart Waycott. Between them, they won every British Experts sidecar title from 1929 right up to the outbreak of war in 1939, with Flook winning no less than six of them.

Harold Tozer's ride in the International Six Days Trial of 1937 was cut short by early retirement on the first day when he crashed off the road, damaging the outfit to the extent of making further progress impossible. It ws a great disappointment.

He made no such mistake in the 1938 event, again held in Wales, when he put up a faultless performance to gain his first ISDT gold medal. In the ill-fated ISDT of 1939, riding in the mixed BSA works team with Jack Amott and Jack Ashworth, Tozer was again without loss when the British contingent was advised to withdraw from the event and make haste for the Swiss frontier.

That year he had made a good start to the season by winning the sidecar premier in the classical Colmore Cup Trial, a good portend of things to come. But with war round the corner, it was to be seven years before this was to come true. Even then, as already noted, it just didn't happen overnight. It was no doubt related to getting the right passenger — or a regular passenger with whom to establish an understanding or rapport. This came in the person of Jack Wilkes, a retiring and modest young man without any former passenger experience at all, who had obtained employment at the Tozer Garage in Selly Oak, Birmingham which had been established during the latter part of the 1930s. After army service overseas and his demobilization in 1945, Harold had used another passenger before Jack Wilkes became available, but by the time they won the Clayton Trophy Trial of August 1946, their team work had developed into a fine art of muted understanding. Neither party was ever heard to shout to the other — unlike many crews.

The partnership of Harold Tozer and Jack Wilkes was a joy to behold, the epitome of perfect understanding, judgement and tactics, with Harold displaying that deftness with the right hand which comes only with experience. It was a calculated, precise and polished performance which stamped them as the artists they were. On one occasion in one of the trade-supported nationals during the peak years of

Standing on the footrests, Harold Tozer climbs a typical Cotswold leafmould-surfaced hill in the 1949 Colmore Cup. He won, yet again, the sidecar premier award, this time with his later outfit 'JOK 536.'

Harold Tozer foots up Fish Hill in the 1949 Colmore Cup Trial. The spectator on the extreme right in a white duffle coat is Ron Watson, managing director of Watsonian Sidecars, himself an expert sidecar competitor.

Tozer, the author recalls watching the sidecar entry on a section in the Bristol area where a short, very steep, slippery climb was preceeded by a rambling approach of gradual gradient littered with an assortment of rocks. Before Tozer arrived, every sidecar competitor adopted speed tactics in an attempt to gain sufficient momentum to surmount the final steep hill, but this meant that they lurched wildly from rock to rock, and all failed with wheel spin. When Tozer's turn came, he trickled up the lane at no more than walking pace, avoiding all the rocks, barely off the pilot jet, in complete control. As he hit the base of the steep climb he turned on the power to rush up as though it didn't exist. It was a masterly and breathtaking performance.

An International Six Days Trial shot of Harold Tozer and Jack Wilkes pressing on during the 1950 event in Wales with the 650 Golden Flash outfit with which they won one of the only three gold medals earned that year by chair outfits. Photo: Birmingham Post and Mail Ltd.

The difference was that those who adopted speed were forced to shut-off at the crucial moment in order to get the outfit lined up for the hill whereas Tozer was in control all the way and able to open up at the correct moment. The incident emphasizes the supreme importance of throttle control and although Tozer knew exactly where to apply power,

he maintained when interviewed during the preparation of this book that the most difficult thing to learn is where to turn it off.

His epic win of the Colmore Cup in 1947 was a combination of throttle control and tactics. On Fish Hill, near Broadway, which had taken marks from the entire solo entry bar two (Nicholson and Colin Edge), Harold kept the BSA just moving with the rear wheel spinning furiously, burning its way over the hard-packed leaf mould and polished exposed tree roots, the throttle mostly against the stop but with intermittent easing off, to surmount the crest of the section amid thunderous applause.

Cleaning that section meant he had completed the whole course without loss of marks and knowing that others might have done likewise, he knew the results of the special test would be decisive. This was the usual down-hill stretch against the stop watch with the time taken related to the distance it took to pull up beyond line 'B'. Time was always the important factor. With so much at stake, Harold and Jack produced their compressed air bottle from the chair and inflated all three tyres board hard in order to reduce the rolling resistance — thus winning the Colmore Cup itself. His superiority that day was so great that the next best sidecar to him — Harold Flook, who thus took the best sidecar award — was a massive 17 marks in arrears.

By then, the main Tozer distinguishing feature — his trade mark almost — was the spare four inch cover looped round the nose of the stubby sidecar body. No, it wasn't merely a spare in the normal meaning of the word. Like the compressed air bottle, it was an aid to tactics; permitting, where the situation was demanding enough, the rear tyre with its three security bolts to be run at zero pressure — say on a decisive hill where the results might determine the outcome of the premier award. The existing cover could be sacrificed and the replacement fitted at the top of the section. More than one trial was won with the aid of that 'spare' cover.

An equally distinguishing feature of the Tozer BSA outfit in those days was the full-throated exhaust note like that of Bill Nicholson's machine — music to the ears of the connoisseur. Who could fail to be stirred by the Tozer outfit on full song — as when storming Town Hall Brae in the centre of Fort William, used daily in the Scottish Six Days. Harold would assault the hill in a thrilling orchestration of sound, the exhaust bellowing from wall-to-wall and over the rooftops beyond, in a glamorous spectacle for all to see and hear. Now the dramatic sound effects have died with the birth of the modern lightweight trials outfits which, in comparison, seem like clockwork mice.

Curiously in 1947, despite his pre-war Scottish experience, Tozer's performance in that first post-war event seemed unusually subdued when he lost the sidecar premier to his old adversary, the one-legged

Harold Taylor (Ariel) who, during the week, had driven with determination and zest. Nonetheless, there was not much in it. With a loss of 25 marks, Tozer was only two marks down on Taylor. Freddie Whittle, in third place with his big 600 Panther, was a solitary mark astern of Tozer, and in fourth place, only two marks adrift of Whittle, was Harold Flook, passengered by his wife.

If Harold Tozer's performance in that Scottish of 1947 could be termed one-degree under, that in the following year's event in 1948 could only be described as devastating, for he destroyed, and probably demoralized, the opposition by increasing his lead every day to finish up with a massive 52 marks lead over runner-up Arthur Humphries (Norton). In other words, with a loss of 47 marks, the runner-up had lost over twice as many. That was just one example of the Tozer magic when he was at his best. Despite losing the Scottish in 1947, it was nonetheless Harold's peak year as was the case with soloist Bill Nicholson, when their joint wins were like a supreme duet. Out of the total of 23 major nationals in 1947, Harold won no less than eleven of them — nearly as many as the rest of the opposition put together. Only Harold Flook, Freddie Whittle and Frank Wilkins managed more than a single win, with Flook and Whittle having three wins and Wilkins two — though both the latter were non-trade-supported (the Cambrian and Perce Simon).

The pattern of wins for 1948 was very similar, with Harold Tozer maintaining his predominance by winning eight of the sidecar premiers in the season's 22 major events. Freddie Whittle with his Panther was next best with four wins and Dennis Mansell — by then Ariel mounted — next with two wins. The other eight events were shared by eight other riders.

The 24 major nationals of 1949 were more equally spread among twelve premier award winners, with Frank Wilkins (Ariel), Freddie Whittle (Panther) and Arthur Humphries (Norton) all winning three each. Tozer topped them all by winning double that number. It would have been ironical indeed if, after such a startling performance, he had failed to maintain such form in the 1950 season, the first year of the ACU 'Championship'. Right from the outset of the season, with the traditional Colmore Cup opener, he was there as usual with the customary best sidecar performance. By the time that first season of the 'Championship' came to an end, with 13 riders sharing the sidecar premier in 25 nationals, Harold Tozer had taken his score to nine victories. Frank Wilkins was next best with three and Arthur Humphries third with two. Yet such was the complexity of the marking system for the new ACU 'Star' that both Wilkins and Humphries were deemed to have tied, with 13 marks each. But there was no mistaking Tozer's victory with a total of 24 marks — nearly double that of the runners-up. He thus scored the first-ever ACU Sidecar Trials Drivers' Star. It was no more than rubber-stamping his known authority.

The anomalous system adopted for marking the 'Star' contest seemed even more ambiguous in 1951 when, at the end of the season, Harold Tozer and Arthur Humphries were deemed to have tied with equal marks scored. Yet during the year, Tozer had won the sidecar premier in ten nationals compared with the seven of Humphries — the latter including the less important, restricted Southern Experts. With only a selected number of events counting towards the 'championship' and with the points awarded in each event determined by the number of sidecars taking part, the result was almost bound to be inconclusive. Having won the sidecar-only D.K. Mansell Trophy Trial three times out of four since the trial was inaugurated by the Birmingham '30' MCC in 1947, Harold Tozer had the bad luck to retire from the 1951 event. This made all the difference. In winning the event, Arthur Humphries — always passengered by brother Harry — collected no less than six points — enough to put him level with his great rival, after completing half the season without a single win.

By this time Harold and Jack Wilkes were using a new outfit first registered in 1949 with the registration number JOK 536. It was fitted with a B34 engine having an alloy cylinder head and barrel. This outfit had replaced HOC 102, registered in time for the Victory of 1947 although it still used the 1939 M24 Gold Star engine previously fitted to the original outfit DOA 664. Using a Watsonian trials body, the sidecar chassis was of BSA manufacture. Recalling his competition days, Harold Tozer pointed out that he did not believe in altering gear ratios or anything else which could render the performance unfamiliar. It was vital to know exactly what the outfit was capable of and how it would behave under certain conditions. In fact the only reason why the original outfit, DOA 664 was replaced at all was after Bert Perrigo had tried it. He thought it was dropping to bits!

In the International Six Days Trial, based at Llandrindod Wells in Radnorshire, he won gold medals in both the 1949 and 1950 events. Dusty and relatively easy in 1949, the severe conditions of the 1950 event were as calamitous for the chair entry as they were for the solos, for of the 31 sidecars to start, a mere seven survived the traumatic week. Of the survivors only three won gold medals: Bill Peacock (350 Matchless s/c), Frank Wilkins (500 Ariel s/c) and Harold Tozer who, with regular passenger Jack Wilkes, crewed a 650 A10 Golden Flash in beige livery.

1952 was Harold Tozer's last year in the saddle. At the end of the season he had won just three trade-supported nationals; the West of England, the Southern and yes, the British Experts for the fifth and last time. By then he had won no less than 54 sidecar premier awards in

Laurence Hands, competitions manager of Champion Sparking Plugs (UK) Ltd (left), entertains the 'BSA Boys'. L to R: Tom Ellis, Ted Fithian (BSA assistant competitions manager) Harold Tozer, Jack Wilkes, Brian Martin and David Tye circa 1953.

national trials — the vast majority being trade-supported — between the Clayton Trophy Trial win of August 1946 and the final Experts win of December 1952. This prolific catalogue of wins included the Experts hat-trick; the Southern Trial four years in succession; the West of England five years in succession, and four wins out of five in the D.K. Mansell Trial.

There are those with a knowledge of motorcycle sport who argue that with smaller entries, it is easier to win a sidecar premier than that of the solo class. A study of the facts, however, does not support this theory for despite the far greater solo entry in any given national trial, only a handful are potential winners. The facts speak for themselves. In 1950, for example, when Jim Alves won the first-ever ACU solo 'Star', eighteen solo riders shared the solo premier awards in the 28 nationals of that year. During the same year, 13 sidecar drivers shared the 25 sidecar national premier awards. Despite the overwhelming predominance of solo riders, a difference of only three winners. Or conversely, from a much smaller total entry of sidecar competitors, there were 13 individual winners.

Harold Tozer had proved to be a worthy champion and a gilt-edged investment by BSA; a true patriarch among the post-war pack of BSA aces.

Chapter Nine

European Champion

DURING THE 1940s, BSA won practically every major trial and scramble, often winning both solo and sidecar premier awards in the former plus capacity class cups and team awards in abundance. But two of the most important continued to elude the BSA experts — the British Experts Trial and the Scottish Six Days. The solo title of the former had not been won by BSA since Fred Povey had last done so in 1934. Then in 1950, as though to redress the situation and start the fifties in the way they meant to go on, Bill Nicholson won the Experts solo title for the first time. That still left the Scottish in which BSA had won the sidecar premier award many times, with the solo premier no closer than Bert Perrigo's one-mark miss of 1937. Then in 1949, prospects suddenly brightened. John Draper, the youngest member of the team, completed the first day without loss of marks, although three other riders shared the lead with him. On the second day, when Draper had added only three to his score, he was out on his own. By Wednesday, the third day, and with Bill Nicholson recovering from a first-day loss of three, Draper shared the lead with him. At long last BSA were leading the Scottish.

But by midday Thursday, the BSA challenge was in tatters, literally swept away by the flood waters of the River Arnisdale. The débâcle cost Draper 34 marks on time, relegating him in one fell swoop from the leadership to the ranks of the also-rans. It was a great disappointment to both BSA and John Draper, not that the ever-chirpy and utterly guileless John showed signs of wilting, for at all times he was untainted by tantrums or inhibitions. He was a rider of natural ability who seemed to tackle all before him without much regard for tactics, relying on determination and quick reaction, always light-hearted, jocular and full of fun.

A farmer's son, the irrepressible John Draper was born on the fringes of Cleeve Hill near Cheltenham, on the western extremes of the

BSA works rider from 1948 to 1951 and from 1953 onwards, John Draper promptly won the 1953 Victory Cup Trial to mark his return to BSA, using the new B34 Gold Star. Photo: Ray Biddle.

Cotswolds, where he lives to this day. It is an area rich in the history of trials and scrambles and of the exploits of such men as Jack Williams and Bob Foster, Indeed, it was the Foster influence which led to Draper's works contract with BSA, for with Bill Nicholson anxious to get in some scrambles practice, he was recommended by Bob Foster to see Harold Draper whose undulating farmland was ideal for the purpose. During the following years Harold Draper played host to a number of clubs who ran their scrambles events there using courses, each different from the other, thanks to the variations in terrain. It was Bill Nicholson, who knew a good rider when he saw one, that first took note of the riding ability of Harold Draper's young son John.

A striking shot of John Draper 'cleaning' the Devil's Staircase in the 1953 Scottish Six Days, an event he won for BSA two years before, to register their first-ever Scottish solo victory. Photo: Ray Biddle.

He was signed-up and his first appearance in the BSA team was in the Kickham Trial of 1948. By the end of that year it seemed that he had not fulfilled his early promise, for he had not won either a premier award or a capacity class cup in any of the national trials of the season. Although he had won a special first class award in the Scottish Six Days earlier in the season — in which he had teamed up with Nicholson and Terry Hill to win the team award for BSA — his best ride was probably in the notorious Scott Trial where he won the Best Newcomer Award. He also made up the BSA winning team in both the Mitchell and West of England Trials. In scrambles, however, his potential was evident from the outset, for in the Cotswold Scramble in June he finished third   115 behind Nicholson and Rist to make it a one-two-three for BSA in the Junior Race. Then in November, in the physically-demanding Lancashire Grand National, he finished fifth as the highest placed BSA man, winning the Best Newcomer Award. Toward the end of the season, having qualified for the Southern Experts Scramble, he finished second to Basil Hall (Matchless), an event held over the famous Sunbeam Point-to-Point course at Weaver's Down in Hampshire, the scene of Bill Nicholson's double triumph of the previous April.

The young Draper again failed to win a single national trial in 1949, but after his sensational two-day lead in the Scottish Six Days, the message was there for all to see. Nonetheless, he did win the 350 Cup in the Hurst Cup, the Bemrose Trophy and the Cambrian in Wales. But again it was in the big-time scrambles that he shone, achieving his first major success in the Junior Race of the Sunbeam Point-to-Point with a brilliant victory. In the same event, with BSA winning yet another team award in the Senior Race, Bill Nicholson had to concede victory to Basil Hall and the big, black Matchless.

It was the 1950 season, however, which really stamped the wiry and pugnacious Draper as the true trials and scrambles champion he became, for he won the premier award in both the Irish Hurst Cup and Wye Valley Traders' Cup Trial. In addition, he won the 350 Cup in the Cotswold Cups and John Douglas trials with a near-miss in the Scott Trial and the British Experts, where he was runner-up in both. In the newly-instituted ACU Trials Drivers' Star contest he was third, with 59 points, behind Rex Young (Norton) on 70 points and winner Jim Alves (Triumph) with 76 points.

Second to Eric Cheney (Ariel) in the Senior Race of the sandy Sunbeam Point-to-Point (with BSA again winning the team prize) Draper also finished third in the Lancashire Grand National on Holcombe Moor in November, winning the 350 Cup in the process. But his greatest win that year came over the summer months when a British team of twelve riders travelled to Sweden for the Motocross des Nations. This international team event had been held for the first time in Holland during 1947, to produce the first of many British victories in the series.

The 1950 event was organized by the Swedes on military ground at Skillingaryd near Varnamo where, in many respects, the course resembled the tree-lined sandy tracks of Bagshot Heath familiar to so many British riders. For the 'Coupe des Nations' the riders were equally divided into two heats of twelve laps in order to whittle down the total field of forty-four riders to one of thirty riders for the seventeen-lap final.

Whilst only a question of qualifying, it was nonetheless indicative of what was to follow when British riders filled the first three places in the

John Draper with 'racing' cap in the disputed 1953 British Experts Trial where after protest and counter-protest, he lost the solo title to arch rival John Brittain. Photo: Ray Biddle.

first heat, with Basil Hall (BSA) leading home John Avery (BSA) and Bill Nicholson, to make it a BSA one-two-three. Heat two produced a similar British boost with Harold Lines (Ariel) heading Brian Stonebridge (Matchless) in second place and Geoff Ward (AFS) fourth. The final comprised the fastest three from the eight nations competing, plus a balance of six decided on time in the heats, irrespective of nationality. This put John Draper in the final line-up alongside compatriots Hall, Avery, Lines, Nicholson, Stonebridge, Ward, Alves, Evans and 17-year-old Graham Beamish. No less than five BSAs in the ten-man British line-up.

Right from the word go in the final, despite a minor collision with Harold Lines, John Draper went straight into the lead, and once having shaken off the initial Belgian opposition represented by Auguste Mingels and Marcel Cox, he drew away until he was out on his own. Basil Hall lay second, with Lines, Evans, Ward, Stonebridge and Nicholson in line astern, with only the odd foreign rider intervening. The British team was in an unassailable position; so much so that team manager Harold Taylor saw fit to display the 'slow down' signal in the interests of conserving the position. John Draper forged ahead and maintained an enormous lead over Basil Hall until the end of the race. It was a resounding victory for the little man from Cheltenham and whilst his reputation at home as a fearless rider had already been established, this success consolidated his   117 reputation on an international basis. He had risen from obscurity to international stardom in just two years.

Earlier that year he had won the Hurst Cup classic in Northern Ireland and later, wound up the season as runner-up in both the Scott Trial and the British Experts. Although Harold Tozer had won the sidecar class of the Scottish Six Days, John Draper, along with the rest of the BSA solo team, had to be content with special first class awards in the 1950 event. The Scottish solo premier still eluded Small Heath.

But just twelve months later, in the Scottish of 1951, John Draper was in the hunt right from the word go, sharing the lead at the end of the first day with Jim Alves (Triumph), with no marks lost.

He fluffed it on the Tuesday by conceding 13 marks, putting him in third place behind Bob Ray (Ariel) on 11 marks and H.R. Kemp (Royal Enfield) on 12. But he fought back on the Wednesday, however, to complete the day without adding to the previous day's total. This put him in the lead with a four-mark margin over Jim Alves and it was a lead he never lost for the rest of the week, to win the premier award with a total of 22 marks. Jim Alves, four marks down on Draper was second with Derek Ratcliffe — brother of 1950 winner Artie Ratcliffe — third on 27.

John Draper had thus secured for BSA their first-ever Scottish Six Days solo victory. It was the last bastion in major British national trials to fall to the BSA brigade. It proved to be Draper's only Scottish victory, yet given normal luck he should have won the Highland classic twice more — again in 1952 when Norton mounted and for a third time in 1957. But like most sports, motorcycle trials riding is full of ifs-and-buts. In 1952 Draper lost only 18 marks on observation compared with the 22 of winner John Brittain (Royal Enfield) but his score was inflated by 19 marks lost on time as a result of tyre trouble.

If it was pure bad luck which robbed John Draper of that Scottish victory in 1952, in 1957 it was merely a case of needing just an extra spoonful of good luck with his riding tactics to achieve the victory which, ironically, again went to John Brittain on that occasion. Having returned to BSA for 1953 after his brief Norton experiment, by the Scottish of 1957 Draper's team mates were Jeff Smith and Arthur Lampkin, all three riding a 500 B34 Gold Star. By the end of the opening day, it was another BSA one-two-three, Draper and Lampkin leading with no marks lost and Jeff Smith in third place with two marks lost.

When John Draper completed the second day with another clean sheet he was out on his own but by then John Brittain had slipped into second place with four marks lost. By the end of Wednesday, John Brittain had slipped to third place with a loss of 12 marks, Jeff Smith on nine taking his place as runner-up. But with a total of five John Draper

John Draper, the supreme scrambler, winning the Junior Race of the 1953 Cotswold Scramble. Second in the Senior Race he also did the Junior/Senior 'double' two years before, winning both races. Photo: Ray Biddle.

was still the undisputed leader. What happened during Thursday and Friday can only be described as pure drama with the lead changing places no less than three times. On Thursday morning came Loch Eild Path, a new section, long, rocky and devious, climbing 1,000 feet from Kinlochleven to the summit. It embraced on the way fifteen observed sections in a 400-yard stretch of concentrated challenge for even the most gifted and it was to this new hill the spectators flocked in droves to witness the spectacle. Of the leaders it was Jeff Smith who tackled the climb first and the fifteen sub-sections cost him seven marks. He was quickly followed by Draper who conceded eight marks he could 119

John Draper winning the 350 Race of the Experts Grand National at Rollswood Farm in 1953, at the time regarded as one of the first scramble courses in the British Isles. Photo: Ray Biddle.

ill-afford to lose, then very soon after, with a superb demonstration of combined balance, throttle-control and speed, John Brittain cleaned all fifteen sections to throw the trial wide open. By the end of that day he led Draper by just one mark, with Jeff Smith third, two marks down on Draper. With the outcome of the trial balanced on a knife-edge, the atmosphere in Fort William was electric, as competitors set out on the fifth day. It remained so as they tackled Grey Mare's Ridge just 22 miles out at Kinlochleven, a climb comprising seven sections of tight hairpin bends with surfaces of gigantic rock ledges combined with severe gradients.

In front of the hushed crowd, Jeff Smith seemed to go to pieces and blew his chances by losing no less than a total of 17 on the hill. Then, with so much at stake, John Draper made a superb climb, dropping only one mark in the first section, followed by cleans in the next five sections, only to spoil it with a stop in the last one. Nonetheless, the hill had cost him only six marks. As John Brittain arrived, the noisy buzz of talk among the excited crowd was replaced by a deathly silence, as he tackled the hill, to lose one mark in an early section, three in a middle one and, like John Draper before him, a stop in the last section. His total loss on the hill was nine. He had lost the lead to Draper who then had a two-mark advantage. Arthur Lampkin, incidentally, did better than any of them by losing only five.

As far as John Brittain was concerned, all was not lost. There were still six more sections to go before the day was out, including old favourites such as the Devil's Staircase and Ravine. But the infamous Staircase had never been in an easier mood. No less than 29 riders mastered it that day — including John Draper. With the Staircase and Ravine failing to take any marks off the BSA ace, Brittain despaired and gave up hope. Then at Camp Hill, the last section on the return run along that picturesque Kinlochmoidart peninsular — a rather innocuous section which rarely gave the average rider much trouble but which occasionally took marks off the experts — John Brittain was told by the observer that Draper had dropped three marks. As far as Brittain was concerned, it was a gift from heaven. It was the last section of the day,

Another fine shot of John Draper airborne in the 1953 Experts Grand National, displaying the tigerish style which brought him the 1955 European Championship. Photo: Courtesy Ray Biddle.

and indeed of the trial. He cleaned it and thus beat John Draper by just one mark. Adding salt to the wound, Arthur Lampkin had a good day to bring his final score into line with that of his team-mate, to share second place with him. Not surprisingly Smith, Draper and Lampkin won the team prize for BSA. Having returned to the BSA camp for 1953, Draper won the 500 Cup in the Scottish of that year, just nine marks down on winner Hugh Viney (AJS) but for 1954 it was a case of the other side of the coin — losing 50 marks on time on the opening day and retiring on the second day with a knee injury sustained after a collision with another rider on the road from Kinlochrannoch. The experience in the Scottish of 1959 is also best swept under the carpet, but for 1960 he was destined once again to finish runner-up, this time to Gordon Jackson (AJS), a mere four marks adrift.

After his memorable Scottish win of 1951, probably John Draper's most outstanding ride was in the 1956 event when, riding as competitor number one, he rode a 149cc Bantam, a model not previously used by the factory in the Scottish classic. No doubt BSA had been impressed by the performance of George Fisher who, with the Francis Barnett two-stroke, had finished runner-up two years running in 1954 and 1955 — on the latter occasion only one mark down on winner Jeff Smith's with the 500 BSA. John Draper on the Bantam did not quite emulate George Fisher, but nonetheless, tied with Sammy Miller (Ariel) for sixth place, putting up a remarkable performance. To this day George Fisher remains the only rider to have bettered John Draper in the Scottish with a small two-stroke of less than 150cc.

Despite John Draper's wide-ranging catalogue of success, he had more than a fair share of hard luck near misses, not confined to being three-times runner-up in the Scottish Six Days, for he was similarly afflicted in the British Experts Trail. In the 1953 Experts event, for example, when Draper's rival John Brittain was announced as the provisional winner, Draper disputed the marks debited against him on a section named Martin's Mill. In due course Draper's protest was upheld and the results amended with his name displacing that of Brittain as the solo title winner. The latter counter-protested and this time the RAC was invited to adjudicate. They overturned the previous ruling and re-installed John Brittain as the solo winner. Just two years later, Draper was runner-up again in the Experts, this time to team-mate Jeff Smith. John Draper never did win the British Experts — expert though he undoubtedly was.

Many of his successes in British national scrambles and Continental motocross bore the print of greatness, such as his victories in the Cotswold Scramble of 1951 where he produced one of his most scintillating and devastating performances ever by winning both the 350

Junior and 500 Senior Races. After a modest start in both events he remorselessly hounded the big guns of AMC in the persons of Geoff Ward (AJS) and Brian Stonebridge (Matchless), whom he picked off in turn with tigerish determination. It was an inspired performance in front of the thousands of thrilled spectators who thronged the grassy hillsides at Nymsfield under a blazing summer sun.

Those few weeks of early summer 1951 produced one of the many peaks of his long career with a versatile performance achieved by few others. Apart from his great Scottish Six Days victory in early May and that ride in the Cotswold Scramble which humbled both Ward and Stonebridge, John Draper crossed over to the Isle of Man to try his hand in the Clubman's TT, his first and only essay into road racing other than by qualifying for that Clubman's ride by competing at Cadwell Park — using his slightly-modified scrambles bike.

As a rider contracted to BSA he was prevented from using the products of the company (a curious rule applied to a rider without normal road racing experience), so with the help and sponsorship of Jack Williams and his company in Cheltenham, he was entered in the Junior Race on a 350 Norton and on a 500 Triumph in the Senior. He delighted both himself and his sponsor by finishing third in the Junior at 74.73 mph with a repeat third place in the Senior at 78.56 mph — being the only rider to get a place in both events. It was a very good debut by any standard and one which proved that he had the ability to learn the intricacies of the most difficult racing circuit in the world.

After his Clubman's TT success and that of the Cotswold Scramble, he won the 350 Race of the Experts Grand National and finished second in the 500 Race, whilst earlier in the season he had won the premier award in the national Mitchell Trial. During 1951 it seemed he could not put a foot wrong when, in Italy during the International Six Days Trial which started from Varese, things started to go awry. He had been going well without loss of marks and on the third day he had done so well that during the afternoon he passed through the time check at Cossato before it was open. This was tantamount to missing a control, but after due consideration he was allowed the lapse but fined 3,000 lire (nearly £2 at the time).

Mileage for the next day, Friday, was split roughly in two: 145 daytime miles with 105 miles making up the night run. The daytime route, running in the area of Lake Como, took in time checks that were all very, very tight. The tracks were extremely narrow and some sections were steep and rocky, with hairpins so close together that they resembled long editions of the famous Devil's Staircase of Scottish Six Days repute. The British motorcycle press reported that no man living could possibly maintain the overall schedule on such going, so that when good

Battling with the dreaded Holcombe Moor, home of the Lancashire Grand National until 1954, John Draper heads for third place in the 1953 event behind David Tye and John Avery, making it another BSA 1-2-3. Note the 'emergency' grab-handle on the front forks. Photo: Ray Biddle.

roads were reached there was no alternative to keeping the throttle wide open, regardless of conditions.

But it was on the night run which followed, running north again to Lecco and Mandello to the head of Lake Como, that John Draper came unstuck. It is not clear to this day exactly what happened but it seems that whilst overtaking another rider in a tunnel he struck a centre-line kerb and came off heavily, sustaining severe concussion. Worse still, the hospital to which he was taken would not undertake an operation to remove a blood clot in his head until BSA had cabled through the medical fees required. This took several days and the delay proved nearly fatal. Meantime his father and Bill Nicholson flew out to Italy to be with him and to bring him home when he left hospital about a week later. For several months after his eyesight was impaired.

Nonetheless, he still finished fourth in the ACU Scramble Drivers' Star for that season and in the early months of 1952 won the Colmore Cup Trial (on a Norton). During the next few years he continued to win both big-time trials and big-time scrambles. In 1953 he won the Victory Cup Trial, the Cotswold Cups and the Southern Experts, with another Junior Race victory in the Cotswold Scramble and in the Experts Grand National.

In 1954 he was runner-up in the Colmore Cup Trial, won the John Douglas Trial, took several 500 class cups and scored two big wins at Shrubland Park in the main Grand National event with a repeat win in the 500 Senior Race. Riding as well as ever, if not better, he showed no effects of his ISDT injury of 1951. By the end of the 1955 season he had scaled yet another peak in his glittering career by winning the European Motocross Championship, the forerunner of today's World Championship series. In national trials he started the season well enough with two early premier awards — one in the Colmore Cup and one in the Hurst cup, both of which he had won before. Curiously, he started the motocross series more modestly with three events in the series concluded before he even scored a point.

It was at Hawkstone Park in the British round, in front of an hysterical home crowd, that the two BSA stars, Jeff Smith and John Draper, dominated both legs of the motocross to finish one-two in that order, in both races. The crowd went wild with delight. Although the result gave Jeff Smith a slight advantage over his team-mate, this was cancelled out in the Belgian round which followed in August, with Draper pulling off an outright win. Les Archer (Norton) secured another win in Luxemburg but a ninth place kept Draper in contention. In the penultimate round held in Sweden it was another victory for Draper. There was just one more round to go to decide the title — the Dutch event in September, and though it produced a win for Sten Lundin (BSA) with fellow Swede Bill Nilsson (BSA) second, John Draper collected enough points with his sixth place to secure the title. The slightly-built and wiry country boy from Cheltenham had aspired to the highest reaches of motocross, gaining for BSA in so doing their first-ever European Championship.

Throughout the fifties John Draper continued to win both trials and scrambles in his own, inimitable, way, seemingly without effort, and like most super riders it was the way in which victory was won that was just as impressive as the victory itself. At the Sunbeam Point-to-Point of 1958, then held on a new course at East Meon in Hampshire, Draper won the 350 Junior Race, his winning style being such that in the muddy conditions the press reported that his style was matched by no other. At one point of the course where other top-liners were forced to use their feet to assist progress, Draper was poised on the footrests, broadsiding feet-up at an incredibly high speed, with a broad grin expressing his enjoyment.

In that race he was followed home by Andy Lee from Cambridge and Peter Taft of Birmingham, to make it another BSA one-two-three. The BSA domination that day was completed by Don Rickman (BSA) winning the Senior Race with Jeff Smith (BSA) third. The BSA team of Brian Martin, John Draper and Peter Taft won the team award in the Junior event. If Draper had humbled the opposition in that 1958 Junior Sunbeam Point-to-Point his performance paled in comparison with that at the same event the following year. Using the same course at East Meon, which the weather had turned into an appalling mess, the report in '*The Motor Cycle*' stating that 'Showers, near-sleet, heavy and torrential rain turned that odd mixture of chalk, clay and grass on which the circuit is laid out, first into a vast, sinuous switchback butterslide and then into near-liquid mud'.

The report went on: 'Draper led the Junior race throughout, building-up a lead that quickly multiplied to over three minutes. Where others slithered and footed at the bottom of adverse cambers, Draper rode feet-up, on top of the camber, at twice their speed. He dashed down gradients, magically reduced speed at the bottom and magically found wheel grip for crashing acceleration. He made it look so easy. But only he could do it. Not yet saturated, the ground was at its worst in the Junior. So bad was it that sections of the course were short-circuited piecemeal. Only Draper could reach the top of the gradient. All other riders simply had to cut off the top loop to keep going. A dozen fell on the first hill on the first lap. Dave Curtis (Matchless) retired, disgusted with the conditions.' So bad were conditions that of the 70 entries only 32 came to the start line. Priase indeed from impartial journalists. In winning the 1959 Junior Race of the Sunbeam Point-to-Point — for the second year in succession — he was followed home, a long way in arrears, by the indomitable Dave Bickers (Greeves), destined to win the 250 European Motocross Championship in 1960 and 1961. Arthur Lampkin (BSA) was third. With Don Rickman winning the Senior race as he had the year before, it was another BSA double.

The evergreen John Draper was as agile in the saddle at the end of the fifties as he had been at the beginning. It has already been noted that a mere four marks robbed him of victory in the Scottish Six Days of 1960, having earlier that season won the Victory Cup Trial yet again. The year before he had finished third in the ACU Trials' Drivers' Star contest. In 1958, the second year of the new World Motocross series that replaced the former shorter European series, — Draper scored points in six of the events, with outright victories in Holland and France. He was

fourth in both Switzerland and Belgium and sixth in Italy and

John Draper in the 1953 Scottish Six Days with two great adversaries, John Brittain (left) and Gordon Jackson, to whom he conceded three Scottish victories – in 1952 and 1957 to Brittain and in 1960 to Jackson. Photo: Ray Biddle.

Luxemburg. But it wasn't enough to stop Belgian René Baeten (FN) winning the World title or the Swedes Bill Nilsson and Sten Lundin beating him into fourth place in the championship.

Notwithstanding his season with Norton in 1952 and a season with Cotton in 1961 (when he won the solo premier award in the Cotswold Cups Trail) the name of John Draper will for ever be associated with that of BSA. Although riding a trials Cotton in 1961, he won the Lincolnshire Grand National that year on a BSA; indeed, he was again BSA mounted when he was sixth in the Senior Race of the Cotswold Scramble in 1962. Although no longer a member of the BSA works team, he was still BSA mounted when he won a first class award in the 1964 Cotswold Cups Trial and if the records are studied closely enough, the name of John Draper will show up from time to time in the list of awards. Today, perky and jocular as of old, he claims he has never retired from riding.

Small, wiry and agile, John Draper was the very epitome of the British works rider of that era. More than most he was able to conceal serious intent with a light-hearted approach to a job which gave him pleasure and enjoyment, with a sparkle even greater than the bottled variety now produced in celebration at the conclusion of major events. He was not unlike a bottle of the best vintage champagne himself; rare and irreplaceable. A legend in his own right.

127

Chapter Ten

Gold Stars Supreme

IN RETROSPECT it seems quite safe to claim that the BSA Gold Star of the 1950s made more impact on world-wide motorcycle sport than any other motorcycle before or since. To catalogue its unparalleled record of success in its entirety would present a reading marathon about as exciting as a railway timetable.

The 350cc B32 and 500cc B34 models in scrambles trim, in particular, proved so functional and appealing that both attracted seasoned riders and pure beginners alike. During that illustrious period every scramble event throughout the United Kingdom was dominated by the Gold Star. Worldwide too, its popularity spread like a fever, to Australia, the USA and Canada; to New Zealand and throughout Europe. Nearly everybody who was anybody in the sport of scrambling rode a Gold Star at one time or another, either as a raw beginner or a seasoned expert.

Writer A. Golland (the pseudonym of a respected BSA engineer) has already revealed in *Goldie**, his development history of the Gold Star, that the M24 Gold Star had been dropped from the 1940 range of BSA motorcycles to be replaced by a new 350, the B29 Silver Sports. This new model featured a cylinder head with integrally-cast rocker boxes that concealed hairpin valve springs and A. Golland recounts how a small batch of these B29s was commandeered by the British Army for dispatch rider duties. During the early war years a military version of the B29, complete with hairpin valve springs and lightweight frame and designated the B30, had been submitted to the War Office for evaluation, but it was rejected in favour of the low compression, 500cc side-valve M20 model with its ability to withstand below average use and maintenance.

During the war years a number of B30 cylinder heads and barrels were cast in aluminium alloy for future use — such as in the 1947 Manx Grand Prix, for example. So it is thus easy to trace the pre-war B29 and

128

*Published by the Haynes Publishing Group, 1978, but now out-of-print.

The 1938/39 M24 Gold Star was one of the earliest standard production models to have an aluminium cylinder head and barrel as standard. Here an overseas visitor collects his 1939 model from the factory just before World War Two.

wartime B30 as the true progenitors of the first post-war B32 Gold Star. This explains why, having been introduced as a 500cc model in 1938, it rcappeared ten years later as a 350cc model. As A. Golland states in his book, 'The Manx Grand Prix of 1947 was used as one of the testing grounds, when that year saw the entry of an experimental high-performance version of a (basically) model B29. Included in its specification was a magnesium-alloy crankcase and a cylinder head cast in aluminium (with, of course, integral rocker boxes with hairpin valve springs) while the compression ratio, valve and ignition timings were, naturally, modified to suit racing purposes.'

Utilizing McCandless swinging-arm rear suspension and a front brake of unusually large proportions, this experimental model was ridden in the Junior race by Bill Nicholson and though performing well enough, it was not fast enough to get on the race leader board. In the race itself, Nicholson missed his scheduled pit stop and subsequently ran out of petrol.

Terry Hill (16) on the front row of the grid for the 1946 Ulster Grand Prix with Artie Bell (11) and Rex McCandless (9). Terry, who initially led the race, was using a 1939 M24 Gold Star. Number 3 is Les Graham, 10 Sam Dalyell, and 14 Ernie Lyons with the Triumph twin on which he later won the Manx Grand Prix.

The true progenitors of the post-war Gold Star were the 1940 B29 Silver Sports model and the aborted wartime B30, the latter shown here in stark war-time livery. The cast-in rocker boxes housing the hairpin valve-springs are the main distinguishing feature.

The hairpin valve springs were subsequently replaced with conventional coil springs and the rocker box reduced in size, with regard to both the alloy cylinder head and also the cast-iron head used on the standard B31 introduced in 1945. It is ironical to recall that originally the new B32 Gold Star was planned for trials application, thus retention of the original valve sizes, their angles and their port diameters tended to inhibit high-performance development. Almost certainly the introduction of the Clubman's TT races in the Isle of Man in 1947 caused a hurried re-think at Small Heath regarding the true role of the Gold Star. The rapid increase in the popularity of scramble events at home, and the motocross counterpart on the Continent, pointed to a 'racing' specification as a priority. Thus from the moment the 1949 B32 Gold Star was introduced at Earls Court in November 1948, development was aimed at producing and making available over the counter a highly-competitive catalogue model suitable for scrambling and all forms of racing at club level.

By the time the 500cc B34 Gold Star followed in the wake of the 350cc model, a whole range of specification options were available. These included cams suitable for touring and trials models, scrambles and grasstrack racing and for road racing. There were no less than four sets of internal gearbox pinions, providing extra close ratios for road racing, a set for scrambles and grass-track racing, those for standard touring, and a wide-ratio set for trials riding. There was also a whole range of sprockets, 16 to 22 teeth for engine, 16 to 19 teeth for gearbox and 42 to 46 teeth for the rear wheel. Even the clutch sprocket with 43 teeth could be made available with 44 teeth to special order. Exhaust pipes also came in for treatment with different lengths for road racing and scrambles. A megaphone became available at a later date.

Peter Rose, who first worked under Jack Amott in 1942 and came to respect both him and his engineering ability, today recalls that when he became involved with the small nucleus of staff building the early Gold Stars the specification variations were such that each model was individually built to the customer's requirements.

As the popularity of the Gold Star gathered pace and orders multiplied, production routine was rearranged and specification options slimmed down in the interests of increasing output and reducing the long delivery delay. All Gold Star engines were, of course, brake tested for power output and the complete machine road tested — either on the public road, the factory's own test track or sometimes at MIRA (then in its early, undeveloped state). Peter Rose himself became involved from time-to-time, but the full-time Gold Star tester was George Statham, no mean rider who raced on short circuits such as Aberdare Park and Cadwell Park.

1952 Junior Clubman's TT winner Eric Houseley (left) with second place man Bob MacIntyre. Second left is sponsor Eric Bowers and second from right sponsor Sam Cooper of Troon. Centre rear is BSA designer Bert Hopwood, with Bert Perrigo on his left and to his right (front row) is BSA export manager Bill Rawson.

Another respected BSA character who later became known as Mr. Gold Star, was Cyril Halliburn who more-or-less took on Jack Amott's duties when the latter left the company. It was he who came to know better than most just how to 'set up' a Gold Star properly, thus earning the gratitude of many riders in the process. Whether or not Gold Star plans were clearly defined at the outset, there can be no gainsaying the fact that once its true role had been identified, racing success multiplied with intoxicating frequency. This can best be judged by the results achieved in the Clubman's TT series in the Isle of Man where a 350cc Gold Star won every Junior race in the series from 1949 until 1956 when the races were discontinued.

By 1956 — when the Junior race was won by Bernard Codd from Lincolnshire, who also won the Senior race — no less than 53 of the 55 starters in that event were Gold Star mounted. That amounted to almost total domination. When Alistair King won the Senior race in 1954 with a new record lap of 87.02 mph, and Eddie Dow repeated his win in 1955, it seemed Gold Star dominance was spreading to that class too. Bernard Codd's win in the Senior race of 1956 made it a BSA Junior/Senior double victory three years running and virtually confirmed it. It was BSA's success that finally killed off the series.

132   As the Gold Star story unfolded with its dominance of the

Clubman's TT so was its success mirrored around the scramble circuits of the world, with these machines frequently finishing one-two-three in both the 350 and 500 classes of major national events. Lower down the scale it was just the same in local restricted-to-centre events and in closed-to-club scrambles run for private clubmen. Despite this success, the early plunger-type frame, acceptable for road use, represented a handicap in scramble events with its weight and limited, undamped movement. The works riders minimised the handicap by using oil-damped conversions, but at best this was no more than a stop-gap compromise. The complete answer came with the introduction of the 1953 models which used a new, all-welded frame with duplex down tubes and swinging-arm suspension. The prototype of this new frame had been used by the works entries during the 1952 scramble season, the first production samples appearing in the International Six Days Trial of that year in the hands of the works riders and some of the British Army team members — the latter including Captain Eddie Dow who had won a gold medal in the Italian event of the year before with the plunger-framed version. Soon after the 500cc Gold Star had been introduced in 1949, early proof of reliability came with the ISDT in

Eddie Dow (227) starts his Gold Star on the first morning of the 1952 International Six Days Trial in Austria. He went on to win a gold medal as did F.E. Lines (Triumph) immediately behind Dow, but Dick Clayton (229, British Vase 'A' team) was excluded on the 4th day. Competitor 228 also retired.

With the B34 Gold Star well 'muddied; Eddie Dow awaits a morning start later in the week during the 1952 ISDT. As a member of the British Army team, Eddie had one of the first Gold Stars with swinging-arm rear suspension.

Wales when no less than ten gold medals went to riders using the new model.

Introduction of the new swinging-arm frame was akin to giving the Gold Star *carte blanche* in road racing and scrambling alike, such were its enhanced characteristics. With the availability of better quality petrol and a logical programme of development, performance was gradually boosted. In 1949 the average 350cc Gold Star with a straight-through exhaust pipe turned out 25 bhp at 6,000 rpm. The 500cc model produced on average 28 bhp at 5,500 rpm. By 1956 the 350cc Clubman's specification model with a megaphone and a 13/16 inch GP carburettor was capable of 32.5 bhp at 7,500 rpm. By 1956 the 500cc version was capable of no less than 40.4 bhp at 7,000 rpm whilst during further development work as much as 48 bhp at 7,500 rpm had been recorded with a 1½ inch GP carburettor and a megaphone exhaust.

Proud managing director of BSA, James Leek, with Alistair King (left) and Phil Palmer, Senior and Junior Clubman's TT winners of 1954 — the first of BSA's hat-tricks of Junior/Senior 'double' victories.

As already pointed out by A. Golland in his book *Goldie*, Manxman Jackie Wood — entered by Geoff Duke — completed a lap at a speed of 91.2 mph during the 1955 Senior Manx Grand Prix, before retiring with clutch trouble, a speed that compared well with the 91.38 mph of winner Geoff Tanner on the Featherbed Norton. In the previous Tuesday's Junior race Jackie had done well on a 350 model by finishing third at 85.54 mph behind Alan Holmes' Norton at 86.84 mph and winner Geoff Tanner's Norton at 88.46 mph. The Gold Star was proving to be a very capable poor man's racer. With a good rider aboard, it was proving more than a match for most of the genuine 'double-knocker' racers. In full racing trim the maximum speed of a 500 Gold Star was in the region of 120 mph: even in Clubman's trim with full lighting the maximum was still around the 112 mph mark. It is salutary to realise that today, 30 years on, the Japanese are only just beginning to match that kind of performance from similar capacity four-stroke singles.

James Leek congratulates Phil Palmer after his 1954 Junior Clubman's TT victory. Of the 41 finishers that year, 34 were Gold Star mounted, such was the BSA dominance.

As previously noted, American Tommy McDermott finished in a creditable sixth place with a prototype 500 Gold Star in the 1949 200-Mile Experts Race at Daytona. It was a race then dominated by the lusty Harley-Davidson and Indian big vee-twins — 73 of the former and 42 of the latter — plus overhead camshaft racing Nortons which totalled 19 in number. Finishing with only three Nortons and two Harleys ahead of him, McDermott's performance augured well for the future; indeed, the following year he rode a Gold Star into third place behind the ohc Nortons of Bill Mathews and Dick Klamfoth. But 1954 was the BSA year at Daytona when they filled the first five places, with a sixth model in eighth position, though it was two Star Twins which headed the Gold Stars home. It must be recognised, nonetheless, that by then genuine overhead camshaft racing models had been outlawed by regulations.

Many were the Gold Star successes throughout the United States. Nick Nicholson won the 50-Mile Amateur Race at Daytona in 1953 with

Better known in later years for his successes with his BSA trials sidecar outfit, Sam Seston of Birmingham thunders along past the scoreboard during the 1953 Senior Clubman's TT. In the 1951 Junior event, Seston finished 12th on his plunger-type Gold Star, on which he also competed in the Senior event.

Robert Winters on another such model in second place, Winters going on to finish second also in the 100-Mile event. Nick Nicholson, who incidentally, visited the Small Heath factory one month later, had won the Catalina Grand Prix on his Gold Star in 1951 when BSA headed all the classes. This was an event where the true connotation of the European 'Grand Prix' title did not apply. Claimed to be one of the world's toughest and most gruelling races, the course consisted of 100 miles of 'rough stuff' over mountain trails, parched countryside and city streets. In repeating a BSA win again in 1956, Charles 'Feets' Minert, in sweltering heat, averaged about 30 mph for the course which, in itself, indicates the severity of the event. Walt Axhelm rode another Gold Star into second place and to make it a BSA one-two-three, C.H. Wheat was third. Although John Gibson on a big twin Harley won the 200-Mile Race at Daytona in 1956 at a speed of 94.21 mph, four Gold Stars chased him home. Dick Klamfoth was second, George Everett third, Tommy McDermott fourth and Eugene Thiesen fifth. In the 100-Mile Amateur event run previously, again with Harley-Davidson the victors, Jack Schlaman was second — a mere three seconds astern of the Harley — and Roger Armstrong was third, both of them on Gold Stars.

It was a BSA victory in the 1957 100-Mile event when Kenny Brown won at 93.87 mph and three BSAs followed him home in fourth, fifth and sixth places. In the main 200-Mile event it was almost a BSA

Captain Eddie Dow on a Gold Star in the 1953 Senior Clubman's TT where, having put up the fastest lap in practice, he retired on the third lap when lying second. He put in a lap at 26 min 51 sec, only three seconds down on the new lap record of 84.49 mph. Photo: The Classic Motor Cycle.

victory too, but in the end Al Gunther had to concede victory to the Harley ridden by Joe Leonard. Even so, both the Gold Star and the Harley shared the fastest lap of 105.5 mph. And so it went on well into the 1960s even after the Gold Star had gone out of production at Small Heath. For example, Jody Nicholas won the 1963 AMA 100-Mile

National Championship at Laconia in the record time 1hr. 35m. 47secs. with Dick Mann third. State-wise, BSA successes were too numerous to record.

On the other side of the Pacific in Australia — the best BSA export market for several years after the war — Gold Star successes were as prolific as in the United Kingdom and just as difficult to chart if boredom is to be avoided. Every State scramble championship must have been won at different times by a Gold Star. In the All-Australian Championships, so often dominated by BSA, there was the occasion of the 1958 Championship held at Evandale, Northern Tasmania where only one machine other than a BSA gained a place in all four capacity classes.

Having finshed 10th in the Senior Clubman's of 1954, Eddie Dow won the 1955 Senior on his Gold Star by the very wide margin of 1 min 18 sec. Here he is rounding Parkfield Corner on the Clypse Course, used that year instead of the Mountain Course.

It was a repeat performance at the 1960 National Championships meeting — held at Arthur's Creek, 30 miles from Melbourne — when BSA won every title, as was the case again in 1963 when the Championships were staged near Brisbane and BSA riders won six of the seven events. The story was much the same at Australian road race

Another fine action shot of Eddie Dow during his winning ride in the 1955 Senior Clubman's TT. A captain in the regular Army, Eddie Dow also rode with distinction in both the Scottish and International Six Days. Photo: The Classic Motor Cycle.

meetings; as on the occasion of the Australian TT held at Mildura, Victoria, on Boxing Day 1956. Here it became a veritable Trevor Pound-BSA benefit when, in the Clubman's Races, he won all three classes; the 350, the 500 and then the 650, all with the Gold Stars. In the 350 race K. Murphy was second and G. Huse third, both on Gold Stars.

Today, the names of Ken Rumble, Trevor Pound, Charlie West and Gordon Renfrew have become woven in the folklore of Australian motorcycle sport, all creating legends together with the name of the Gold Star. Throughout the world, where motorcycle sport thrived, so did the Gold Star; in New Zealand, South Africa and nearer home in Spain, France and Holland. Norway, Sweden and Denmark too all had their regional or national champions who made their mark with the Birmingham-made cosmopolitan product. But most of all the Gold Star became virtually a status symbol in the British Isles and the Irish Republic, a passport to a sweeping vista of victories too many to record in detail. Only the main features can be picked out, such as the results of the Thruxton Nine Hour Race of 1955 which was won by Senior Clubman's TT winner Eddie Dow, partnered by Eddie Crooks, at a speed of 67.73 mph. They were ahead of a 350 Gold Star in second place ridden by Ken James and Ivor Lloyd, with Ron Langston and J.F.Righten fifth on yet another 350 Gold Star.

The performance of BSA in the 1956 event was overwhelming, with Gold Stars filling the first six places, the overall winners — Ken James and Ivor Lloyd — completing 236 laps at an average speed of 72.3 mph **with the smaller 350 model**. Bernard Codd and F.A. Rutherford (499 BSA) were second; H. Argent and E.P. Eacott (499 BSA) third; Derek Powell and Tony Godfrey (348 BSA) fourth; W.J. Hill and D.G. Chapman (499 BSA) fifth and G.H. Turner and R. Lawrence (499 BSA) sixth. In comparison, the highest placed 650 model was the Triumph of Percy Tait and Ken Bryen, who completed 222 laps at a speed of 68.01 mph. Such was the superiority of the Gold Star.

In the world of British scrambling this superiority can only be conveyed by typical example. Although Geoff Ward (AJS) was the first-ever winner of the ACU Scramble Drivers' Star in 1951, six of the first ten in the contest were Gold Star mounted (6 BSA, 2 Norton, 1 AJS, a Matchless). In 1952, when John Avery took the title with his Gold Star, three more BSAs finished in the top ten. In 1954, seven out of the top ten were Gold Star mounted. In 1955, when Jeff Smith won his first Scramble Star, four of the top six were BSA. When Jeff Smith won again in 1956 it was almost a BSA grand slam with Dave Curtis riding the only machine other than a BSA in the first six. He won the title in 1958, with BSA filling the next five places. To round off the fifties in appropriate fashion, Arthur Lampkin won the Scramble Star for 1959, on the still defiantly competitive Gold Star.

The Gold Star shone with greater brilliance in some events more than others. In that popular Good Friday classic, the Hants Grand National, BSA won no less than eight times from 1947 to 1960. In the Sunbeam Point-to-Point over the same period (though the 1960 event was cancelled) BSA scored 16 victories without counting the runner-up placings. In the Cotswold Scramble the BSA success was breathtaking for during the period 1946-1960, taking into account all classes, the total was a staggering 28 victories.

The Experts Grand National at Rollswood Farm, Warwickshire was another BSA happy hunting ground where again from 1949 (when it was established) to 1960, no less than 26 victories were scored. In the 1956 event it was almost a BSA massacre of the opposition when they finished first and second in all five events, the sole exception being the 250 Race where Arthur Shutt (Francis Barnett) managed to stave off John Avery, who finished second.

Hawkstone Park in Shropshire, with its steep climb and fast sandy circuit where the bellowing Gold Star was really in its element, was

The 500 Gold Star in International Six Days trim was symbolic of the classic British bikes of that era used by British riders. This B34 was used by Brian Martin in the 1954 and 1955 events, a model Brian regarded as the ultimate tool for the job. Photo: The Classic Motor Cycle.

another circuit where Jeff Smith, John Draper, John Avery, Brian Stonebridge, Phil Nex, Brian Martin and John Burton trounced the opposition time and again to the delight of the huge crowds who flocked to that circuit in those days. Between them, from 1951 to 1960, they won 22 races.

In the old established Lancashire Grand National — transferred from its traditional home on Holcombe Moor to Curden Park near Preston where the event was revamped into shorter, capacity-class events from 1955 — BSA won the Grand National event seven years in succession, from 1956 to 1962. Going farther north the Cumberland Grand National was dominated by Arthur Lampkin and BSA for years. In 1958, for example, BSA were one-two-three in the Senior Grand National; one-two-three in the Junior Grand National and one-two-three in the Senior Invitation Race. It was much the same in the event of 1959 when only one Triumph and two DOTs broke the BSA monopoly.

It was a monopoly in every sense of the word, with Gold Star wins in national scrambles alone so numerous during the 'fifties as to render the actual total purely academic.

The glory was not confined to scrambles, however, for with BSA winning both the solo and the sidecar title in the 1950 British Experts Trial, the ACU Solo Trials Star for 1951 and 1952; and the 1951 Scottish Six Days, it was a barn-storming start to the fifties. After Bill Nicholson's win of the Experts in 1950 and that of Tom Ellis the

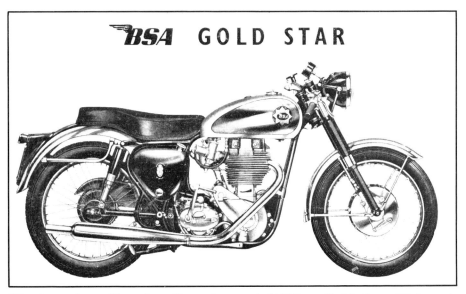

The last of an illustrious line, the 1956 DBD34 Gold Star Clubman's model, one of the greatest of British big singles. The model received little or no further development until its demise in 1963. Later factory sales catalogues stated that the Clubman's model was not intended for use on the public highway!

following year, BSA went on to win the British Experts solo title four years in succession in 1954, '55, '56 and '57. They won the Scottish Six Days again in 1955 — this time with Jeff Smith the victor — and during the course of that season won a further seven trade-supported national trials.

Organized by the Birmingham MCC, the Victory Cup Trial was very much a BSA speciality, as though regarded as 'playing at home' by the riders, for from 1946, when Fred Rist made best solo performance, BSA riders made best solo performance on nine occasions between then and 1956, with six victories in succession. The notorious Scott Trial in Yorkshire was another such event where BSA riders reaped a lavish harvest of success, with eight outright wins from 1946 to 1960 and making fastest time many times over.

The versatility of the Gold Star, proved the world over in the multi-field of competition, was never more profound than in the Isle of Man Clubman's TT series where the dominant results achieved are, today, indicative of the model's success. During the ten-year history of the series from 1947 to 1956, of the 20 Junior and Senior races collectively, BSA won nearly twice as many as any other manufacturer, with a total of 11 victories. Norton were next best with 6 victories, whilst Triumph, HRD and Velocette had only one victory each.

The orthodox ohv four-stroke single had made a lasting impression in trials, scrambles and road racing like no other, justifying and rewarding the faith placed in it and the methodical programme of development pursued at Small Heath. The Gold Star was killed off by both politics and fashion. Today, like a martyr, its memory is perpepuated by the tangible activities of the Gold Star Owners Club.

What other individual motorcycle can lay claim to such an honour?

Chapter Eleven

Star Galaxy

LIKE MOST British manufacturers BSA relied on a team of works riders of the calibre of Fred Rist, Bill Nicholson and John Draper, able to apply their versatile skills equally in trials, scrambles and six-day events. Most riders of that ilk 'cut their teeth' with trials riding in which they learned the basic arts of balance and throttle control — the latter of immeasurable value in scrambles where the elements had been at work.

In the immediate post-war years the time-honoured pattern and character of British scrambles changed, for there emerged a new generation of scramble riders attracted to the short, fast courses sited on private land where events were organized for paying gates. To such men it was a new sport, glamorous, exciting and challenging. There was born, as a result, a long line of riders whose activities were confined to the sport of scrambling, and in which trials riding played little or no part. It was yet another example of the specialization which came in with speedway racing twenty years before.

The specialist scramble experts of those days are best exemplified by such hallowed names as those of Eddie Bessant, Harold Lines, Les Archer, Geoff Ward and Basil Hall. The list is endless. None did more than Harold Lines and Basil Hall to spread the fame of this new breed of fearless riders for, during the immediate post-war years, they travelled the Continent, going from national meeting to national meeting with considerable success. Soon, the names of Harold Lines with his dope-tuned Ariel and Basil Hall, a big fair-haired farmer from Hertfordshire who rode a Matchless, became legendary in France where at meetings such as those staged at the famous 'Chalk Pit' course near Paris crowds of up to 80,000 were commonplace. They were besieged after every win by huge crowds of excited fans on a scale unknown in England, revered with an adulation reserved today for pop idols. Once described by free-lance journalist Ralph Venables as 'scrambling's   145

An airborne Basil Hall on his way to second place in the Experts Grand National of 1953 at Rollswood Farm, Warwickshire. Photo: Ray Biddle.

greatest gentleman', Basil Hall was typical of that new generation of scramble specialists, fast and utterly fearless, with a great will to win. Nonetheless, Basil's determination was tempered by clean and fair tactics, reflecting a temperament as generous as his size.

Born in 1921 among the rural surroundings of Markyate, north of St. Albans, Basil's first British national scramble was the infamous Lancashire Grand National of 1947 on Holcombe Moor, won by Bill Nicholson and BSA. Riding a 500cc Matchless of less than pristine condition, his performance throughout that season had been such that for 1948 he was taken on by AMC and given a works 500cc Matchless. The transition from novice to the point of achieving works status had been swift and sure, for he had not even ridden a motorcycle until he was brought into contact with them during wartime Home Guard service.

As the war came to an end, he spectated at a locally-organized scramble and succumbed to its appeal. As a result he set about building a

With his familiar handkerchief mouth-mask, Basil Hall lines up for a right-hand turn in the Italian Motocross Grand Prix circa 1953 with Eric Cheney (Ariel) following astern.

250 Special, using a JAP engine once raced by Eric Fernihough at Brooklands. Riding this Special for the first time in 1946, he soon learned that a large person like himself would be better off with a large bike. So a 500 Matchless followed, with the help of his father-in-law Bert England, who ran a motorcycle business in Dunstable and Luton.

In two short seasons he had become a works rider and in his first ride in that capacity in the Junior Race of the Sunbeam Point-to-Point, he finished third behind winner Bill Nicholson (BSA) and Bert Gaymer (Triumph). Then in June came his first trade-supported national scramble win in the Senior Race of the Cotswold Scramble, after a race-long scrap with Bill Nicholson who eventually went out with mechanical trouble. He rounded off his first season as an official works rider with a victory in the Lancashire Grand National. In 1949 it became a season-long duel between Bill Nicholson and Basil Hall, with the Matchless ace drawing first blood by winning the Senior Race of the Sunbeam Point-to-Point. Nicholson reversed the order in the Cotswold Scramble where, having won the Junior Race, he pushed Hall into second place to win in addition the Senior Race. Basil Hall won the Junior Race at Shrubland Park but was second-best to Nicholson in the Senior Race.

Bert Perrigo had recognised the need to strengthen the BSA team 147

With serried ranks of spectators crowding the amphitheatre slopes in the background, Basil Hall leaves the opposition far in arrears in a French motocross meeting near Lyon, circa 1953.

Basil Hall works on his Gold Star in the paddock of a Continental motocross in 1954, with BSA competitions manager Dennis Hardwicke lending moral support.

with additional scramble riders of the new school and the performance of Basil Hall had convinced him that here was the first recruit. To get Hall onto a BSA had the added advantage of reducing the strength of the main opposition. So from 1950 Basil Hall was Gold Star mounted, alongside Rist, Nicholson and Draper. During that first season with the BSA he won the Junior Race of the Cotswold Scramble, with a second in the Senior; won both the Junior and Senior at Shrubland Park; won the Experts Grand National at Rollswood Farm, was second in the Motocross des Nations in Sweden — behind team mate John Draper — and second in the French Motocross Grand Prix behind his old friend Harold Lines. During the next four years he won many races, including the Senior Race of the Sunbeam Point-to-Point yet again in 1954. The previous year he had won the Swiss Motocross Grand Prix with a second place in the British round and a sixth in Belgium.

Although his riding experience had largely been limited by conditions encountered on scrambles courses, he was nevertheless entered by AMC in the 1949 International Six Days Trial in Wales when, riding like a veteran and justifying the faith placed in him, he won a gold medal with a faultless ride. So much so that in 1950, when BSA mounted, he was selected by the ISDT team selectors to ride in the British Vase 'B' team alongside Dick Clayton (Norton) and Tom Ellis (Royal Enfield). Sadly it proved an ill-fated team. Dick Clayton retired on the fourth day, Tom Ellis on the fifth day and Basil Hall on the last day. Notwithstanding Basil's retirement, his performance was one of the most gallant of the week, for having been delayed several times with a magneto problem, he had ridden like the wind to keep on time. Finally the engine began to go sick with loss of compression and could only be restarted by energetic pushing, to expire within striking distance of the final speed test at Eppynt. The magneto, specially prepared by Lucas, had been assembled with an excess amount of bearing grease which fouled the HT slip ring. Overcoming the delays thus caused by using maximum rpm in each gear, his desperate race against time probably led to the trouble which caused his eventual retirement for when the engine was stripped, one of the valve seat inserts was found to be cracked.

Although it was a retirement, Basil Hall's performance showed the kind of determination in the face of adversity which impresses team selectors, so it was no surprise when he was again nominated for the British Vase 'B' team for the Italian event in 1951. Again fate intervened. Competing in the Swedish Motocross Grand Prix during the summer, he came off heavily and broke his right leg and was prevented from taking part.

During his five years with works Gold Stars, Basil Hall — a true gentleman who would never dream of commencing practice at any

Continental motocross meeting without first shaking hands with the principal officials — won many top-grade events at home and on the continent of Europe. It was whilst riding in a national motocross meeting in Belgium in 1955 that his right leg became entangled with the footrest and kickstart lever, to suffer yet another break. He bowed to medical advice and retired from the sport. He was but the forerunner of a long line of scramble specialists recruited by BSA to campaign the Gold Star in support of the works-employed all-rounders.

If the reign of Basil Hall had been comparatively short, it was typical of those whose active riding career had been shortened by the war years. Gradually a new generation emerged, young men little more than boys who were maturing as the war ended and were thus able to enter the sport without such constraints (though subjected to National Service at a later date). One such young man was John Avery of Oxford who, with a privately-owned BSA, shot to the top in four short seasons to win the 1952 ACU Scramble Drivers' Star — at the same time finishing third in the European Motocross Championship behind the Belgian giants Victor Leloup and Auguste 'Man Mountain' Mingels.

Though classified as a scrambles specialist, John Avery did in fact start off with some trials riding — and not without success, for as early as 1948 he had won a class cup in a national trial — the 250 Cup in the Manville Trial run by the Coventry & Warwickshire MC. He won another 250 Cup in the Mitchell Trial of 1949 as well as winning a first class award in the Scottish Six Days of that year. It was soon after the Mitchell Trial in 1949 that he decided to convert his 1939 B21 250cc BSA into scrambles trim in order to try his hand at the mushrooming sport. He had already fitted BSA 'C' group telescopic front forks in place of the old girder forks and with a bit of home tuning, he promptly won the 250 Race in the national Shrubland Park Scramble near Ipswich. From 1947 until 1949 his activities were somewhat inhibited by National Service but nonetheless, he had already tasted enough of scrambling to know that when he was free from the confines of khaki, his energies could be channelled in that direction. After being released from the Army in 1950 he won the 250 Race of the Cotswold Scramble, beating the redoubtable Fred Rist in the process. He repeated his 250 win in both the Shrubland Park national and in the Experts Grand National at Rollswood Farm. With an additional 500 model — fitted with Cheshire swinging-arm rear suspension — he finished second in the Lancashire Grand National, headed only by Brian Stonebridge on a Matchless. His form during the season had been such that he was selected for the British Motocross des Nations team, that year held in Sweden, where he finished second to Basil Hall in the first heat. He was likewise selected for the British Motocross team in 1951 and 1952.

After yet another Continental motocross victory, Basil Hall is congratu-lated by a fellow Gold Star competitor from Holland. Picture circa 1953.

The 500cc model he acquired for 1950 was basically a B34 with an iron cylinder head and barrel, but having already attracted the attention of the factory, the engine was subjected to a degree of attention by both Cyril Halliburn and Jack Amott. The rear suspension — fabricated by Fred Cheshire of Cheltenham — was based on the McCandless principle but claimed to have additional features like increased wheel movement. During the 1951 season that remarkable pre-war B21 250 saw service in both trials and scrambles, for not only did John Avery win four 250 class cups in national trials (Cotswold Cups, Greensmith, Southern and West of England) but he was also second in the 250 Race of the Experts Grand National. That, however, was the last year in which the faithful B21 saw service as a trials model. Thereafter it was used solely to contest national scrambles 250cc races, winning that class of the Experts Grand National of 1952; a win he repeated in the 1954 event. He won the 250 Race of the Cotswold Scramble of 1953 and again in 1954. At Shrubland Park that year, however, he had to be content with second place in the 250 Race — a position he had to settle for in three other events that day.

John Avery's peak year was undoubtedly 1952, his first year as a fully-fledged BSA works rider on factory-prepared Gold Stars. That year he won the 350 Race at the Hants Grand National; the Senior Race of the Sunbeam Point-to-Point; the Senior Race of the Cotswold Scramble; both the 250 and 350 Races at the Experts Grand National and both the Junior and Senior Races at Hawkstone Park in Shropshire. He finished third in the gruelling Lancashire Grand National and overseas won the Swedish Motocross Grand Prix with a third place in the French round. He was sixth overall in the Motocross des Nations at Brands Hatch. It was fitting that he should head the ACU Scramble Drivers' Star contest for that year; to follow it up with a third place in 1953.

A rare picture of Basil Hall (right front row) on a 650cc BSA A10 twin at an international team event in Holland in May 1951. After a few rides the A10 was considered 'too vicious' and discarded. Also in line-up L to R; front row Brian Stonebridge, John Avery and Geoff Ward with team manager Harold Taylor.

John Avery's riding ability and competitive instinct were hereditary to some extent for his father Harold, — passengered by his wife — won the British Experts Car Trial in a Singer Le Mans during 1933, when John was just five years old.

Right from the outset his aggressive and tigerish style was manifest, the stocky, fair-haired John seeming to thrive on difficult courses which abounded in steep banks and hollows, precipitating massive leaps through the air. No rider hurled himself higher in the air than John Avery. He was not nicknamed 'Clem' without justification ('Clem' being short for Clempson, the French birdman who, with home-made wings attached to his person, tried to be the first man to achieve natural flight).

The ill-fated British Vase 'B' team at the start of the 1950 International Six Days Trial. L to R; team reservist A.B.N. Taylor (AJS), Basil Hall (BSA), Dick Clayton (Norton) and Tom Ellis (Royal Enfield). Clayton retired on the 4th day, Ellis on the 5th day and Basil Hall on the 6th day, when within reach of the finish.

Very much an extrovert by nature, John had a flamboyant riding style in contrast to the more modest standards of the era. In truth, he was a true professional who recognised the value of public relations and showmanship. He never arrived at a scrambles meeting with bikes that were other than spotless and shining and had riding gear to match. His was an immaculate turn-out; a credit to himself and the BSA name.

During the mid-1950s, with works Gold Stars at his disposal, he continued to score top-level victories at home and abroad — another Junior Race victory in the Hants Grand National, the Cotswold Scramble and at Hawkstone Park. Then after taking second place in the 350 Race of the Experts Grand National in 1957 he had a severe prang which shattered his right arm, the scars of which show to this day. It was time to hang up his riding-gear and devote all his time to the motorcycle business he had established in Oxford in 1949 and which he runs to this day. Though now devoted to cars, the business is modern and smart, like John Avery and the Gold Stars he rode in his heyday.

Of his contemporaries, nobody contrasted with the flamboyant John Avery more than Phil Nex, an introvert by nature, modest and a loner by reputation. Nonetheless, Avery and Nex had two things in common; both were superb riders and both were fastidious with their appearance and in their machine preparation. Coming from Fareham in 153

Pre-war BSA 250s (with post-war telescopic forks) finished 1-2-3 in the 250 lightweight Race of the 1950 Cotswold Scramble, with winner John Avery (right), Fred Rist runner-up (middle), and a very young Brian Povey (left) 3rd. Note the machine examiner taking petrol samples.

Hampshire, Phil Nex first achieved prominence in national scrambles when he finished second to Ray Scovell (BSA) in the Hants Grand National of 1949. At the time he was Ariel mounted like his close friend Eric Cheney but by 1950 he was riding a Gold Star — with which he won the Hants Grand National three years in succession from 1952 to 1954. From then on he remained loyal to BSA. His early successes were eclipsed, without a doubt, in 1952, when he finished second to the great Brian Stonebridge in the first-ever British Motocross Grand Prix at Hawkstone Park. It placed him amongst the top-flight of the sport. But it was a feat he surpassed just two years later at the same venue when he won this great international contest outright. Between times his principal victories included the 500 Race at the Experts Grand National of 1953; the Senior Race at the Cotswold Scramble of 1954 and 350 Race wins in the Hants Grand Nationals of 1954 and '55.

His best season was 1954 when, by virtue of safe, consistent riding, he finished second in the ACU Scramble Drivers' Star and though fifteen marks down on winner Geoff Ward (AJS) he headed a phalanx of BSA Gold Star riders who filled the next six places. Apart from Geoff

An airborne Brian Stonebridge (Matchless) in close company with a landing John Avery on his Gold Star at the Berkshire Grand National circa 1951.

Ward, the only other non-BSA rider to get a look-in that year was Dave Curtis (Matchless) in ninth spot.

In addition to winning the British Motocross Grand Prix of 1954 he also gained several good placings in the European counterparts, such as second place in the Italian Grand Prix of 1953; a fifth in the Swedish round that same year; another fifth in Switzerland in 1954 and a sixth place in Luxemburg 1955. Not surprisingly, he was one of the king-pins of his own Southern Centre where he won the Centre Solo Championship two years running in 1953 and 1954. Then, on the latter occasion, as though to prove his versatility and ability to learn fast, he wheeled out a sidecar outfit, completed a couple of practice laps of the course at Old Idsworth, near Horndean, in Hampshire, and proceeded to storm to victory in the Sidecar Championship. According to journalist Ralph Venables, it was Phil Nex's first essay with a sidecar, and according to Nex's life-long friend, Peter Ryall, that unique achievement in the Southern Centre has never been repeated. Neither, it seems, did he lack talent in trials for he won the 500 Cup in the 1960 national Hoad Trophy Trial.

Over the years he had competed in many French national motocross meetings together with his friend Eric Cheney and almost certainly his last such trip to France was in 1960, having earlier that year taken part in the newly-inaugurated Brian Stonebridge Memorial Scramble at Hawkstone Park (Brian had been tragically killed in a car accident). Sadly, Phil Nex too was destined to die under tragic circumstances. The complex personality of Philip Alan Nex is best summed-up by his close friend Peter Ryall who wrote:

John Avery battles for the lead with Phil Nex in the 1952 Berkshire Grand National. Avery's iron-engined B34 is fitted with Cheshire swinging-arm rear suspension.

'Phil was born at Bexhill-on-Sea in 1928. He came to Fareham at the age of 11 years in 1939 where he spent all his adult life until he married. He lived with his parents at The Lodge, Bishopswood, Fareham, the official residence of the Bishop of Portsmouth. His mother was cook/housekeeper to the Bishop. It was for this reason he was nicknamed 'The Bishop', which typified his character, a man of placid nature with a total commitment to his work and the sport of motorcycling. He was always immaculate in his appearance: his riding gear and machinery alike. His aim in life was always perfection and

A rare picture of frame builder Fred Cheshire (clutching bike cover and goggles) with John Draper (left) and John Avery at a Churchdown scramble near Cheltenham circa 1951.

success in whatever he attempted, and failure never entered his mind.'

He emigrated to Australia in 1965 but returned to England in April 1969 when he bought a very old half-timbered cottage at Denmead, Hampshire. It was here that he died on 30th December 1971.

One of the youngest riders to hit the post-war headlines was Graham Beamish of Portslade, Sussex. At the tender age of 17, astride a brand new B32 Gold Star, he shook the established masters by finishing second in the Junior Race of the 1950 Sunbeam Point-to-Point behind the stylish Brian Stonebridge (Matchless) and ahead of the mighty Basil Hall and other factory riders strung out astern. The very next day in a centre event at Marlow in Buckinghamshire, he beat them all; Bill Nicholson, Basil Hall, John Avery, Geoff Ward and Jack Stocker. Later that season, in July, he tasted victory again at the then famous 'Chalk Pit' circuit at Montreuil, near Paris, scene of many French motocross epics. Just twelve months previously at the age of 16 he had ridden a Bantam in the International Six Days Trial in Wales but was forced to retire on the fourth day, troubled by a knee injury and front wheel problems.

His riding form in 1950 had been such that he was selected to ride in the British team in the Motocross des Nations held in Sweden. At 17 years of age he was the youngest rider ever selected for the British team   157

In 1952 John Avery won BSA's first Scramble Drivers' Star by winning seven national scramble events during the year. Here he takes his Gold Star round the normally dusty circuit at Shrubland Park in 1952.

— and still is, Graham claims. His main successes thereafter included a second place behind John Avery in the 350 Race of the Hants Grand National of 1953 and a win in the Senior Race at the Dartmoor Scramble of the same year, thus winning the massive and valuable Patchquick Trophy. In 1954 he scored another second place in the 350 event of the Hants Grand National, this time behind Phil Nex.

By the mid-1950s, the BSA Gold Star scramble team strength was at its zenith with an incomparable line-up of talent never before mustered under one factory banner. By 1953 David Tye had been on the Small Heath payroll for two years and John Draper — after one year with Norton — had returned to the BSA fold bringing Jeff Smith with him. Together with Tom Ellis, the Yorkshire trials rider recruited for 1951, the whole team became a Bert Perrigo legacy to BSA as, by the end of 1953, that shrewd judge of riding talent had departed to take up an appointment as sales manager of Ariel Motors at Selly Oak. Taking his place as competitions manager at Small Heath was journalist Dennis Hardwicke of the weekly publication *Motor Cycling* — a Londoner who had moved to the Midlands some five years previously to be close to the

John Avery (1) and Geoff Ward (AJS) in close combat at Hawkstone Park circa 1953/54. In 1952 Avery did the 'double' by winning both the 350 and 500 races at this popular Shropshire circuit.

heart of the motorcycle industry. Whilst his appointment caused some surprise in certain quarters, it was the result of a recommendation made by Bert Perrigo.

Very quickly Dennis Hardwicke showed that he had every intention of pursuing the Perrigo policy of maintaining — even increasing — rider representation in depth. One of his first 'captures' was the tall, lanky Brian Stonebridge (known to his rivals as 'Strawberry') enticed from the Associated Motor Cycle stable like Basil Hall before him. Matchless mounted, he had gained an enviable reputation as one of the safest riders in the sport and had been able to see off the best of the BSA boys. For three years, from 1954 to 1956, he joined the legendary Gold Star line-up.

It is true that some of the greatest battles took place during the early 1950s involving Brian Stonebridge (Matchless) and Geoff Ward (AJS) who fought tooth-and-nail with the Gold Star boys. To some extent the 159

John Avery on the way to winning the 1952 Swedish Motocross Grand Prix, his first International motocross victory.

glamour was dulled when Stonebridge defected to BSA, and even more so when Geoff Ward changed sides for the 1956 season. Basil Hall, Brian Stonebridge and Geoff Ward had been the three superstars who had kept the AMC flag at full mast during nearly ten years of furious racing against the BSA camp up and down the country. It was the most glamorous and stimulating period in the history of British scrambling. With the defection of both Stonebridge and Ward, the main AMC thrust thereafter came from Dave Curtis who more than maintained the tradition. Curiously he first came into prominence when riding a BSA, being thus mounted when he finished eighth in the ACU scramble Drivers' Star contest of 1953.

John Avery proudly displays one of the biggest and most valuable trophies in British scrambles — the Patchquick Challenge Trophy awarded annually at the Dartmoor Scramble which Avery won in 1954.

Hailing from the broad acres of Cambridgeshire, Brian Stonebridge had distinctive style and seemed to 'lope' along in a high gear like a swift-footed panther pursuing its prey — unspectacular and deceptive. He achieved his best, it must be admitted, when riding the big, black Matchless, before joining BSA. By then he had won the first-ever British Motocross Grand Prix at Hawkstone Park in 1952, a prestigious victory

John Avery was not labelled 'Clem' without justification for few flew through the air with the greatest of ease than the irrepressible Oxford flyer.

he repeated the following year. He led the British team to victory in the 1952 Motocross des Nations held in Holland where he was the individual winner.

Although Brian Stonebridge had finished fifth in the 1949 Lancashire Grand National on a privately-owned BSA, he first rose to prominence in 1950 when he won the Junior Race of the Sunbeam Point-to-Point on a works Matchless vacated by Basil Hall. He went on

An in-flight action shot of Phil Nex who, among his major victories on BSA, achieved an outright win in the 1954 British Motocross Grand Prix at Hawkstone Park. He was also second in the first-ever 1952 event.

to win the Junior Race in both the Cotswold Scramble and the Experts Grand National, rounding off his first season on a works Matchless by defeating the rigours of Holcombe Moor to win the Lancashire Grand National. He repeated this feat the following year to become the only rider ever to win the Holcombe Moor classic two years in succession after the war.

During his last Matchless-mounted season in 1953 he won both the Junior and Senior Races of the Sunbeam Point-to-Point in addition to the British Motocross Grand Prix victory. In comparison, his three seasons on the Gold Star seemed less spectacular though his first win came soon enough with the 500 Race at Hawkstone Park during the early months of 1954. He was second to Geoff Ward in the Junior Race of the Cotswold Scramble, with another second place, this time to Jeff Smith, in the Experts Grand National. In 1955 he won the Junior Race of the Sunbeam Point-to-Point — that year held on a new course at Golding

'The Bishop', as Phil Nex was nicknamed by his contemporaries, a placid introvert by nature, totally dedicated to the sport of scrambling. Here he adjusts the rear chain of his Gold Star, with Brian Martin lending moral support.

Barn near Shoreham-on-Sea — where he was followed home by Paul Jarman and Terry Cheshire to make it another BSA one-two-three. That Junior Race victory of 1955 was the first of five consecutive BSA victories in that specific event. With a second place behind Geoff Ward yet again in the 500 Race at Hawkstone Park, his only other wins that year were with the diminutive 150cc Bantam when, somehow wrapping his long legs round that bread-and-butter lightweight, he won the Lightweight Race at the Experts Grand National as Bill Nicholson had done before him in 1950. He repeated that Lightweight win at Shrubland Park. In 1956 he had to concede victory in the Lightweight Race of the Experts Grand National to teamster John Draper but he made sure of victory with the Bantam in the Lightweight Race at Shrubland Park for the second year in succession. The record suggests that after four successful seasons on a Matchless, Stonebridge may have been slow in adapting to the unfamiliar Gold Star; on the other hand it may have been the ever-increasing competition, with the addition of such new names as Dave Curtis, Jeff Smith, David Tye and the Rickman brothers making success all the more difficult to come by. Nonetheless, his best placings in the ACU Scramble Star contest were achieved in 1955 and 1956 whilst Gold Star-mounted, with a sixth place in 1955 and a joint sixth place with Peter Taft (BSA) in 1956.

For 1957 Brian Stonebridge moved on from BSA to Greeves, from then on campaigning the lightweight two-strokes from Thundersley,

Graham Beamish of Portslade, Sussex, leaps his Gold Star on his 'home course' at Golding Barn circa 1955. At 17 years of age he was probably the youngest-ever rider selected for the 1950 British Motocross des Nations team.

Essex until 29th October 1959. On that fateful day the motorcycle world was shocked by the news of his tragic death in a car accident near Retford, Nottinghamshire. Brian Stonebridge was a man of stature, both physically and by virtue of his personality, respected and regarded as one of the all-time greats by his fellow competitors. He was an outstanding rider during the greatest era of British scrambles.

Geoff Ward was an equally dominant AMC rider during the early

165

Another Midland Centre win in the Inter-Centre Team Scramble of 1954 at Hawkstone Park. L to R: Jim Bray, Jeff Smith and Brian Martin — all BSA mounted — being presented with the trophy by AJS works road racer Bill Doran. George Rowley (left), the pre-war all-rounder, looks on. Photo: Ray Biddle.

fifties campaigning the AJS 'look-alike' alongside the Stonebridge Matchless. Between them, they made every BSA victory hard-won and worthwhile, in the process over-and-over again thrilling the crowds with nerve-tingling excitement as ding-dong battles raged as never before. Whereas Stonebridge was elegant in style, almost majestic, pacing himself with head tilted to one side and not appearing to indulge in cut-and-thrust racing. Geoff Ward was the opposite, aggressive, spectacular and courageous in style. Broad and well-built, he lived life to the full with an easy-going manner, and a ready willingness to help fellow competitors when in trouble. Like Stonebridge, when riding for the 'opposition' he gave the BSA men a great deal of trouble, winning the ACU Scramble Star two years in succession in 1953 and '54, and preventing a BSA grand-slam in both cases. In the 1953 contest he was chased home by four BSA riders and the following year no less than seven BSA men trailed him.

From 1951 through to 1955 he had his fair share of victories in the major events that mattered — the Sunbeam Point-to-Point, Hawkstone Park, Cotswold Scramble, Shrubland Park, and the Experts Grand National — the latter being won two years in succession — though he never bettered his fourth place in the old Lancashire Grand National on Holcombe Moor.

Andy Lee of Cambridge who, among his notable rides, finished second in the Junior Race of the 1958 Sunbeam Point-to-Point. Here he is seen with his immaculate Gold Star at Arrington, Cambridgeshire in 1955.

Paul Jarman (1) who won the 350 Race in the 1954 Dartmoor Scramble here receives the winner's trophy at another West Country event, with Peter Taft (91) second and Brian Martin (81) third. Frank Jarman senior (right with trilby hat) looks suitably pleased.

In view of earlier trends, it was no surprise when it became known that Dennis Hardwicke had persuaded Geoff Ward to join the BSA camp for 1956, adding to that already powerful Gold Star line-up. But again, as with Brian Stonebridge, the change to BSA seemed to stem the flow of success. Maybe it was tantamount to changing horses in mid-stream. Nonetheless, there was nothing amiss with his opening ride on the Gold Star in the Sunbeam Point-to-Point, the season's first trade-supported national scramble, organized by the Sunbeam Club on yet another new course on the South Downs near Shoreham-on-Sea. As with the course at Golding Barn used in 1955 — which did not prove popular — the new one at Tottington Mount was laid out on land belonging to the Beamish family. Using the folds of the South Downs like a natural amphitheatre, the 2,300-yard circuit, super-fast, spectacular and dusty, was more like a mountain grasstrack than a scramble course.

Geoff Ward, using a reverse-cone megaphone on the 350 Gold Star and a rev. counter as did other BSA works riders, was in his element. He stormed to a Junior Race victory after a great tussle with David Tye (BSA), who finished second, Phil Nex's third making it another BSA one-two-three. It was a similar story in the Senior Race when Jeff Smith brought a 500 Gold Star to victory, ahead of Les Archer on his 500 overhead camshaft Norton, with speeds of over 90 mph being reached across the floor of the amphitheatre bowl and round a large segment of its rim. That course was probably the fastest and most spectacular ever used in the United Kingdom. It was fitting that a BSA Gold Star should have dominated both races.

Despite that impressive win at Tottington Mount, Geoff Ward failed to maintain form for the rest of that season; thereafter doing no better than two second places at the Shrubland Park national. Toward the end of the season, however, he did win the 350 Junior Race of the Lancashire Grand National which, the year before, had switched to a new course in Cuerden Park near Preston when separate capacity class races had been initiated. Curiously, this course too, like that of the Sunbeam Point-to-Point described above, was a super-fast, two-mile circuit of smooth grass and bumpy gradients where speeds of up to 80 mph were reached, giving rise to lap speeds of around 45 mph. In contrast to Holcome Moor, it was a case of from the ridiculous to the sublime.

Prior to joining BSA, Geoff Ward's best Continental motocross performance had been in the 1954 Motocross des Nations in Holland, where he finished second to the Swedish champion Bill Nilsson, who rode a works BSA. Thereafter on BSA, Ward had a third place in the

French Motocross Grand Prix of 1956, a third in the Belgian round, and

Fly-away Peter (left) fly-away Paul (right); the Birmingham Taft brothers who did a Rickman-like double act on Gold Stars in the fifties with considerable success. In these shots it is a case of 'spot the difference.

Jack Mathews (14) and Paul Taft (6), both on Gold Stars, lead the pack in the North v South Scramble at Pirbright, Surrey in May 1959 with John Burton (4) close astern on another Gold Star, Number 5 is Ken Messenger, 16 Roger Kyffin and 15 Dick Rix.

'Big John' Burton of the British team powers his Gold Star through the sandy terrain, typical of Dutch courses, in the Motocross des Nations of August 1961. Belgium beat the British team into second place. Photo: The Classic Motor Cycle.

a fifth place with the British team which won the Motocross des Nations in Belgium. He finished fourth in the ACU Scramble Drivers' Star for 1956 as he had the year before.

The Ward/BSA partnership had dissolved by the end of 1956. For 1957 he was back on AJS and twelve months later he changed horses again, this time to Norton, before retiring to pursue a very successful business career in the West Country. He had come a long way since his early days on BSA (he had started on a BSA, being thus mounted when he finished third behind Basil Hall and Don Evans in the first-ever Experts Grand National Scramble of 1949) to finish as one of the all-time greats of British scrambling, an inspiration to many younger riders who strove to emulate his dynamic style.

With few exceptions, nearly every top-line scrambler during the golden fifties had been linked with BSA at some stage in his riding career, including the articulate and redoubtable Rickman brothers from New Milton, Hampshire. They subsequently achieved even greater fame with their home-brewed Metisse specials, assembled in their own workshop, before going on to fabricate their own twin-loop, all-welded frame on a commercial basis. Yet, both Don and Derek Rickman had established their reputations on a Gold Star over a period of seven years (with a break of one year on Royal Enfield in 1955) with an ability which saw them frequently sharing top honours in the same event. Their national event successes began with the 1952 Hants Grand National in which Derek finished third on his privately-owned BSA. Two years later brother Don finished second in the same event. They virtually dominated that popular Good Friday national event in 1957 when Derek won the main Grand National event with Don the runner-up; in the 350 Race Don was the victor with Derek the runner-up.

In those days, the popular and likeable Rickmans were a dominant force in the centre events of the southern counties, though less well known in northern climes. Nonetheless, they travelled north to Cuerden Park near Preston in 1957 for the re-vamped Lancashire Grand

John Burton leading Don Rickman (Metisse) in the Thirsk Grand National of September 1963, his last season on works BSA.

National, where Derek finished third, and Don fourth, headed by winner Jeff Smith and runner-up Brian Martin. Adding to the successes of these two BSA big guns, they made it a BSA one-two-three-four. At the same meeting Don was also third in the Senior Race behind Jeff Smith (BSA) and Dave Curtis (Matchless). In 1958, the Rickmans' final year on BSA, Derek secured another win in the Senior Race of the Hants Grand National, with a second in the Grand National itself. Soon after, in the Sunbeam Point-to-Point held for the first time on the East Meon Valley course in Hampshire, Don Rickman achieved his biggest BSA success by snatching the Senior Race from Dave Curtis (Matchless) and third-place man Jeff Smith. Finally at Shrubland Park, Don was runner-up to Jeff Smith in the Senior Race.

John Burton leads Vic Eastwood (Matchless) in the 1962 Experts Grand National at Rollswood Farm, when he was second to Jeff Smith in the 500 Race. In 1961 John was 5th in the World Championship and in '62 second in the British Championship.

Whilst history will relate the name of Rickman to that of the specials they went on to manufacture and market in a very professional way during the years which followed, Don and Derek had established their riding reputations on a Gold Star like so many others, including Jim Bray and the Taft brothers, Peter and Paul, of Birmingham, Paul and Neil Jarman of Taunton, John Burton of Lutterworth, Andy Lee of Cambridge, Dave Bickerton and Terry Cheshire from Lancashire, Jerry Scott from Dorset, Keith Hickman and many more.

John Burton (16) neck-and-neck with diminutive Vic Eastwood in the West Wilts MC BBC TV Scramble of October 1963, on two of the most famous 'big bikes' of the British scrambles scene.

One of the most successful of those early privateers was the young Terry Cheshire (no relation to the Cheltenham Fred Cheshire who made the Cheshire frame) who, after a season of two on a DOT, first made his presence felt in 1954 by winning both the 350 and 500 Races in the Cumberland Grand National. This double victory was repeated in the Newcastle Grand National where he won the 350 Race and the 20-lapper called the Belmont Grand National - all on his 350 Gold Star. His consistent performance that year put him in fifth place in the ACU Star contest, headed only by Geoff Ward, Phil Nex, David Tye, and Jeff Smith. His performance in 1955 was even more remarkable for by the end of the season he was headed only by Jeff Smith in the ACU Star contest, beating Dave Curtis, Geoff Ward, Phil Nex and Brian Stonebridge in the process. That year he had won both the 350 Race and

173

A 1965 shot of Jerry Scott on a Cheney-BSA Gold Star landing nose first in disarray — how not to do it! Photo: Motor Cycle News.

the Grand National event of the Kidstone Scramble, outriding Dave Curtis in both. He repeated this performance in the Cheshire Grand National where he outrode Brian Martin to win both the Grand National event and the main race called the Hatherton Scramble.

With a works 499cc Gold Star at his disposal he won the Isle of Man Grand National in June, then the Yorkshire Grand National including the All-Comers at the same meeting, before again going farther north to repeat the 1954 double victory at the Newcastle Grand National.

Hailing from Lancashire, Terry Cheshire was more active in northern events than others. Nonetheless, he did come south for the

Hants Grand National and the Sunbeam Point-to-Point where, in the former, he was second in the 350 Race of 1955 and 1956. In the latter, he was third in the Junior Race of 1955 behind winner Brian Stonebridge and runner-up Paul Jarman, making it a familiar BSA one-two-three.

Before going over to Royal Enfield for 1957, Terry Cheshire rounded off his BSA contribution with a splendid gold medal in the 1956 International Six Days Trial, that year staged around Garmisch-Partenkirchen in Germany. He was using a prototype 250cc Gold Star developed by Roland Pike, then with the Small Heath development staff. It was rumoured that the Roland Pike 250 developed more bhp during a first run on the test bed than the much-vaunted, four-valve overhead camshaft 250cc MC1 racer of 1952/53. It has been suggested that the sole reason for the one-off 250 Gold Star of 1956 was to take advantage of the capacity speed schedules in enduro events such as the ISDT and Welsh Two Days. As in the case of the MC1 racer, the 250 Gold Star project was not pursued.

Not quite as successful as Terry Cheshire — who finished third in the ACU Scramble Star contest of 1956 — but nonetheless equally determined young men who rode Gold Stars with considerable aplomb were Midlanders Peter and Paul Taft and Jimmy Bray. All proved quite capable of ousting the top stars in national events, Peter Taft finishing fifth in the ACU ratings of 1956. By 1957 Peter had really matured to win the Junior Race of the Sunbeam Point-to-Point, held that year at Hankon Bottom near Winchester. Peter was also second to Jeff Smith in the Senior Race which followed. Earlier in the season — for that year the famous Sunbeam Club event took place in September instead of the customary April — Peter Taft had been runner-up to Dave Curtis in the Junior Race of the Cotswold Scramble. In the Experts Grand National he won the 500 Race, beating Andy Lee from Cambridge who had already won the 350 Race with his B32 Gold Star.

During the early 1950s, the big-framed Jimmy Bray had won the 1952 Isle of Man Grand National Scramble and finished second to John Avery in the 350 Race at Hawkstone Park — a position he repeated the following year in 1953, that time behind Geoff Ward. In the 1954 Kidstone — won by David Tye — Bray was second to Tye in the 350 Race, ahead of Welsh champion Tom Wheeler, to make it a BSA one-two-three twice over that day.

During the 1958 season Peter Taft had to be content with placings only in the trade-supported nationals — one second place and two thirds — and in the Lancashire Grand National of 1959 the Taft brothers emulated the Rickmans by Paul finishing second in the Senior Race ahead of Peter in third place, with the order reversed in the Grand National — Peter second and Paul third. With both races won by the

175

Taken just nine months before he was fatally injured in the North v South Scramble at Boltby, Yorkshire, during July 1966, Jerry Scott demonstrates the right way to do it with the Cheney-BSA Gold Star. He was on his way to winning the first heat of a championship meeting in Hampshire. Photo: Motor Cycle News.

remarkable Arthur Lampkin, it was a rather familiar BSA one-two-three in both events. Only the year before, Peter Taft had finished third in the Junior Race of this northern classic.

One of the most widely-known of the Gold Star scramble élite —

Keith Hickman, star rider of the day with the Cheney-BSA Gold Star, won the two main races at the North Hants Scramble in January 1966. Photo: Motor Cycle News.

one who acquired works-rider status in 1960 — was 'Big John' Burton of Lutterworth. As the nickname implies he was built on generous lines like Basil Hall, with fresh, fair complexion and blue eyes, the son of pre-war speedway ace 'Squib' Burton. His fame became widely known because when he reached his riding peak toward the end of the Gold Star saga it coincided with the early days of televised scrambles. Along with Arthur Lampkin, he became one of the stars of the small screen. Not that he failed to make his mark before then for as early as 1954 he had gained a second place in the 350 Race of the Lincolnshire Grand National. Nonetheless, it was 1960 before he really hit the top by finishing runner-up to Jeff Smith in the ACU Star contest (tying with Don Rickman on 20 points). During the year he had performed the hat-trick at Hawkstone Park by winning the 350 Race, 500 Race and the unlimited Grand National event. In June that year he had finished second to Dave 177

A Gold Star 'blitzkrieg' of devastating talent circa 1954 with L to R: John Draper, Jeff Smith, Brian Martin, David Tye, Phil Nex, John Avery and Brian Stonebridge. Between them they won everything worth winning.

Curtis (Matchless) in the Junior Race of the Cotswold Scramble — a meeting at which Jeff Smith finally ended Dave Curtis's long sequence of wins in the Senior Race. Burton also scored two second places in the Experts Grand National.

Tying with John Giles (Triumph) and Don Rickman (Metisse) in the 1961 Star contest (in 4th place), John Burton won the 350 Race at Hawkstone Park, the 500 Race at the Experts Grand National classic, and a second place in the Lancashire Grand National. In 1961 he was also the highest placed British rider in the World Championship series, in fifth place, the title that year going to Swedish ace Sten Lundin (Lito).

His best rides in the nationals of 1962 produced only placings, such as a second in the 500 Race of the Experts Grand National and a third in the Grand National at Shrubland Park behind winner Jeff Smith and runner-up Arthur Lampkin — making yet another BSA one-two-three. Nevertheless, his performance throughout the season was enough to put him in second place in the Star contest, with 16 points, well down on the 40 scored by title winner Jeff Smith. John Burton's last BSA success was at Hawkstone Park in 1963 when he finished second to Jeff Smith in both legs of the 500 Race. By 1964 he was riding a Triumph-engined Metisse produced by the Rickman brothers.

The list of riders who helped to immortalize the Gold Star name in British scrambles is endless, many such riders confining their activities to events of less than national status — riders who became local heroes to the thousands of fans who went from meeting to meeting with their support. Such riders are too numerous to mention. But no list could be considered without including the names of Jerry Scott and Keith Hickman, both of whom established themselves with a Gold Star and continued on to ride the new generation of Victor scramblers. Keith Hickman, who eventually became an official works rider, stormed to a double win in the Southern Scott Scramble of November 1963, winning both the main 500 races. Jerry Scott, destined to be one of scramblings rare fatalities, won both legs of the 1964 Experts Grand National in convincing style. Not surprisingly, he was selected for the British team to ride in the Motocross des Nations, at Namur, Belgium in the August of 1965.

Born in Coventry in 1939 but residing in Parkstone, Dorset in adult life, Jerry Scott died from fatal injuries sustained whilst taking part in the North v South Scramble at Boltby, Yorkshire on 31st July 1966.

Jerry's best season in 1965 saw him in fourth place in the ACU Star contest (the year before the introduction of the new-style British Championship) and in eighth place in the World Championship. Just one month before his tragic death, Jerry had joined the BSA factory team. Happily, such accidents are rare in scrambles and motocross in striking contrast to the spectacular mode of the sport.

Those incomparable Gold Star riders who ravaged the opposition throughout the 1950s immortalized both themselves and the models they rode. It was a veritable galaxy of shining stars.

Chapter 12

Trials Riding Supporting Cast

IN COMPARISON with the array of scramble riders recruited to supplement the front-line works-employed experts, expansion of the trials riding team was modest indeed. This was undoubtedly a result of the domination of Bill Nicholson during '47, '48 and '49 and his ACU Trials Drivers' Star wins of 1951 and '52. When Jeff Smith followed Nicholson to win the Star in 1953 and '54 it meant that BSA had won the solo 'championship' four years in succession.

Nonetheless, there was need for additional support from time to time and initially Bert Perrigo made use of the dynamic Terry Hill from Belfast. For 1951 the long-legged and nonchalant Tom Ellis from Ripley, Yorkshire, joined the factory line-up and from 1954 one-time Norton works teamster Rex Young also turned out on a works B34. Before riding a works Norton he had ridden a BSA on which he finished runner-up (tying with Geoff Duke on another BSA) to the incomparable Bill Nicholson in the 1947 Scott Trial.

As mentor to Bill Nicholson during his early riding days, it wasn't long before the beguiling Terry Hill had been singled out for BSA works support. From time to time, when needs dictated, he was included in the official works team — such as in the 1948 Scottish Six Days, where he replaced Fred Rist who had been prevented from taking part. On that occasion Terry Hill was teamed-up with Nicholson and Draper, to win the manufacturers' team award; and with Nicholson and Tozer to win the mixed-team award — two team awards for BSA in the one event. Two years before he had teamed-up with Nicholson and Fred Rist to win the team award in the 1946 Scott Trial, at the same time winning the Best Newcomer Award. In the Scottish Six Days of 1950, Terry was best of all the BSA runners, winning the Latimer Trophy with a loss of 28 marks.

A man of considerable versatility embracing trials, scrambles,

*The BSA works team for the 1952 Scottish Six Days with Tom Ellis (left)
David Tye (centre) and Brian Martin. David Tye was runner-up, just
three marks down on the winner; Tom Ellis won the 500 Cup and the trio
collected the team prize for BSA. Photo:* Ray Biddle.

grasstrack and road racing, Terry Hill was a great character, a man of
infinite charm yet tough as old boots and as enduring as a piece of
granite. He went on competing in both the Scottish and International
Six Days for many years; indeed, he competed in no less than 28 of the
former — finishing in 25 — and won a total of seven medals in the
International. One of his rare failures in the International Six Days was
in 1950 when, riding an A7 Twin in the Irish Vase team, he retired with
fellow Irish teamster T.J.B.Stronge, joining the other 132 casualties that
year. Amongst them was Tom Ellis and it was the latter's retirement
which led to his recruitment by BSA.

Riding as a member of the Royal Enfield works team for the
previous three seasons. Tom Ellis had maintained a clean sheet in that
ISDT of 1950 until the fifth day, when mechanical trouble with the bike
forced his retirement. He was so fed-up with his rotten luck that he left
his bike at the roadside and forlornly trudged to the nearest pub for
solace and refreshment. Who should be there but Bert Perrigo and BSA
sales manager George Savage, who invited Tom to join them. Having
unburdened his soul, Tom was a little taken a aback when Bert
suggested, with his usual dry humour, that all he needed was a 'decent' 181

Cigarette-smoking Tom Ellis on his way to victory in the 1951 British Experts Trial, held in the Buxton area of Derbyshire. It was BSA's second-in-a-row solo Experts win.

bike and, if he cared to think about it, to give him a ring at the factory. Which he did.

So for 1951 Tom Ellis turned out on a works B34 for the first time, during the course of the season winning the 500 Cup in the Bemrose, Mitchell, Clayton Trophy and St. Davids trials and his first premier award in the Alan Trophy Trial. Then right at the end of the season,

Relaxing in the warm sunshine of the 1953 Scottish Six Days, spectators watch Tom Ellis, 'clean' Kinlochrannoch, 112 miles out from Edinburgh, on the first day. Photo: Ray Biddle.

almost as a big thank-you to BSA, he won the British Experts — BSAs second in succession.

Born in 1924, Tom had been too young to do any public-road riding before the war. So it was not until 1946 that his active competitions career commenced when, riding a Matchless, he began to make his mark by winning a special first class award in the first post-war Scottish Six Days of 1947. He finished tenth in order of merit, with a loss of 47 marks. In the 1948 Scottish, by then mounted on a works Royal Enfield, he was actually leading the trial by the end of the Tuesday, tying with John Draper. Although failing to maintain that form throughout the week, he collected another special first class award, finishing eighth, one mark in front of Bill Nicholson.

A young Brian Povey, entrusted with Brian Martin's works B32 (registration BSA 300), weighing-in for the 1953 Scottish Six Days, an event won by his father, Fred Povey, in 1938. Photo: Ray Biddle.

Thereafter he was a good consistent performer, winning the premier award in a number of nationals such as the Mitchell of 1952, the Irish Patland Cup of 1955, and in the same year finishing runner-up to Jeff Smith in the international Austrian Alpine Trial. 1956 saw him victorious in the St. Davids of South Wales and many were the 500 class cups he won over the years, including that of the 1952 Scottish Six Days.

The bad luck which had put him out of the 1950 International Six Days — and steered him in the direction of BSA — persisted; indeed, it had struck even before then for though he had been selected to ride in the 1949 British Vase 'B' team a broken ankle sustained prior to the event prevented him from even starting. In 1948, with the International based at San Remo and riding in the Enfield team, he had the bad luck to drop one solitary mark, which relegated him to silver medal standard.

Despite these ISDT setbacks and without a gold medal to his name, the ACU team selectors still had confidence in him as an ideal team man, again selecting him for the 1951 British Vase 'B' team, the event that year being based at Varese, in Northern Italy. Whilst hitherto it had been merely capricious bad luck that had dogged Tom Ellis's previous ISDT rides, that encountered during the 1951 ISDT was of the most savage kind.

For most of the week all had been well, with Tom riding swiftly, safely and with confidence. On the fifth day, still with a clean sheet, his ride came to a sudden and violent end without any warning when he was flung over the handlebars and down a steep precipice on the route between Luino and Laveno. On that fast, downhill section of winding road, where unrestricted visibility encouraged rapid progress, a hidden tree root had caught between the spokes of the rear wheel, tossing Tom over the top and down the hillside with the bike following him. There

With accentuated body lean, Brian Povey battles with the rockery above Flook's Corner on Mamore in the 1953 Scottish Six Days Trial. Photo: Ray Biddle.

One of the great Irish all-rounders, Terry Hill of Belfast, winning the 1958 Northern Ireland Boxing Day Trial with the rear sprung 500 Gold Star on which he won many awards.

were but two clumps of young saplings on that bare hillside, one ensnared the bike and the other arrested his flight. Bruised and battered he climbed back to the bike, by which time local villagers had rushed to the scene. Some of them rushed back to the village to get saws and ropes with which to release the bike and haul it back on to the road. Remarkably, the bike was less battered than Tom and with the resolve typical of the good ISDT team man, he pressed on, bruised but undefeated, to complete the week. He had missed yet another gold but the bronze medal he did win was more justly earned than any gold, where troubles have not disturbed the rhythm of riding.

Terry Hill also endured a similar desperate situation that week when, having taken a nasty spill, he fractured his jaw, knocked out some teeth and injured his spine. Thus injured and severely concussed, he nonetheless managed to remount and ride the bike back to Varese where he collapsed at the official control. Like his companion Johnny Draper, already hospitalized with severe injuries as recounted in a previous chapter, Terry spent the rest of the week under medical care.

All was not gloom in the BSA camp, however. As captain of the British Trophy team Fred Rist had won another gold medal — as already described — as had David Tye who, like Rist, rode a 650cc A10 twin. Two British riders of A10 Gold Flash sidecar outfits — George Buck and R. Wagger — also won gold medals as did three Gold Star solo riders — S. Frost, E. Arnott and Eddie Dow of the British Army team. Even more praiseworthy was the gold won by Britisher F. Allen, mounted on a humble 123cc BSA Bantam.

Frank Darrieulat and passenger Dave Warner with the BSA fitted with Reynolds pivoting front forks at the start of the 1956 Cotswold Cups Trial. It was one of nine national trials they won that year, including the British Experts.

Functional engineering but stark and ungainly! The FN-type trailing-action pivoting front forks fabricated and used by Frank Darrieulat on his Gold Star outfit during 1957/58. Photo: Motor Cycle News.

With the BSA works team reduced by injury, compensation came with the success of the BSA team entered by the Dutch importers under the name 'BSA Holland' with J.Flinterman, P.Knijnenburg and J.Roest all winning gold medals and a team prize.

Finally, at his fifth attempt, Tom Ellis succeeded in his objective and won his first International Six Days gold medal in the mountains of Austria in 1952 when conditions were at their worst. He was then riding for the first time a new swinging-arm Gold Star. With the ISDT back in Wales for 1954, Tom earned another gold with an incident-free ride (he did not ride in the 1953 event staged in Czechoslovakia when Great Britain won the International Trophy once more). But in 1955, with the event again taking place in Czechoslovakia, the gremlins struck once more, forcing Tom to retire on the third day.

That proved to be his last International Six Days Trial so it was a pity it ended on such a dull note. Nonetheless, Tom Ellis went on competing in trials until 1963, by which time he had ridden in the notorious Scott Trial 14 times, winning in the process twelve first class awards — the silver crested tea spoon that is probably the most

Frank Darrieulat with passenger Dave Warner winning the sidecar premier award in the 1957 West of England Trial using his unconventional pivoting front forks. Note also hydraulic steering damper anchored on the sidecar chassis. Photo: Motor Cycle News.

highly-prized award in the sport. He had completed 17 active years in trials riding when he withdrew from active competition — though he had participated in scrambles to a lesser degree, including the Sunbeam Point-to-Point on one occasion. Today he is as active as ever with the administration of the sport in various official capacities.

To describe any rider as playing a 'supporting role' is somewhat derisive, for every man was as good as the next. Nonetheless, some can be seen as having been more successful than others, although they still needed good back-up if the coveted team prize was to be won. No British manufacturer won more team prizes than BSA. When victory in the sidecar class was added to a solo class victory, publicity was all that more powerful. In that respect BSA were particularly fortunate during the Harold Tozer era. Once he had retired, it never seemed quite the same, although that remark too, seems unfair. His immediate successor with a BSA outfit — one Frank Darrieulat with passenger Dave Warner — won no less than 32 major sidecar awards.

BSA: Competition History

Although Londoner Frank (of French parentage) first made his mark with an ex-Tozer BSA outfit in the D.K.Mansell Sidecar Trial of 1952, in which he won the 500 Class Cup, his best year was clearly 1956 when he made best sidecar performance in no less than nine nationals. These included the prestigious British Experts title and ACU Sidecar Drivers' Star in the one season. He had already won the British Experts in 1954 when, with a loss of 29 marks, he handsomely beat runner-up Jack Stocker (Royal Enfield) who lost 47 marks and third place man Frank Wilkins who lost 51. Born in 1914 Frank Darrieulat was one of the earliest pioneers of the lightweight, two-stroke trials outfit, when he used a 197cc DOT outfit in a number of trials during 1955 before he returned to a Gold Star outfit and his best season in 1956.

For the British Experts Trial of November 1958, Frank Darrieulat had reverted to the Reynolds pivoting front fork — in this shot with a broken damper unit. Darrieulat won the Experts title in 1954 and 1956. Photo: Motor Cycle News.

Darrieulat was also noted for the ungainly, trailing-action pivoting front forks he constructed and used. Though ugly in appearance he swore by them, claiming to be able to tackle rocker terrain at twice the speed possible with conventional telescopics. True or not, he reverted to the Reynolds leading-action pivoting forks he had previously used.

Darrieulat's last effective year with the BSA outfit was in 1958 when he made best sidecar performance in eight national trials, his last win being the sidecar class of the Colmore Cup in 1959 — an event he had not won before. The Beggars Roost Easter-time national in north Devonshire was one of his favourites which he won five times; four of them in succession from 1955 to '58. He also competed in sidecar scrambles when one of his main victories was in the Shrubland Park national of 1958 (where Jeff Smith also won the Grand National and Senior events).

Toward the end of the Darrieulat era two new names showed up in the list of sidecar class winners — both with BSA outfits — one being Sam Seston of Birmingham who made best sidecar performance in the national Vic Brittain Trial of January 1958. The other was that ever-popular London motorcycle dealer Bill Slocombe, who won the

Popular London motorcycle dealer Bill Slocombe with passenger Frank Ball climbing a section on Weavers Down, Hampshire, in March 1960, the year in which he won the British Experts sidecar title. The Slocombe Gold Star outfit is fitted with Reynolds pivoting front forks made to individual order.

sidecar cup in the Mitcham Vase in November the same year. Sam Seston, always passengered by Harry Nash, went on to win his class of the St. Davids Trial of 1959, then the Victory Cup and Bemrose Trophy in 1960. He had devoted all his younger years to riding solo in grasstrack racing events, and had several rides in the Isle of Man Clubman's TT. Indeed, in the Clubman's of 1951 he finished 12th in the Junior Race on a Gold Star at 71.91 mph (also 32nd in the Senior that week on the same

BSA: Competition History

model), with his pal and future passenger, Harry Nash, 14th on another Gold Star at 71.40 mph.

Then at a time in life when most men decide enough is enough, Sam Seston came out with the BSA trials outfit to do better than he had ever done solo. His most notable win came in the 1960 Scottish Six Days, the last time the Highland classic catered for a sidecar entry. Thus the names of Sam Seston and Harry Nash go down in the pages of history as the last of a long line of Scottish Six Days sidecar winners. An injury later that season robbed him of the chance of winning the ACU Sidecar Star; and in the following February, whilst riding round the Colmore Cup course (though not competing) he collapsed with a fatal heart attack.

The Slocombe outfit with BSA telescopic forks turned 180 degrees to bring the front brake inboard. Note also the speedo head mounted in the sidecar nose and the sidecar wheel brake lever mounted on grabrail.

Bill Slocombe with his later BSA outfit climbing Camp Hill in the 1963 D.K. Mansell Sidecar Trial run in the Colmore Cup Trial territory of the Cotswolds. Photo: The Classic Motor Cycle.

With one of the most handsome ever BSA sidecar outfits — prepared by Alec Wright (today, manager of the Kawasaki off-road operation) — Bill Slocombe went on to win the Hoad Trophy of 1959 (a win he repeated in 1961), the Beggar's Roost of 1960, then at the end of that season he hit the jackpot by winning the sidecar title in the British Experts Trial with a clear margin of 12 marks over runner-up Peter Roydhouse (Norton) on 59 marks and third-place man Frank Darrieulat (BSA) on 63.

During the mid-1960s, Arthur Pulman (who had won the ACU Sidecar Star for 1959 and 1960 with a Matchless) competed with a 350cc B40 outfit, winning the Southern Trial in 1963, the John Douglas in 1964 and, in 1965, the important Victory Cup Trial and the West of England at Newton Abbot. Other riders to win sidecar premier awards with BSA outfits included A.C.Kelly, who won the Reliance Trial of 1952 and the Alan Trophy of 1954, J.S.Oliver who won the class in the 1958 Scottish Six Days (included for the first time since 1950), London Policeman Ernie Small who won the Southern Trial of 1961 and the Mitcham Vase of 1963, Bernard Checklin of Mansfield who won the Greensmith Trial of 1966 and Peter Mountfield, who won the Welsh Trophy Trial in 1965 and the Allan Jefferies of 1966.

Sam Seston with passenger Harry Nash on their way to finishing second in the sidecar class of the 1959 British Experts Trial, just five marks down on winner Frank Wilkins (Ariel). Photo: The Classic Motor Cycle

Sam Seston and Harry Nash struggling among the boulders of Flook's Corner on Mamore in the 1958 Scottish Six Days, the year in which the sidecar class was reintroduced — and won by Jack Oliver (BSA)

Here 'cleaning' a section in the 1958 Scottish Six Days, Sam Seston etched his name in the record books by being the last sidecar premier award winner. After his victory in the 1960 event, the class was dropped from this classic.

It must be conceded, however, that during the 1960s, Ariel ruled the sidecar roost until in 1971 along came Ray and Derek Round to break the sequence, a look-alike duo with Ray doing the driving and Derek the passengering. Emanating from the Black Country, they firstly strove for the top with a Gold Star outfit but by 1968 they had replaced the ageing Gold Star with a works-supplied 441cc Victor, that year enjoying their best season to date with a win in the Belgian Lamborelle Trial, the Greensmith Memorial, the Sam Seston Sidecar Trial and the Southern. Their successes in 1969 included premier awards in the Vic Brittain, Colmore Cup and Knut Trophy Trials and with a loud knocking on the door, a third place in the British Experts.

Finally, with their well-prepared 441 Victor outfit, Ray and Derek Round received the ultimate success by winning both the British Experts and the ACU Sidecar Star for 1971, repeating both title wins in 1972, to make it a double victory two years in succession. In winning both the Experts and the ACU Star in the same season they joined the exclusive BSA company of Harold Tozer and Frank Darrieulat who had achieved it before. Furthermore, they had broken the ten year monopoly of Ariel in the sidecar class with their 1971 British Experts victory, to make BSA the most prolific four-stroke winner of the sidecar class of that 195

Bearded Ray Round with brother Derek (normally bearded also) mastering the rocks of Crump's Brook in the Greensmith Trial circa 1971 with his 440 Victor outfit. Photo: Terry Smith.

old-established classic. Up to and including 1970, Ariel and BSA had been level pegging with 13 wins each.

The Expert wins of Ray and Derek Round made the BSA score 15. With the additional 12 solo titles, the joint BSA total amounts to an astonishing 27 titles in that classic. The only other British manufacturer to get within distance of that was Ariel, with a joint total of 19 wins. Norton came third with a joint total of 10 wins. Under the harsh light of close scrutiny no other make will stand comparison. Royal Enfield and AJS are next, with three solo victories each, Matchless and Velocette had two wins each and Triumph and Greeves but one each. It is sobering to admit that Triumph never won a single solo or single sidecar title in the British Experts after the Second World War.

In that context — thanks to the main and 'supporting' cast — BSA were giants indeed.

Another graphic shot of the Round brothers taken in the Greensmith Trial. They won the British Experts sidecar title and ACU Sidecar Star two years running in 1971 and 1972, thus breaking the Ariel monopoly. Photo: Terry Smith.

Chapter 13

Supporting Role

WITH THE comprehensive range of models produced and marketed by BSA to fill plant capacity and provide the valuable franchise sought by world-wide dealers, it is logical that BSA would select and use for competitions activity the type most suited for the job. With certain exceptions, the minimum size considered 'man enough' for trials and scrambles pre-war was one of 250cc, but by 1939 the 350cc model had become regarded as the ideal. Thus after the war the 350cc single-cylinder four-stroke was the dominant type with the bigger 500cc variant increasing in popularity as the months went by. So all the major entrants — Ariel, AMC, BSA, Norton and Royal Enfield — fielded teams of riders mounted on their four-stroke single cylinder products.

Nevertheless, all the trade-supported national trials of the immediate post-war years contained entries from James, DMW and Royal Enfield — plus, at a later date, Francis Barnett — with their riders mounted on small-capacity, two-stroke models. In the case of Royal Enfield their 125cc lightweight entry was merely an adjunct to their big-bike entry. These small two-stroke models were but slight variations of the standard road model and as such, when competing alongside the experts of the day using big four-strokes, they had no chance of winning outright. In the eyes of the big-bike competitor, such machines were a joke; the riders to be pitied, denied as they were the potent performance required for such hills as Henwood in the Cotswolds. Indeed, the sort of performance that made trials riding worthwhile.

Capacity class cups seemed the most they could win but, overall, the main objective was publicity; to prove that mundane lightweights were quite capable of coping with the same conditions encountered by the bigger models.

When BSA announced in June 1948 the introduction of a new 123cc two-stroke lightweight named the Bantam, a competitions version must

The great Bill Nicholson trying the original prototype 123cc trials Bantam around the rough hillocks to the rear of the BSA sports ground and test track. Ridden by George Pickering, it won its class cup first time out in the 1949 Colmore Cup Trial.

have been furthest from the thoughts of BSA management at that time. Weighing in at a paltry 153 lbs, this stylish, mist-green newcomer was displayed to the British public for the first time at the Earls Court Motorcycle Show of November 1948, marked-up at £79.7.6d including speedometer and purchase tax — the latter in those days levied on so-called 'luxury' goods.

The Bantam was a huge success from the outset, with production reaching 100,000 in the brief space of five years. At that price and light weight, the private clubman recognised its potential as a bread-and-butter trials model straight away and in no time the factory was inundated with requests for a trials variant, with some enthusiasts converting the standard model themselves.

With Fred Rist, Bill Nicholson and John Draper competing with the 'real' models, Bert Perrigo had to look around for another rider when the first Bantam trials prototype had been prepared. He did not have far 199

Works tester George Pickering riding the 1950 trials Bantam in a typical Midlands quagmire mudbath. During 1949/50 Pickering won six 125cc class cups in national trials.

to look, for among the factory road testers was one George Pickering, a wartime Army dispatch rider who had done a little competition riding pre-war and post-war with another of those pre-war 250cc B21 models on which Fred Rist and John Avery had done so well.

Although no newcomer to trials, George had no time to practise with the unfamiliar lightweight before the Colmore Cup came round as the model's first try-out. It was very much a case of suck it and see. To the delight of all concerned George won the 125cc Class Cup and in so doing became the first man to win a national trial capacity class cup with the Bantam. Initially, specification variations from standard were little more than a larger rear sprocket, raised saddle, lighting set removed and standard 2.75 inch tyres replaced with a 3 inch front and 3.25 inch rear. In due course, with Jack Amott and Reg Wilkes developing the engine performance, and modifications to the rear sub-frame allowing the use of a 4 inch tyre — with an even bigger rear sprocket to counter the latter — the little Bantam became more competitive, though with a top gear of 11.1 it was less fun to ride on the open road.

George Pickering repeated his capacity class win of the Colmore Cup in the Wye Valley Traders Cup which followed and in the Red Rose in Lancashire later that season. Later still, with production models

George Pickering (19) and F.W. Osborne (James) under starter's orders on the first morning of the 1950 International Six Days Trial in Wales. Both riders retired on the 5th day with Pickering unpenalized at the time. Number 23 is F.G. Smith on another Bantam who retired on the 2nd day. Photo: The Classic Motor Cycle.

Brian Martin trying out the prototype 150cc trials Bantam with swinging-arm rear suspension and 'heavyweight' 'C' Group front forks. The venue is the rough hillocks to the rear of the factory at Small Heath. Photo: The Classic Motor Cycle.

available, R. Porter won the 125 Cup in both the Alan Trial and newly-inaugurated Allan Jefferies Trial. C. Horn won the class in the Travers Trial in Northumberland and G. Jones likewise in the Reliance in North Wales. It was a pretty good start by any standard and during the next three years Bantam riders won as many 125cc class cups in national trials as any other make; indeed, during the 1950 season it was best 125 in no less than nine national trials, mostly of trade-supported status, with George Pickering winning three of then as best individual.

John Draper winning the 150 class cup with the 150cc Bantam Major in the Mitcham Vase Trial of 1955. Draper also won the 150 cup in the Manville that year and finished 6th in the Scottish Six Days of 1956, repeating his Bemrose Trophy class cup award.

During the 1952 season, after an early Bantam success in the Kickham when R. Jackson won the 125 Classic Cup and George Pickering repeated this performance in the Victory Cup, a new name came into prominence in the lightweight class. In quick succession, he won the 125 class with a privately-owned Bantam in the Beggar's Roost, the Cotswold Cups and the Wye Valley Traders. This name was George Fisher who went on to become a Francis Barnett 'works' rider and one of the most successful lightweight competitors. Whilst history will always

associate the name of George Fisher with that of the Coventry-made lightweight, the fact remains he began his competition riding career on a Bantam.

Success with the Bantam in the International Six Days Trial was rather more perfunctory than in the sporting nationals. Not one gold was won on a Bantam until F. Allen did so in Italy in 1951. With no official factory entries in the ISDT of 1949, there were a number of private entries with Bantams, four of which completed that dusty week in Wales to win medals — R.W.Wagger with three marks lost and C.Clegg with six marks lost, to gain silver medals. In gaining bronze medals, D.J.Hughes lost 14 marks and C.Cooper 33.

However, with the 1950 ISDT again staged in the mountains of Wales, Bert Perrigo entered two Bantams officially, one to be ridden by Mrs P.Hughes and the other by works tester George Pickering who had won a gold medal in 1949 with his privately-entered pre-war B21 250 model. Additionally, seven private Bantams were entered. It was a disaster. Mrs Hughes retired on the first day and by the fifth George Pickering was the sole Bantam running, still without penalty. Then, he too, struck disaster when suspect route marking put him off course as it did a number of early riders. By the time he had regained the course and reached the next check, his time allowance had expired. Only 81 competitors had survived the horrific conditions and there was cold comfort in the fact that not a single 125cc lightweight had won a gold. Austrian rider E.Beranek (125cc Puch) was the best of the class, with a loss of 19 marks. If publicity and the proving of reliability were the main objectives, then the 1950 ISDT results were counter-productive relative to that lightweight class. Lightweights of that era — including those of foreign makers — were not man enough for events of that severity.

Until the introduction of the larger capacity 150cc Bantam Major of 1955, George Pickering continued to ride a 123cc Bantam, winning the occasional class cup; then with the International Six Days back in Wales for 1954, George had his last Six Days ride on a Bantam. As in 1950, he was clean for most of the week before trouble again struck. This time, one of the many rocks encounted daily among the Welsh mountains had damaged the bottom chainguard. This threw the chain off the rear sprocket which them jammed between the final-drive sprocket and engine casting. By the time he had rectified the trouble, he was several minutes late at the next time check. Thus at the conclusion of the event he had to settle for a silver medal only.

Well before then, however, the Bantam had been exposed to its baptism of fire in national scrambles, in the first instance in the Cotswold Scramble of 1950, ridden by Bill Nicholson. The organizing Stroud Club had included a 125cc Lightweight class in their national since 1946 and indeed, the class had been won by privateer T.Barker on a

Bantam in 1949. In 1950 Bill Nicholson romped away to victory on the factory Bantam, and with Nicholson also winning the Senior Race, Basil Hall the Junior Race and John Avery the 250 Race, the Bantam win helped achieve a BSA grand-slam that day. The prospect of winning all four classes had encouraged racing the Bantam. It provided yet another opportunity of underlining BSA supremacy.

It is probably true that competition in that ultra-lightweight class during the immediate post-war rears was rather less severe than during the years which followed. Nonetheless, competition there was. Speedway rider and all-rounder Roger Wise had won the class in the Cotswold Scramble of 1946 with his Royal Enfield with B.Harris winning in 1947 on an Excelsior. With Jack Plowright aboard, Royal Enfield won it again in 1948.

By virtue of the Bantam, BSA enjoyed a similar grand-slam string of victories when winning every race at Shrubland Park in 1950. At the Experts Grand National meetings of 1955 and 1956 with the Bantam winning its class on both occasions, only the 250 race eluded BSA when they won all else. The win by Paul Taft in the event of 1957 made it a Bantam hat-trick in the lightweight class.

One of the most convincing Bantam wins was that in the Experts Grand National of 1956 with both Brian Stonebridge and John Draper contesting the class. After a disastrous start with Stonebridge and Draper last away from the line, they literally ran through the field of riders to head the screaming pack by the end of the opening lap with Stonebridge leading Draper until the last lap when the man from Cheltenham nipped past to win.

However, all concerned knew that the 123cc Bantam had its limitations for it was never taken very seriously as it struggled in the shadow of the mighty Gold Star. Even so it was evident that a small two-stroke was an increasing force to be reckoned with in both trials and scrambles. As early as 1951 Bill Lomas — who went on to win the 350 World Road Racing Championships of 1955 and '56 — had won the Travers Trophy Trial with a 197cc James and thus became the first man to win a post-war national trial with a two-stroke. By 1955 John Haughton had won no less than four nationals in the season on a similar model. Eric Adcock was doing well for DOT, with Bill Martin and Arthur Shutt doing well on Francis Barnetts. The latter actually beat Draper to win the coveted Scott Trial in 1953 and, two years later, won the Northern Experts of 1955.

When the Bantam was increased in capacity to 148cc it was designated the D3 Bantam Major and a little later endowed with swinging-arm rear suspension, to make it a little more competitive. In the 1955 season competitions manager Dennis Hardwicke prevailed

The most successful trials Bantam, the 175cc D10 ridden by Dave Rowland into second place in the 1967 Scottish Six Days. He is seen here negotiating the rockery of Grey Mares Ridge during that sensational ride.

upon the lightweight John Draper to have a go with the prototype when, first time out, he won the 150 Class Cup in both the Mitcham Vase and the Manville. In the following January Brian Martin tried the model in the Vic Brittain Trial and won a first class award. The main objective, however, was the Scottish Six Days Trial, but before departing for Scotland John Draper had won the 175cc Class Cup in the national Bemrose Trophy Trial in Derbyshire.

In the Highland classic, John Draper's performance exceeded all   205

Another shot of Dave Rowland surmounting the rock ledges of Grey Mares Ridge with the competitive Bantam in the 1967 Scottish. Veteran journalist Ralph Venables (extreme right) displays mute approval. Photo: Motor Cycle News

expectations, for in winning the 175 Class Cup he finished overall in sixth place, tying with Sammy Miller (Ariel) with a loss of 38 marks. Even then the Bantam Major was still outclassed, overtaken by the rapid strides being made in the development of the 175cc two-stroke — and later the 250cc — for use in competitions by those makers without comparable four-stroke models. Still with its three-speed gearbox, the Bantam Major remained essentially a basic utility lightweight for daily commuting.

In national events the Bantam featured less frequently in results. In 1957, however, D.H.Barrett won the 150 Cup in the Welsh Trophy Trial and in 1959 Ken Sedgley won the 175 Cup in the Victory Cup Trial. By 1964, during which time the engine had been increased in size yet again, and the machine redesignated the D7 Bantam Super, Tony Davis of Gloucester had won the 175 Cup in the Welsh Trophy Trial. But the model was still handicapped with only three speeds. By then the Bantam had fallen between two stools — it was no longer a true utility model or one of sporty character.

1967 heralded the introduction of the D10 Bantam, which had a sports specification that included a four-speed gearbox, a higher-compression engine with a claimed power output of 10 bhp, and stronger front forks. Brian Martin, by then competitions manager, felt for the first time that the Bantam had a true potential as a trials model, capable of taking on the 250 Greeves and Bultaco which had by then started to dominate results. With his own brother Michael having prepared the engine at the Redditch factory (where Bantam engines had always been made) Brian Martin had the prototype completed by December 1966 and tried it himself in a local trial run by the Solihull Motor Cycle Club called the Half-Crown Trial. No longer active in trials riding Brian was gratified to finish runner-up to Ken Sedgley, who lost seven fewer marks with his 250 Bultaco.

In the New Year both Brian Martin and Jeff Smith rode the new Bantam in the national St. Davids Trial in South Wales and then the Victory Cup Trial, with first class awards in the former; second class in the latter.

In March Mick Bowers — another BSA development department engineer — rode the D10 in the Cotswold Cups Trial and won the 200 Class Cup; then with the Scottish Six Days not far away one such model was handed over to the young Dave Rowland from Lancashire for use in that event. This newcomer had first achieved prominence during 1963 by winning both the Red Rose and Clayton national trials on the BSA 250cc C15T, to finish the season with a very creditable fifth place in the British Experts. From then on he was a very consistent winner of 250 class cups as well as being runner-up in the Allan Jefferies (1965) and Kickham (1966).

When Dave Rowland on the D10 Bantam finished in second place on the opening day of that 1967 Scottish, right behind Sammy Miller on a Bultaco, nobody was more elated than Brian Martin. But as Brian well knew, a day is a long time in the Scottish and anything could happen. Nonetheless Dave remained in contention all the week, never dropping below third place, and at the end of the week, he was runner-up to the great Sammy Miller. Just one super rider had prevented a Bantam from winning the Scottish Six Days. Mick Bowers, on another D10, had a good ride to win a special first class award with a loss of 79 marks. Sidecar expert Colin Morewood, taking his annual solo fling in the

After his superb performance with the Bantam in the 1967 Scottish Six Days, Dave Rowland went on to achieve outright victory with it in the Allan Jefferies Trial in July and the Mitchell Trial in October. It proved to be the trials Bantam's swan-song. Photo: Motor Cycle News

Scottish, also won a special first class award with his 148cc Bantam Major.

Rowland's success created enthusiasm at the factory with hopes of a production replica model, but the financial problems of the company were already manifest, creating the need for a reduction of short-run, non-standard specification models. Almost as a grand-finale, before that season was out, Dave Rowland won the premier award in both the Allan Jefferies and Mitchell Memorial Trial.

It was a fitting Bantam swan-song (if such a metaphor is permissible). Born to fulfil the humble role of a bread-and-butter utility model, the Bantam was quickly overtaken by events. It soon became a horse for all courses for apart from its application in trials and scrambles, there were those who decided to adapt it for road racing at private clubman level. Over the years a number of individuals came to specialize in Bantam tuning, such as Fred Hadley of Dudley in the West Midlands (who today is a partner in the Omega piston specialist firm) and George Todd of Bristol, who later joined the development staff at Small Heath on two-stroke projects. Fred Hadley was responsible for tuning the D7 Bantam raced by Don Wolfindale when, throughout the 1965 season, well able to use the Bantam's maximum of 90 mph, Wolfindale finished within the first five of every 250 class in which he competed. Even as early as 1951 a 123cc Bantam had finished 9th in the Isle of Man Ultra-Lightweight TT at a speed of 56.38 mph with L.B. Caldecut in the saddle. Twelve months later Harvey Williams finished 7th in the Ultra-Lightweight TT at 58.03 mph.

As good as the Bantam was in British events, it was those great enthusiasts and do-it-yourself innovators in Australia who really created the legend of the BSA Bantam by developing it to a remarkable degree. With engines tuned for alcohol fuel they achieved performance and reliability levels of a sufficiently high standard for this mundane model to humble the genuine double overhead camshaft racers of Mondial and MV. The most famous Australian Bantam tuner was Eric Walsh, whose models over a period of years were considered invincible.

In 1953 for example, Maurice Quincey actually won the Victorian TT Championship at Fisherman's Bend, near Melbourne, with the little 125cc Walsh-tuned Bantam. During February that same year, Ken Rumble — as adept at road racing as he was at scrambling — destroyed the opposition at an AJS Club scramble at Fisherman' Bend when he won four out of five races, all with the 125 Walsh-Bantam. These included the 250 Scratch Race, the 350 Scratch Heat and the Scratch Final, but in the Unlimited event, up against all the big four-strokes, he was forced to retire with an injured hand after putting in what proved to be the fastest lap in the race.

Never intended to fulfill a competitions role, the little 123cc Bantam, introduced in 1948, was the most successful post-war British lightweight. Here Sir Anthony Eden (later Lord Avon) examines the 100,000th model at the 1953 Earls Court Exhibition with various BSA personnel looking on.

In November in the Victorian Scramble Championship at Moe, some sixty miles from Melbourne, Ken Rumble set out to defend the three titles he had won the year before. He led the field from the opening lap in all four races he contested, aided by the appalling weather conditions in which a freak storm of gale-force winds and rain produced the wettest and coldest Victorian day for 40 years. He won both the 250 Lightweight and 350 Junior Race on the Bantam — in the former finishing a mighty 1 min 40 sec ahead of the second finisher. The 125 Ultra-Lightweight Race, however, was won by K.Emmett with P. Crozier second — both on Bantams.

Results throughout 1954 were very similar, with the Walsh-tuned Bantams winning almost every 125cc race it contested and many victories in the larger-capacity classes. Ken Rumble won the 125 Class at the two-day road race meeting at Fisherman's Bend in April, whilst the Australian Scramble Championship meeting in August at Sheidon Park, near Adelaide, was a positive BSA benefit, Ken Rumble won the 125 Title with B. Watson second and B. Ashendon third — a Bantam one-two-three — and in the 250 title race Rumble, using a 150cc Walsh-Bantam was third.

The saga continued unabated throughout the fifties and sixties. In the Australian TT of Boxing Day 1957 at Mildura, Victoria, the 125 Race was dominated by Walsh-Bantams, with Don Cameron and Ron

Miles finishing first and second. In the Australian Scramble Championship of May 1958, held at Evandale, Northern Tasmania, the 125 Race was won by A.Lee, with K.Richards second and G.Bowling third, all on Bantams. And at the Australian Scramble Championship of 1963, held in the tropical climate of Queensland, near Brisbane, Stan Jones won the 125 Title Race on a Bantam — a BSA victory repeated in the big capacity classes which followed; 250, 350, 500 and Unlimited. In retrospect, it would seem that the humble Bantam achieved more glory in Australia than anywhere else in the world.

Today, the non-territorial Bantam Racing Club of Great Britain, formed many years ago for members to enjoy the thrill of racing on a shoe-string budget, remains a tangible reminder of one of the most remarkable utility lightweights ever made. Never intended for competition greatness, it nonetheless had a degree of greatness thrust upon it. Few would disagree that the BSA Bantam was probably the most versatile lightweight two-stroke ever made in Great Britain.

Chapter 14

Star All-Rounders

MOST FACTORY riders in the old days were adept and skilful in most aspects of motorcycle sport, capable of procuring top honours for the firm they represented. Going right back to the early days, the list of such riders is long and fascinating, revealing as it does that sometimes the jack of all trades was master of them all. Names such as Geoff Davison, George Dance, Bert Kershaw, George Rowley, Vic Brittain, Jack Williams and Bob Foster, to name but a few, illustrate the point. There were many others but today specialization has eroded such versatility.

Even during the post-World War Two years, many of the most successful riders possessed that all-round ability in trials, scrambles and six-day events. No factory fielded more top-grade all-rounders than BSA; indeed, that coterie of BSA experts of the 1950s must represent the most potent team of all-rounders ever assembled. Bill Nicholson, Fred Rist, David Tye, Brian Martin, Jeff Smith, Arthur Lampkin, Allan Lampkin and John Harris all played their part in flying the BSA flag in all kinds of events. With the exception of the Lampkin brothers, all had one thing in common: they worked within the factory complex at Small Heath.

The exploits of Rist and Nicholson have already been recorded in earlier chapters and close on their heels come those of David Tye, hailing from the hills and dales of Derbyshire near Matlock; a man of charm and courtesy with a constant smile. A man brim-full of impish good fun and humour, yet highly principled and motivated. One of the great characters of the sport.

It is probable that David Tye's first national trial premier award — the 1949 Reliance Trial in North Wales — went unnoticed by BSA, notwithstanding the fact that he was riding one of the recently-introduced production B34 competition models, for he was an unknown private rider at the time. When later he began winning the odd 350

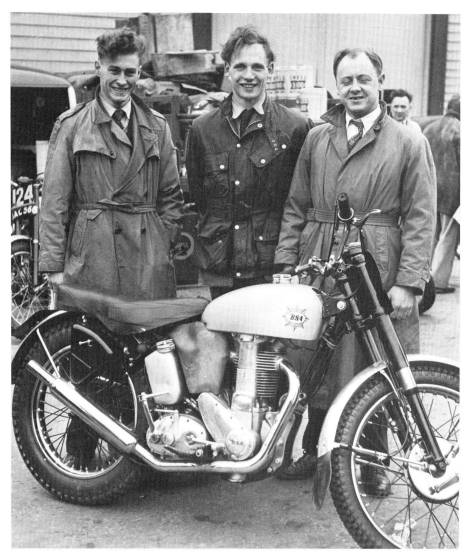

David (Tye) with his B32 'BSA 350' at the start of 1952 Scottish Six Days in which he was runner-up to winner John Brittain (Royal Enfield) by the small margin of three marks. Left is Brian Martin and right Peter Hammond of the Triumph works team. Photo: Ray Biddle.

capacity class cup on a 350 Douglas twin, people began to take notice, including Bert Perrigo, always on the lookout for promising talent.

When approached, it did not take David long to make up his mind, and by December 1950 he had left the Douglas company for whom he worked as a sales representative to join the hallowed ranks of the BSA competitions department. He promptly won the Northern Experts, to notch up his first win as an official BSA works rider.

After completing National Service with the Parachute Regiment, David had worked for a steel company in Sheffield. Still living in the family home near Matlock, it meant a daily round trip of 60 miles, initially with a KTS Velocette. In due course the KTS was replaced by a new BSA B34, suitable for both personal transport and for trials riding. It was with this that he won the 1949 Reliance Trial. He had progressed from being a B34 private owner to a Douglas works rider and then a BSA works rider in just twelve months.

For the 1953 Scottish Six Days the works team of Tom Ellis (left), David Tye (centre) and John Draper were mounted on the new all-welded frame Gold Stars. John Draper won the 500 Cup. Photo: Ray Biddle.

It was during his first full season with BSA in 1951 that David Tye launched into scrambling and right from the outset he proved to have a natural ability for it was this type of event to which his exuberant style was most suited. Nonetheless, that first year on a works BSA produced a number of trials successes; three 350 class cups (in the Victory, Mitchell and Southern Trials) a premier award in the Cleveland Sporting Trial, and a fourth place in the Northern Experts he had won the year before. In national scrambles he won the 250 Race at Shrubland Park and was second to Basil Hall in the 350 Race. Then in the punishing Lancashire Grand National he was runner-up to Brian Stonebridge — this, his first season at the sport. He was second again in 1952, finally winning that great classic in 1953 to lead home John Avery and John Draper in a BSA one-two-three.

His only trials premier award for 1952 came in the Kickham Trial

Even in the middle of 'cleaning' the Devil's Staircase in the Scottish Six Days of 1954, David Tye still displays his habitual charming smile. Centre lady in group of three among spectators is John Brittain's mother, Mrs. Vic Brittain. Photo: Ray Biddle.

— a win he repeated two years later — with the Beggar's Roost his only national trial win of 1953. He won several class cups, however, and he excelled in the Scottish Six Days by finishing runner-up to winner John Brittain (Royal Enfield), making up the BSA factory team to win the team prize.

It was in scrambling that he really excelled with his attitude of pressing-on regardless.

Like the occasion at a Burton-on-Trent Club scramble where David was leading the third race, having won the two before, when a terrific purler broke his left handlebar clean off. His sort doesn't give up that easily. Quickly remounting, he held the broken bar against his thigh to facilitate clutch-lever operation, and completed the remaining five laps still to finish second. It was not a question of financial motivation, for the monetary rewards in those days were little more than nominal.

David Tye put his heart and soul into everything he did, an attitude which produced his best season in 1953 when he finished runner-up to

David Tye being chased by Brian Stonebridge (Matchless) in the 1953 Cotswold Scramble in which he was 7th in the Senior Race. At the end of the season David Tye was runner-up in the ACU Scramble Drivers' Star. Photo: Ray Biddle.

Indicative of the conditions, David Tye (right) and T. Barker (both BSA) plastered with wet matted grass and mud at the finish of the 1953 Kidstone Scramble near Builth Wells, Wales. Contrast this with the sartorial elegance of Lt. Commander Home-Kidstone, whose name graces the event. Tye won, with Barker second.

216

Geoff Ward in the ACU Scramble Star, just seven marks down. Apart from his Lancashire Grand National victory that year, he also won the Tirley Championship Race in the Gloucester Grand National and soon after he achieved a tremendous triple win in the muddy Kidstone Scramble, winning the 350 Race, Unlimited and the Kidstone Grand National. He had a third place at Hawkstone Park; a fourth in both the Junior and Senior events of the Sunbeam Point-to-Point and a seventh in the Senior Race of the Cotswold Scramble. At the conclusion of the season he was third in the Southern Experts Trial.

David Tye winning the notorious 1953 Lancashire Grand National on Holcombe Moor, leading home John Avery and John Draper in another BSA 1-2-3. Photo: *Ray Biddle.*

Although David Tye had taken part in the 1950 International Six Days Trial in Wales on the works Douglas — when he retired on the third day — his first ISDT ride for BSA was in the 1951 event, run in the dusty sunshine of Italy, when he rode the big 650cc A10 Golden Flash. Although the event caused havoc with John Draper, Terry Hill and Tom Ellis, David never put a foot wrong to win his first gold medal.

He repeated his success the following year at Bad Aussee in Austria, riding one of the new swinging-arm Gold Stars, despite coming off   217

David Tye tackling a loose-stone track among the Welsh hills during the Welsh Two-Day Trial of 1953. Photo: Ray Biddle.

during the final one-hour speed test when overdoing his cornering on a surface of stone sets.

For the 1953 event staged in Czechoslovakia, David was selected to ride in the British Vase 'B' team. Riding a 500 Gold Star as in 1952, this time his luck deserted him, for on the fourth day he suffered front spoke breakages which, in turn, punctured the tube. Sorting out that problem cost him nine marks on time, dropping him to silver medal standard.

With the ISDT back in Wales for 1954, David's last ISDT ride for BSA produced another gold medal, with a faultless ride in company with fellow BSA teamsters Jeff Smith and Tom Ellis. In addition, three British Army riders on Gold Stars also won golds — these being the reliable Captain Eddie Dow, Lance Bombardier E.B. Crooks and Terry Cheshire, a craftsman in REME doing his National Service.

David Tye (259) with John Brittain (Enfield 215) and Peter Hammond (Triumph 226), the British Vase 'B' team in the 1952 International Six Days Trial, held in Austria. Right is team reserve Tom Ellis (BSA) who won a gold metal, as did David Tye, but both Brittain and Hammond retired. Photo: The Classic Motor Cycle.

David Tye with the swinging-arm Gold Star at the weigh-in for the 1952 International Six Days Trials in Austria. British team manager Len Heath looks quizzical as he makes notes, whilst George Rowley (right) 'keeps his distance'. Photo: The Classic Motor Cycle.

BSA: Competition History

Like John Draper before him, David Tye was attracted to the Isle of Man Clubman's TT and like Draper, under contract to BSA, was prevented from riding a Gold Star, so for the 1952 Senior event he acquired a Triumph twin. Although he had to retire on the last lap of the event when lying sixth, he put in some excellent lap times, over the 80 mph mark. With an opening lap of 81.81 mph, he was positioned in fifth place which he held until the third lap — increasing his speed to 82.18 mph, just 21 seconds down on leader Bernard Hargreaves. Eventually Jack Bottomley (Triumph) stormed through from behind to finish third, in the process dropping David into sixth spot before he retired.

Baulked by stalled and struggling foreign riders in the 1953 International Six Days in Czechoslovakia, David Tye, still smiling broadly, rides round the obstacle feet up.

A study of David Tye apparently 'praying to Allah' in the 1953 International Six Days — to no avail for he dropped 9 marks on time to win only a silver medal. Photo: The Classic Motor Cycle.

David Tye throws up plumes of sand in the forests of Czechoslovakia in the 1953 International Six Days as a member of the British Vase 'B' team. Fellow Vase team member John Giles (Triumph) also dropped to silver medal standard but the third member of the team, Stan Holmes (Ariel), won a gold medal.

There can be little doubt that had David Tye elected to pursue road racing seriously, he would have made the same indelible mark he had made in trials and scrambles.

In 1954 he left BSA employment to establish his own motorcycle business in Cromford, near Matlock, and during the years which followed he developed an enthusiasm for sub-aqua diving to the extent that he decided to do it professionally. He sold the Cromford business and moved north to the inspiring and rugged beauty of Argyllshire where he established a diving centre at Oban.

Davie Tye did not achieve the tally of wins of Nicholson, Draper and Jeff Smith, but by virtue of his bold and courageous style and, perhaps above all, that endearing and cultured charm, he was one of the finest ambassadors BSA ever had.

With his bold and courageous style, endearing and cultured charm, David Tye was one of the finest ambassadors BSA ever had. Photo: The Classic Motor Cycle.

Before David Tye had departed from Small Heath, both Brian Martin and Jeff Smith had joined the BSA band of all-rounders. Fred Rist had already gone in 1952 and with David Tye went the great Bill Nicholson. Nonetheless, John Draper was back in the BSA fold and during 1954 came the emergence of Terry Cheshire, so the balance of strength seemed preserved. However, when a new name came to the fore during the early months of 1956, Dennis Hardwicke did not hesitate to take advantage of it.

That new name was one Arthur Lampkin, the eldest of three brothers who, between them during the next two decades, would etch the family name into the history books of motorcycling as a remarkable

*Four of the great BSA all-rounders, L to R: Brian Martin, David Tye,
John Draper and Jeff Smith circa 1956, David Tye's last scramble season
with the Gold Star. In the rear background is Phil Nex.*

*A youthful Arthur Lampkin (left) joins the aura of three of BSA's greats.
L to R: Jeff Smith, John Draper and Brian Martin circa 1956 at
Hawkstone Park when Smith won both the main events.*

trio. Each one in turn won the Scottish Six Days Trial, with Martin, the youngest, achieving a hat-trick of wins in that great classic (though not with BSA).

Hailing from Silsden on the Yorkshire moors between Ilkley and Keighley, Arthur Lampkin, blunt and down to earth, had his first success with a factory BSA in the Scottish Six Days of 1956, when he

Yorkshire all-rounder Arthur Lampkin with the 250cc scramble C15 circa 1962. That year he was third in the 250 European Motocross Championship after being runner-up the year before.

won the 500 Cup by finishing fifth overall. In August that year he won the premier award in the Clayton Trophy Trial which, curiously, proved to be his last national trial premier for a period of four years. Then in November 1960 he achieved what must be the ambition of all competition riders — not least of all Yorkshire men — by winning the fabled Scott Trial, beating, in the process, Jeff Smith who had made fastest time. Thereafter for several years, that Everest-like event became Arthur Lampkin's favourite playground.

One of Arthur Lampkin's most memorable wins was his victory in the 1963 Scottish Six Days with the 250cc C15T. Here he is rounding the lower hairpin on the Devil's Staircase, by then denuded of the trees which shrouded the hill in former years. Photo: Motor Cycle News.

BSA: Competition History

He won the Scott Trial again in 1961, for the second year in succession, making both best performance on observation and fastest time, a full 13 minutes quicker than Jeff Smith had managed the year before. He again made fastest time in the event of 1963, and in 1965 it was outright victory, again best on observation and fastest time. When brother Alan won the event in 1966 it was Arthur who yet again made fastest time.

Arthur's other great victory was his win of the Scottish Six Days of 1963, a feat which brother Alan emulated just three years later, both Lampkin wins being achieved with a 250cc C15T BSA. The Alan Lampkin victory was significant, not only as the last BSA victory in that Highland classic, but as the last British four-stroke win also.

After a season with Cotton in 1964, Arthur Lampkin returned to the BSA fold for 1965 to make second-best performance in both the Bemrose and Scottish Six Days, and later to win the Manx Three Days Trial. Although he won the Northern Experts of 1963, luck was against him in the British Experts itself, his best placing being third in 1963.

Arthur Lampkin negotiates the Derbyshire rockery in the 1962 Bemrose Trophy Trial. The BSA team of Jim Sandiford, Jeff Smith and Dave Langston won the team prize for BSA, mounted on C15Ts. Photo: The Classic Motor Cycle.

Arthur Lampkin on the 440 Victor GP pursued by Don Rickman (Metisse) as they charge through the drifting sand at Hawkstone Park in the 1965 British Motocross Grand Prix.

It was in televised scrambles events that the name of Arthur Lampkin became most widely known, sharing with Jeff Smith and John Burton many of the BSA victories enjoyed in those specially-organized events. In the genuine national events, he first achieved prominence in the 1957 Lancashire Grand National by finishing third in the 350 Race. Then with good, consistent rides throughout 1958 he tied with Jeff Smith for third place in the ACU Star contest. It was again consistent riding which earned him the ACU Scramble Star for 1959. His most remarkable performance during that period was surely in the Cumberland Grand National run at Brownrigg Fell near Penrith. For three years in succession he won all three main races — the Junior Grand National, Senior Grand National and Senior Invitation, a feat tantamount to nine wins in a row from 1958 to 1960.

227

He had a similarly rewarding day at the Gloucester Grand National of 1961 when he won the three main events — the 250 Race, the 500 Race and the Tirley Grand National. In 1963 he was third in both legs of the British Motocross Grand Prix, placing him second overall. That year he achieved his highest placing in the 500 World Motocross Championship, with a fifth.

During the later sixties he was still capable of producing wins, doing

Brothers-in-law and comrades in arms, Jeff Smith (right) and John Draper, after their brilliant victory in the 1955 British Motocross Grand Prix at Hawkstone Park. With Smith the winner, they were first and second in both legs, with ten of the first twelve placings being BSA-mounted. Smith and Draper were without doubt two of BSA's greatest all-rounders.

228

just that in the West of England Trial of 1966, as he had over the summer months when he won the Belgian Motocross Grand Prix at Namur. In 1968 he contributed to a most impressive BSA one-two-three-four in the 750cc class of the BBC Grandstand TV Trophy series, finishing fourth behind John Banks, Vic Eastwood and Keith Hickman.

Riding for the British Vase 'B' team in the International Six Days Trial of 1962 in Germany, Arthur won a gold medal, but twelve months later in Czechoslovakia, again in the British Vase 'B' team, he dropped to silver medal standard as a result of a most unusual problem. The felt sealing washer in the air cleaner became detached and was sucked into the induction tract. Extracting it cost him 13 marks on time. Finally, when riding a BSA/Triumph hybrid for the British Trophy team in Sweden in 1966, he won another gold medal.

The story of Alan Lampkin reads very much like that of brother Arthur, as does that of Martin who began riding BSA with prominence in 1967. It is a story of three brothers with that versatile ability to win top honours in trials, scrambles and six-day events in the true traditions of motorcycle sport.

One other such BSA rider was John Harris, who worked in the competitions shop from 1958 until he departed at the end of 1963. During that period he won a number of class cups in national trials, and had several impressive wins in national scrambles such as in the Lancashire Grand National of 1961 when he won both the 250 Race and the Grand National event. He achieved a double victory in the 1962 Kidstone Scramble by winning the 500 Race and Grand National event, and he won the 500 Race of the Cotswold Scramble in 1963.

He won two gold medals in the International Six Days — one in Wales in 1961; and the other in 1962 as a member of the British Vase 'B' team, when the event was in Germany. In 1962, when the event was staged in Czechoslovakia, he retired on the first day with oil pump trouble. Perhaps his greatest claim to fame was his moral and practical support of Jeff Smith in the world motocross series of 1964 where, it seems, his tactical advice contributed in no small way to Jeff's world title.

There can be little doubt that BSA deployed more top-grade all-rounders than any other British manufacturer; a phenomenon like the Gold Star itself, indicative of versatile adaptability.

Chapter 15

The Third Man

WHEN BRIAN Martin was appointed competitions manager in November 1960 he could not have guessed he was destined to fill that role during a period of great change in what proved to be the final years of the company. During the previous 15 years there had been just two men; Bert Perrigo and Dennis Hardwicke. Thus Brian Martin became the third and last manager, spanning the final 25 years of BSA competition history.

On reflection, it is clear that Brian Martin was given the job during an interim period created by senior management marking time on Gold Star development for several years past, and concurrently dragging their feet over the provision of a newly-engineered replacement. As an accomplished and talented rider in both trials and scrambles, nobody would be more conscious of the immediate shortcomings and needs than Brian. A new generation of highly-potent lightweight two-strokes was coming to the fore in world scrambles, with similar purpose-built models showing signs of doing the same in trials.

The events and aftermath of the power struggle which took place within the BSA boardroom in 1956 culminating in the dismissal of Sir Bernard Docker as chairman of the board lie outside the scope of this book. Nonetheless it sparked off a chain of events which led to the transfer of Bert Perrigo from his post as Ariel sales manager back to Small Heath as chief development engineer, with joint responsibility for competitions activity.

With Perrigo assuming his new duties by the November of 1956, Dennis Hardwicke continued in his role as competitions manager until the early months of 1957, when he was appointed Power Unit sales manager – the division of the company marketing stationary engines for industrial application. With the departure of Hardwicke, and new products taking up the time of Bert Perrigo, the affairs of the

A youthful Brian Martin passengering Bill Howard in a Midland Centre Group Trial of 1946. Brian's younger brother Michael also did a stint as Bill Howard's passenger when Brian was old enough to go solo.

competitions department were increasingly delegated to Brian Martin who, having worked within the department since 1954, showed great aptitude for the job with its balance of riding, engineering and administraton. During his brilliant riding days of the 1950s, with a string of successes in both trials and scrambles, Brian had been rather more than just a fitter working on the team bikes. Dennis Hardwicke had come to rely on him for organizing, chasing, fabricating and developing non-standard components for the works bikes, such as the pivoting front forks tried by some of the works team in the British Motocross Grand Prix at Hawkstone Park in 1956. These had been developed by Brian through practical experience, getting the damper units right by trial and error in several events.

231

Signed-up by BSA for 1952, Brian Martin took over 'BSA 300' previously used by John Draper and which he used throughout the 'fifties until replaced with a 250cc C15T. Here he weighs-in for the 1952 Scottish Six Days. Photo: Ray Biddle.

When it became the responsibility of the factory to produce 12 sample sets – for use on the team bikes – a number of things proved incorrect. During practice at Hawkstone Park some of the riders complained bitterly, for with a lighter rider in particular, the damping proved too hard. In a panic, standard telescopic forks were substituted for the racing and the pivoting forks were buried for ever. Brian considers the judgement made was over-hasty, and the fork condemned for the wrong reasons. He points out that the bought-in high-grade damper units provided superior damping to that of the telescopic forks of the period. A potential advantage had been lost.

Brian Martin was first signed-up as a BSA works rider for 1952 as a direct replacement for John Draper, who had gone to Norton. First time

Brian Martin's name will always be linked with the remarkable BSA Maudes Trophy win of 1952 when he rode one of the standard Star Twins. Here, with ACU observer John McNulty, he readies for yet another day in the Austrian Alps.

With the plunger rear suspension working overtime, Brian Martin swoops downhill among the pine forests of Austria in the 1952 International Six Days, used as a part of the ACU Certified test.

out, on the former Draper 350, Brian Martin won the 350 Cup in the Colmore and a week or two later he won the premier award in the Victory Cup Trial – with John Draper on a Norton second. The latter must have regarded it as rather ironical to be beaten by 'his bike'. That was the first of many such BSA wins for Brian Martin and having completed an engineering apprenticeship with a small Birmingham engineering company, he joined the BSA payroll in August that year.

At the time, Bert Perrigo, Fred Rist and Ted Fithian were working on the operational details of the remarkable ACU Certified Test which involved three standard 500cc Star Twins. Brian Martin was thus in a position to ride as the third member of the team.

He was a relatively green beginner and, as a Francis Barnett works rider, had ridden their 125cc model in the International Six Days of 1951 in Italy where by sheer bad luck alone he lost his gold medal. At one time check, with ample time to spare, he emulated the way of the experts by using the time before clocking in for cleaning and checking over his bike. He became so absorbed in the job that he suddenly realized his time had expired. To confess to AMC team manager George Rowley just how he had lost vital marks caused young Martin acute embarrassment.

234   Whilst 1951 was Brian Martin's first season as a works rider, his

*Brian Martin (202) paddles his way along one of the typical 'main roads'
encountered in the 1952 International Six Days which wreaked wholesale
havoc on all but the BSA Star Twins.*

experience in national trials went back to 1946, when he passengered Bill
Howard in many trials. By 1947 he was learning the hard way, with an
ancient 1934, 150cc Triumph solo. Then, having saved enough pocket
money raised by acting as a 'pusher' at Birmingham Speedway (where
his father also officiated), he purchased a pre-war BSA B25 350 on which
to go scrambling.

By 1950, Brian's talent had caught the eye of Bert Perrigo's friend
and rival, George Rowley of AMC, who signed him up to ride a works
125cc Francis Barnett for the 1951 season. Thus began one of the most   235

With rear wheel airborne, Brian Martin sweeps along an Austrian forest track on the way to one of the three gold medals won by the standard Star Twins in the 1952 International Six Days.

successful lightweight partnerships of the British scene. During that memorable year Brian Martin won no less than eleven 125 capacity class cups in national trials, the majority of them having trade-supported status.

When his talent came to the fore during 1951, it is clear that Bert Perrigo regretted not having secured him before his friend George Rowley, and it was that life-long friendship which inhibited events for a time. Eventually it was Bill Nicholson who reconciled things by acting as go-between and a Martin/BSA tie-up was agreed for 1952.

When subjected to the events leading to the BSA Maudes Trophy success of 1952, the young, inexperienced, Brian Martin justified the faith placed in him by Bert Perrigo, and having ridden the Star Twins from Newcastle (after disembarkation from the Norwegian boat) to

The 'backdoor' exit out of the square at Fort William. Brian Martin climbs M & D in the 1953 Scottish Six Days with the Army B34 he rode as a member in one of the Army MCA teams. Photo: Ray Biddle.

L to R astride the bikes: John Houghton, Brian Martin and W.A. Bell of the Army MCA team with the Meteor Trophy won in the 1953 Scottish Six Days. Taken outside the BSA office entrance at Small Heath, the group includes Captain Eddie Dow (who also rode) and Bert Perrigo (right).

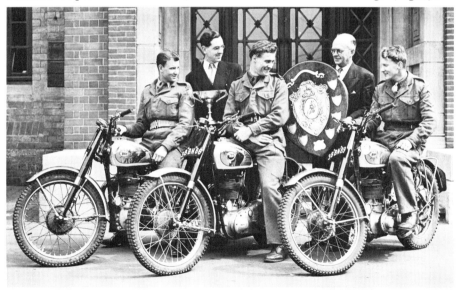

Birmingham, the party arrived back at the factory on the afternoon of Thursday, October 2nd. It was the weekend of the West of England Trial. By prior arrangement Brian's 350 B32 had been taken down to Newton Abbot by road with Bill Nicholson, leaving Brian to make his own way there by rail on his return from Norway. Without any practice whatsoever he went out to win the premier award. Then immediately after that success he dashed back to the Midlands to take part in the Worcestershire Grand National, to gain another victory in the main event.

Brian Martin conquering the rocks above Flook's Corner on Mamore, whilst riding the Army MCA-entered B34 in the 1953 Scottish Six Days during his period of National Service. Photo: Ray Biddle.

It was a string of victories which earmarked him, still only 20 years of age, as a rider of great potential, but first there was the question of National Service, deferred for a month or two to facilitate his participation in the Maudes Trophy attempt. So for the next two years he did his military service, though, as a private in the 8th Battalion of REME, motorcycles were never far away. He represented the Army Motor Cycle Association in the Scottish Six Days of 1953 and took week-end leave to ride in civilian national trials, during which period he won the 350 Class Cup in the Cotswold Cups, the Bemrose and Hoad Trophy Trial.

Free from the constraints of military routine, and back in the
competitions shop at Small Heath by the autumn of 1954, he set about

Brian Martin (81) doing battle with fellow BSA teamster John Avery in the September 1953 Hawkstone Championship Scramble amid the clouds of dust which blighted the Shropshire course in those days. Photo: Ray Biddle.

With broken front mudguard, Brian Martin controls a leaping Gold Star. It is plastered with the mud and grass of a typical British scramble circuit primed by a wet British summer circa 1956. Photo: Motor Cycle News.

A panoramic view from the top of Hawkstone's famous hill with Brian Martin (23) opting for the outside line up the hill when leading the Midland Centre to victory in the October 1954 Inter-centre Team Scramble. Photo: The Classic Motor Cycle.

making up for lost time, though despite the soldiering handicap of that year, he had finished 8th in the ACU Trials Star. Thereafter he seemed somewhat slow off the mark for his first full season of 1955, winning but one premier award, that of the Irish Experts Trial, although he did win in addition three capacity class cups. During the next three seasons, however, he had an impressive catalogue of wins in both trials and scrambles. In the former he won the Victory Cup again, the Southern Trial, the Lamborelle in Belgium, the Irish Experts again, the St. Cucufa Trial in France, the international Host Trial of Gothenburg in Sweden, the Southern Experts, the Wye Valley Traders Trophy Trial and innumerable class cups. In 1956 he was third in the ACU Trials Star behind Gordon Jackson (AJS) and winner John Brittain (Royal Enfield), twelve points ahead of fourth place man Jeff Smith.

He won the Vic Brittain twice on a 350 B32 – 1954 and 1958 – then repeated the win in 1960 with a 250cc C15T. As late as 1963, when deeply involved with development work on the world motocross models, he was still quite capable of winning as he did that year in the Bemrose Trophy Trial. His performance in scrambles was equally consistent, riding always with intelligence and safety and rarely falling off. He secured his best placings in the ACU Scramble Star contest in 1958 and

1960, with a fifth place on both occasions. Third in the 1956 Lancashire Grand National, he won the 350 Race in 1957, with a second place in the Grand National event. But he won the Grand Natonal in 1958 and won the Senior Race too.

Brian Martin 'cleans' the Devil's Staircase in the 1956 Scottish Six Days with the rear-sprung B32 on which he won three national premier awards that year. Photo: The Classic Motor Cycle.

During 1958 he won the 350 and 500 races at Hawkstone Park, and having been eighth in the British Motocross Grand Prix of 1956, was seventh in the 1958 event after being placed third in the first heat. In 1960 he finished third in the 250 Race at the Hants Grand National, then later that season won the 250 Race at Hawkstone Park, with a second in both the 500 Race and the Grand National event on the same day.

After his brilliant ride in Austria in 1952 on the standard Star Twin, he was unable to take part in the 1953 event held in Czechoslovakia, but with the International Six Days back in Wales for 1954 he was selected for the British Vase 'B' team. Unfortunately, after four days unpenalized, he lost six marks on the fifth day as a result of coming off whilst riding on the top limit to make up time lost after being delayed with waterlogged ignition. This was poor consolation indeed for his good Samaritan act the previous day when, pressing on between Corris and Tal-y-Llyn, he came across Dutchman M. Rosenberg stranded without petrol as a result of not filling-up his BSA that morning. 241

A dramatic picture of Brian Martin (264) demonstrating the expert's ability to surmount a hill choked with stalled and exhausted riders in the 1954 International Six Days Trial in Wales. He was riding as a member of the British Vase 'B' team. Photo: Ray Biddle.

Ignoring the risk to himself, Martin dashed back to a nearby inn, borrowed an empty bottle, rushed back to the stranded rider and transferred petrol from his tank to the Dutchman's. Ironical indeed that Rosenburg went on to win a gold medal. That action was typical of Brian Martin's constant willingness to help others whenever he could. With the 1955 ISDT held in Czechoslovakia and Martin again riding for the British Vase 'B' team he made amends by winning a gold medal for a faultless performance. He gained another gold medal in 1956, this time as a member of the British Trophy Team when the event was based at Garmisch-Partenkirchen in West Germany. The British team finished third in the Trophy contest.

The 1957 ISDT, held yet again in Czechoslovakia, was not supported by the British industry (with only four private British riders taking part), but for 1958 it went back to Garmisch-Partenkirchen and the forested beauty of Bavaria.

Once again selected for the British Trophy Team, Brian Martin suffered his great disappointment when, on the second day, he was forced to retire with a severely water-logged magneto. At one of the time checks the Gold Star refused to re-start, despite Brian stripping the ignition system to dry it out. He kicked and pushed until he had

With no time for the ethic of 'ladies first', Brian Martin eases past a stalled Mollie Briggs (Triumph) at a river crossing in Wales during the 1954 International Six Days Trial.

exceeded the time limit which results in automatic exclusion. There was not a spark of life. Returning later that day with transport to collect the silent Gold Star, the kickstart crank was given a nonchalant swing, whereupon the engine burst into life with a clean and even beat. There were those who were superstitious enough to believe the registration number of POK 175 had something to do with it, adding up as it did to the ominous total of 13.

A rare picture of a night-run check point taken during the 1955 International Six Days Trial in Czechoslovakia with Brian Martin (236) waiting to check out. As a member of the British Vase 'B' team he won a gold medal. Centre (without hat) is British team manager Jack Stocker. Photo: The Classic Motor Cycle.

Brian Martin (150) again storming past stalled riders in an International Six Days, this time in the forests of Germany in the 1956 event when he rode for the British Trophy Team. He won another gold medal. Photo: The Classic Motor Cycle.

Riding 'BSA 300' Brian Martin tackles a taped hazard in the BBC TV Team Trial staged at Purbright in February 1958 as a member of the Midlands team. Photo: The Classic Motor Cycle.

*All in a day's work! Ron Watson (of Watsonian Sidecars) at the wheel of a Land Rover during Victory Trial course plotting with posse of works riders. L to R: George Wilson (*The Motor Cycle *journalist), Bill Howard with chair outfit and Michael Martin as passenger, Brian Martin and John Brittain (Royal Enfield). Photo:* The Classic Motor Cycle.

Brian Martin descending 'Cheeks' in the 1959 Bemrose Trophy Trial on the new 250cc C15T model which he introduced to national status events in the 1958 British Experts Trial. Photo: The Classic Motor Cycle.

Brian Martin's wide-ranging competitions experience, allied with his knowledge of engineering and production methods, made him an ideal candidate for the role of competitions manager. Only those who have worked within a large motorcycle manufacturing plant can understand the complexities when the priorities of a competitions shop can be very much at odds with the overall priorities of a plant committed to volume output. Where work had to be placed with various sections of the plant, it was often looked upon as an irksome nuisance, interrupting normal production routine.

Against this background it came as a great surprise to Brian Martin to learn of the dramatic effect the series of televised scrambles had on the average shopfloor operator. Quite suddenly many sections of the plant were able to identify themselves with the BSA success on the small silver screen. One did not need to be a regular scrambles fan to respond to the excitement of Jeff Smith wearing down the opposition, lap-by-lap, to take the lead from the last bend on the last lap and win by a short head.

Quite suddenly where sections had shown indifference, there was an

Brian Martin being presented with the premier award for his win in the 6th Trial de St. Cucufa in November 1957, near Paris.

enthusiasm to do all they could; to share in the BSA glory. They saw it as a collective victory. Which of course it was.

Brian Martin – rider, engineer, administrator – the third and last man to head BSA competitions during the final quarter of a century, had probably the more difficult task of the three, one he accomplished with glowing distinction, producing as he did, the peak of BSA competitions achievement.

On the BSA stand at the 1960 Earls Court Motor Cycle Show, Brian Martin is congratulated on his formal appointment as BSA competitions manager by chief development engineer Bert Perrigo, with director and general manager Bob Fearon looking on.

Chapter 16

From Humble Beginnings

ALTHOUGH THE lightweight two-stroke model had first made its mark in British national events as early as 1951 — joined by the 149cc four-stroke Triumph Terrier in 1952 — the big four-stroke continued to dominate national trials.

In the prestigious Victory Cup Trial for example, BSA won the premier award no less than nine times during the period 1946-1956. Most such events, like the Hurst Cup and the Scottish Six Days, continued to be the domain of the big four-stroke throughout the fifties. But straws in the wind soon became more plentiful. Although Jeff Smith had won the British Experts solo title three years in succession, from 1955 to 1957, by the latter half of the decade BSA success in trials was less frequent. Admittedly Jeff had won the Perce Simon in 1957, with Brian Martin winning the Wye Valley Traders Cup with his 350cc model, and in 1958 Martin had won the Vic Brittain Trial at the beginning of the season with Jeff winning the John Douglas later on. But by the time John Giles, Artie Ratcliffe and Roy Peplow had won a number of national events during 1958/59 with a 199cc Triumph Cub, Brian Martin knew that BSA needed a similar, smaller and lighter model. The three-speed Bantam was not the answer long term and neither was the 250cc C11G/C12 model. But when in the summer of 1958 BSA finalized plans to tool-up for a 250cc version of the Triumph Tiger Cub, Brian Martin recognized the prospective model as the answer to his problem. Designated the C15, technical details of this new model were announced in the motorcycle press of September 1958 as the first of the models came off the production line. Prior to this no prototypes had existed, which meant that no trials specification development had been possible. All Brian Martin could do was grab a production model and apply the basic requirements as quickly as possible.

Jim Sandiford of Bury climbing the Devil's Staircase in the 1959 Scottish Six Days with a standard production 250cc C15T. It proved to be the only C15T to finish that year, the rest blighted with stripped distributor gears.

With Jim Sandiford climbing 'Foyers' in the 1961 Scottish Six Days, the grand vista of Highland scenery illustrates the vivid magic of the event. Sandiford won the 250 Cup and with John Harris and Tony Davis the team prize for BSA. Photo: The Classic Motor Cycle.

To get more ground clearance from the standard production frame, the 17 inch wheels were replaced with a front one of 20 inch diameter and a rear of 18 inches. The former was shod with 3 inch section tyre, and the latter with one of the customary 4 inch. To accommodate the bigger section tyre, a wider-than-standard pivoting fork had to be fabricated. Standard Triumph Cub front forks were replaced with BSA 'C' group forks, which permitted the use of a smaller, $5^{1/2}$ inch, single-sided brake, in the interests of weight saving. Initially, standard gear ratios had to be used until wide-ratio gears became available. With an upswept exhaust pipe and alloy petrol tank, the prototype trials model

Jim Sandiford conquering the rocks of Laggan Locks on the third day of the 1962 Scottish Six Days, riding the ex-Jeff Smith works C15T. The works team of C15Ts again took the team prize. Photo: The Classic Motor Cycle.

scaled 250 lbs with oil in the tank and the engine developed 15 bhp.

Having first used the new C15T with BSA 'C' group forks, these were replaced by standard Triumph Cub forks complete with the heavier cast-iron, full-width hub when it was established that the 'C' fork was to go out of production.

First time out on the new prototype, in the Sixth Midland Centre Group Trial organized by the Leamington Victory MCC on 2nd November 1958, Brian Martin threw away the premier award through stopping to help Brian Povey stuck at the roadside. Nonetheless it was a promising start. Twenty-eight days later the new C15T had its first airing in a major trial; the British Experts no less, on 30th November. Brian Martin was again in the saddle, the rest of the works riders using the big 500cc B34 models. Brian was sufficiently gratified to finish eighth overall, ahead of all his team mates. Soon after the Experts he won the 250 Cup in the Mitcham Vase — the C15T's first national trial award — followed by the 250 Cup in the Knut Trophy Trial, then a third place in the Irish Experts Trial. Right at the end of December, Brian won the Southern Experts, to register the model's first premier award.

Gloucestershire farmer Dave Langston, one of the most successful trials riders with the C15T, who won at least 17 principal national trials awards — without one national premier!

Such early success may have induced a false sense of security for, strictly speaking, the model had not been properly developed. This became only too obvious in the Scottish Six Days Trial of May 1959 when it had been decided to enter all works riders on the 250 lightweight. Before the Scottish, however, the new model earned fresh praise when Jeff Smith won the premier award in the St. Davids Trial and the 250 Class Cup in both the Victory Cup and Cotswold Cups.

Dave Langston on the C15T demonstrating the art of avoiding the worst on Camp Ditch in the Colmore Cup Trial, an event in which he won the 250 Cup in 1961 and was runner-up in 1964, 1965 and 1967.

In the Scottish Six Days, in contrast, it was embarrassing disaster, with John Draper retiring with a seized piston on the first day, only a few miles out from Edinburgh before even reaching the first observed hill. On the Tuesday Jeff Smith retired with distributor-drive trouble, and if that was not bad enough, both Tom Ellis and Arthur Lampkin retired with identical trouble on the Wednesday. Thus all the works C15Ts had had been eliminated.

For quite some time trouble persisted with the skew gear driving the long distributor shaft until Bert Currie — a skilled toolmaker of the old school and foreman of the BSA model room — produced gear replacements with a revised tooth form.

Whilst such short-term problems arose from insufficient development time, the basic cause was tantamount to putting the cart before the horse. Whereas the Gold Star had been engineered for competiton applications, the C15 — and later the 350cc B40 — was intended for the use of the average man-in-the-street. In other words, it was never intended to be other than a value-for-money utility lightweight for volume production. It was up to the competitions department to make it more adept for sporting application at a minimum of expense.

253

A shot of Dave Langston tackling 'Upper Hall' in the 1963 British Experts Trial won by Jeff Smith on another C15T. Photo: The Classic Motor Cycle.

By 1962, for example, a roller bearing big-end had replaced the original plain metal bearing on the trials and scramble variants (C15T and C15S), an improvement extended to the standard C15 for 1964. In due course the external distributor had been replaced by a contact breaker assembly driven by the camshaft and housed within the engine casing. By the time the standard C15 went out of production in 1967, it even had a Hoffman ball bearing on the timing side shaft.

Tony Davis of Gloucester was another very successful C15T rider, here seen in the 1961 Colmore Cup Trial in which he was runner-up. In 1963 he won both the Perce Simon and Hoad Trophy Trials with a C15T. Photo: The Classic Motor Cycle.

In 1963 the standard, rather mundane, single-loop frame with bolted-up rear sub-frame used on all C15 models was replaced on the scramble and trials variants with an excellent all-welded frame with twin loops running from the bottom cradle to the rear of the top tube. Heavily reinforced with gusset plates where strength was paramount, the frame was used on a number of subsequent models; indeed, it became the basis of the frame used on all single-cylinder models from then on. The new frame also featured BSA 'B' group front forks, having solid fork ends with a pull-out spindle and 7 inch single-sided front brake.

Notwithstanding the poor showing in the Scottish Six Days of 1959, the C15T went on to secure two premier awards and several class cups during the remainder of the season, with Jeff Smith winning the Perce Simon Trial and John Draper the Mitcham Vase. Dave Langston was

Dave Rowland in trouble in the top section of Grey Mares Ridge in the 1963 Scottish Six Days in which he finished 4th best performer. He won the Best Newcomer Award with the new, all-welded frame C15T. Photo: Motor Cycle News.

Dave Rowland navigates the rocks of 'Washford' in the notorious 1963 Scott Trial in which he was runner-up and best 250. Also with a C15T, Arthur Lampkin made fastest time and, for good measure, Jim Sandiford won the 350 Cup. Photo: Motor Cycle News.

fourth in the Southern Experts, but the greatest success of all was Jeff Smith's victory in the Scott Trial, in so doing making fastest time. The little C15T — not even in existence just twelve months before — had overcome its initial teething troubles to become fully competitive.

It would be easier to recount what the C15T failed to win during the next few years rather than to catalogue its many victories, for in addition to winning 28 national trials, it won countless capacity class and runner-up awards, not to mention team awards. Of the many victories,

A fine study of World Motocross Champion Jeff Smith competing in the 1965 Scott Trial on a C15T, making second fastest time and finishing 4th overall to win the 250 Cup. He won the Scott in 1954 and 1959 and made fastest time on at least four occasions.

none were more prized than the 'big three' — the Scottish Six Days, the Scott and the British Experts. The former victory was secured by Arthur Lampkin in 1963, redeeming the ignominy of 1959, and yet again in 1966 by brother Alan. Having won the British Experts three years in succession with the 500cc B34, Jeff Smith again won the prized Skefko Gold Cup in 1963 (with Arthur Lampkin third and Dave Rowland fifth). In a space of five years the C15T had scaled the three principal peaks of the trials world. Two years after Jeff Smith, Scott Ellis took the British Experts solo title with this model.

It was in the Scott Trial where the 250 BSA was at its most convincing, with a hat-trick of victories from 1959 to 1961 — Jeff Smith the winning rider in 1959 and Arthur Lampkin in 1960 and '61. Jeff Smith made fastest time in 1959 and 1960 but Arthur Lampkin returned fastest time no less than four times, in 1961, '63, '65 and 1966 — the last occasion when brother Alan won the premier award. That Alan Lampkin victory of 1966 was BSA's eleventh Scott Trial win since 1946, during which time they also won nine manufacturer's team awards.

The BSA policy of fielding additional riders for scrambles and motocross was then applied to trials for the 1960s, for with Jeff Smith devoting most his energies to scrambles and motorcross with considerable success, there was a need for new blood within the orbit of trials. Before long the BSA team of riders on the C15T was as strong as it had ever been, with such names as Dave Langston, Tony Davis, Scott Ellis, Dave Rowland, Jim Sandiford and Alan Lampkin, between them producing a considerable crop of victories. One of the most successful was Scott Ellis who, having previously ridden a works Triumph Cub, switched to the BSA for 1965. First time out in a national trial he finished third in the Colmore Cup. His first premier award came a couple of weeks later in the all-important Victory cup Trial. During that season he won the Dick Farquharson Trial in Dorset and was runner-up in the Belgian Lamborelle Trial. He finished off his first season on a C15T in the best possible way by winning the British Experts — BSA's eighth solo win since the war, and their last. He was runner-up in the Victory Cup in 1967, winning the premier award in the West of England later in the year. During his period he won a host of 250 class cups on a C15T.

If any C15T rider won more 250 class cups than any other rider it must have been Dave Langston (brother of all-rounder Ron Langston) who won a considerable number without ever winning the premier award in a trade-supported national — despite three near misses in the Colmore Cup where he was runner-up no less than three times in 1964, '65 and 1967. He was also runner-up in the Victory Cup of 1962 and the Perce Simon of 1966. His first 250 class cup on the C15T came with the

Riding the one-off works 343cc B40 first used by Jeff Smith, Jim Sandiford 'cleans' the top section of Grey Mares Ridge in the 1964 Scottish Six Days in which he finished 9th. Jim Sandiford now owns 776 BOP.

Colmore cup of 1961 and he finished tenth in the British Experts of 1966. Needless to say he shared in a number of BSA team prizes over that period.

Another of the more successful C15T riders was Jim Sandiford from Bury, who won the 250 Cup in the Scottish Six Days of 1961 and achieved fastest time in the Hurst Cup Trial of 1963. He had his first premier award in the Greensmith Trial of 1961, with another premier award the following year in the Clayton Trophy. Then in 1965 he won both the Allan Jefferies and Travers Trophy.

In addition to the award of a number of 250 class cups Jim Sandiford had an admirable record in the International Six Days Trial, in which he won four gold medals in succession in the events of 1961 (Wales), 1962 (Germany), 1963 (Czechoslovakia) and 1964 (East Germany), In the two latter events, however, he was mounted on the larger 343cc B40. In both 1962 and '63 he represented Great Britain as a member of the Vase 'A' team and in 1964 as a member of the Trophy team.

Tony Davis used the works B40 — '776 BOP' — before Jim Sandiford, and won the Mitchell and West of England Trials with it in 1962, plus about seven 350 class cups during that period.

Other premier awards achieved with a C15T included the Vic Brittain Trial of 1961 won by Brian Povey, and the Perce Simon and Hoad Trophy of 1963 both won by Tony Davis of Gloucester — the latter having been runner-up in the Colmore Cup of 1961 and again in 1962. Prior to Alan Lampkin winning the Scottish Six Days in 1966 he had already won the Bemrose Trophy that year and in 1963 he had won the Travers Trophy. Then, in the wheeltracks of brothers Arthur and Alan came Martin Lampkin, the third of that illustrious trio. He started his winning sequence in 1967 with the Best Novice Award in both the Victory Cup and Scottish Six Days on a C15T, with other high placings that season.

The B40, a 343cc version of the standard C15, was launched at Earls Court in November 1960. By December Jeff Smith was riding a prototype B40 in trials specification in the Southern Experts that month. The new model had a unit-construction layout like that of the C15 and was similar to the smaller model in almost every respect, including the stroke dimension of 70mm. Despite weighing some 20 lbs more, it had a good power-to-weight ratio.

There could not have been much wrong with the prototype trials model because after riding it for the first time in the Southern Experts of 1960, Jeff Smith promptly won the St. Davids Trial in January 1961, followed by best 350 performance in the Bemrose, Cotswold Cups and the Scott Trial. Tony Davis proved to be the most successful with the B40, however, winning both the Mitchell and West of England in 1962, the runner-up award in the John Douglas and the 350 Cup in the Cotswold Cups and Hoad Trophy. Then, in 1963, he won the 350 Cup in both the Victory Trial and Wye Valley Traders. Jim Sandiford also tried the model, winning two 350 class cups in the process.

It was a case of mixed fortunes with the B40 in the International Six Days. It has already been noted that Jim Sandiford won two of his gold medals with this model but whilst doing so other were less fortunate. Arthur Lampkin had dropped to silver medal standard in Czechoslovakia in 1963 through that air cleaner problem, and in 1964, with John Lewis nominated in the British Vase 'B' team, he was penalized 20 marks for failing to start his B40 in the prescribed time at one of the controls. An ignition fault was responsible. Scott Ellis riding for the Vase 'A' team had worse luck, retiring on the fourth day with a broken gearbox mainshaft. In contrast, Pat Slinn — a BSA employee riding privately — won a gold medal with his B40.

If the B40 fortunes in the ISDT of 1963 and 1964 had been mixed, experience in the Isle of Man during 1965 proved nothing less than an unmitigated disaster with dreadful weather conditions to match. Five BSAs were entered amongst the British national teams, three of 343cc capacity and two enlarged to 441cc (later designated B44 Victors). Arthur Lampkin (441 model) and Sammy Miller (343 B40) were Trophy Team nominations, with Alan Lampkin (441 model) and Jim Sandiford

Jim Sandiford with the works 343cc B40 on which he won a gold medal in the 1963 International Six Days Trial in Czechoslovakia whilst a member of the British Vase 'A' team. His was the only BSA gold medal that year.

262

(343 B40) Vase 'A' team nominations. Scott Ellis (343 B40) was nominated team reserve and Pat Slinn was again riding in a private capacity. During the course of the unfortunate week every single BSA works bike retired with alternator failure. There was no comfort to be had from the fact that of the 299 starters only 82 survived, a mere 18 winning gold medals. It was an ignominious and embarrassing failure for all concerned, posing many questions in its wake. Subsequent investigation revealed that Lucas had supplied a batch of special alternators for fitting to both BSA and Triumph works models. The special components had been supplied together in the same box and whereas those fitted to BSA models had all failed, those fitted to the Triumph had run faultlessly. Explanations at the time were never conclusive, being attributed to differing engine operating temperatures which can be influenced by various factors.

Jim Sandiford cornering a B40 in the 1965 International Six Days Trial in the Isle of Man as a member of the British Vase 'A' team. He retired on the 4th day with a defunct alternator, as did all the other works BSAs. It was a black week for BSA.

BSA: Competition History

The experience did a lot of harm — if only amongst senior management — who, in a mood of defeatism, sanctioned the preparation of BSA/Triumph hybrids for the 1966 event in Sweden. With Arthur Lampkin riding in the British Trophy Team and Alan Lampkin the Vase 'A' team, they were supplied with BSA models fitted with overbored Triumph twin engines of 502cc. After a trouble-free ride and a gold medal each, this unusual precedence appeared to have been justified. Nonetheless, Pat Slinn also won a gold medal. He was riding a 441cc Victor of original BSA specification. This success alone makes it difficult to condone the hybrid decision which seems even more illogical now than it did at the time.

The functional scrambles 250cc C15 with which BSA contested the European 250 Motocross Championship of 1960, 1961 and 1962. Jeff Smith was runner-up in 1960 and 1962, with Arthur Lampkin the runner-up in 1961. Note the pre-production all-welded frame and alloy front hub.

When the C15 came along, Brian Martin welcomed it with open arms for, hitherto, with only the 350 and 500 Gold Star available, he had been unable to contest the 250cc class then being dominated by the Greeves, CZs and Husqvarnas in British scrambles.

In addition, to competing in events in the British Isles, a concerted effort was made to win the European 250 Motocross Championship with the C15S when, in 1960, 1961 and 1962 BSA had almost made it. In 1962, a mere two points separated Jeff Smith from the title, which went to Torsten Hallman of Sweden with his Husqvarna. But for 1960 and 1961 it was the brilliant Dave Bickers of Ipswich who thwarted BSA's ambitions when he won the European title two years running with the potent Greeves. Jeff Smith was runner-up to Dave Bickers in 1960, with Arthur Lampkin runner-up in 1961 when Smith finished third.

Good though the C15S performance had been in scrambles and motocross, the time came when it had to be admitted that it had its limitations now that two-stroke technology was advancing rapidly, to give riders of such models an increasing advantage. Facing up to the facts of life, Brian Martin and his team switched their time and energies from the 250 C15 to the 343 B40. When the latter new model arrived in 1961 the Gold Star was still competitive, Jeff Smith winning yet another ACU Scramble Star — his fourth with the Gold Star — and using the

The first prototype 343cc B40 scrambles model circa 1961 — a podgy adolescent leading to the glamorous world-beating 440 Victor Grand Prix and later the full-blown 499cc B50.

Goldie in the Motocross des Nations of 1962 when team mate Arthur Lampkin reverted to a 352cc B40.

Nonetheless, competitive or not, the Gold Star was by now obsolete by engineering standards, although perhaps no longer fashionable might be a more apt description. Engine and gearbox in unit construction was now the vogue with 12 volt AC electrical equipment replacing the antiquated 6 volt DC systems of the past. Already the electrical equipment makers had given notice of discontinuing production of their 'old fashioned' components such as magnetos and dynamos. As such, the Gold Star, with its separate gearbox and 6 volt electrics, had been under 265 sentence of death for years; and with sales declining to a relative handful (particularly after the demise of the Clubman's series in the Isle of Man from 1957) continued production could no longer be justified.

The irony was that with the Gold Star clinging to life, there was no planned replacement, so when the 343cc B40 arrived, Brian Martin clutched at it like a drowning man. It was a case of any port in a storm.

During the early months of 1961, Brian and the competition shop busied themselves with preparing the first 343cc B40 prototype, using the excellent C15S frame, and by the Easter Monday Brian was able to give the model its first airing at the famous Red Marley Freak Hill Climb. Running the machine on alcohol fuel, he won both the 350 and unlimited classes, just missing the standing hill record in the process.

Later that season Jeff Smith tried the model for the first time in an important trade-supported national scramble, that at Shrubland Park, near Ipswich, winning every event he contested, the 350 Race, the 500 Race and the Grand National. In doing so he beat a string of stars on full 500s including John Burton, Arthur Lampkin, John Harris and Freddie Mayes, all on gold Stars, plus Don Rickman on the big Metisse.

At that time the B40 engine developed 27.2 bhp at 7,000 rpm, with a compression ratio of 12:1 and a $1^1/8$ inch Amal Monobloc carburettor. With the unit painted black in the interests of heat dissipation, in no time at all it had acquired the pseudonym of 'Black Bess'. Lacking the gutsy glamour of the Gold Star, it looked starkly functional and almost innocuous; very much the ugly duckling which grew into a beautiful swan. Indeed, at that time what proved to be a world-beating model was merely at the hatching stage. With original engine dimensions of 79mm x 70mm, well over-square, there was ample scope for a longer stroke and before long an experimental engine with a bore and stroke of 80mm x 86mm had been tested at Hawkstone Park. It was at that stage that Brian Martin was blessed with a stroke of good luck when he found a set of con-rod dies once used for a long-since forgotten experimental engine which were just right for the 86mm stroke envisaged. Reverting to the standard bore of 79mm with a distance piece under the base of the cast-iron cylinder (replaced with one of light alloy soon after) an engine with the curious capacity of 421cc was created, and with it another chapter in the BSA story.

The first 421cc prototype scrambler was raced by Jeff Smith at Matchams Park on Good Friday 1962 when he won the Hants Grand National for the third year in succession. Although the C15 camshaft had been retained, the crankshafts and flywheels had been replaced by heavier, hand-made components; and likewise the gearbox and clutch had been stiffened to cope with the increased power output.

By 1964 the Grand Prix models, with a total dry weight of 228 lbs,

The works 420cc Victor scrambles model as used by Jeff Smith in the 500 World Championship title series in 1963 and 1964 — producing BSA its first world title.

produced 29.9 bhp at 6,000 rpm with a compression ratio of 11:1 and with a 1^{15}/$_{31}$ inch Monobloc carburettor. Having proved the bigger engine throughout 1962, with Jeff Smith again winning the ACU Scramble Star for the third year running in what proved to be a long sequence of six such wins in a row, another 421cc model was built for Arthur Lampkin with which to partner Jeff Smith in a serious bid for the 1963 500 World Championship. But the opposition from those iron men from Sweden proved too great, with the 1962 champion Rolf Tibblin (Husqvarna) again winning the title with compatriot Sten Lundin (Lito) — Champion in 1961 — runner-up. Arthur Lampkin finished fifth in the championship and eighth — on one of the 'old' Gold Stars — was John Burton. Jeff Smith finished in third place, just two points down on Lundin.

With reliability achieved the result was highly encouraging, with further development planned for the 1964 season. This consisted mainly of a new frame with a large diameter top tube to be used as the engine oil container, with the space vacated by the displaced oil tank being filled by an extra-large air filter. The front forks incorporated new two-way damping and the contact-breaker assembly was housed within the timing case.

The dramatic details of the epic 1964 season are recounted in the next chapter. Suffice it to say that by the penultimate round in East Germany Jeff Smith was on level terms with World Champion Rolf Tibblin, leaving but the final round at San Sebastian to decide the title 267

With two World Titles to its credit by 1965 — when this shot of Jeff Smith was taken whilst competing in the Hampshire Grand National — the 440 Victor Grand Prix was trim and sleek, without an ounce of surplus weight.

for 1964. Although it is now 21 years since that dramatic sequel, events are still vividly clear in the minds of those old enough to remember when Jeff Smith became the first British 500 Motocross Champion of the World.

At the Earls Court Motor Cycle Show, in November 1964, the company launched a production replica of the Jeff Smith model bearing the inspired name of Victor Grand Prix. By then, using an even longer stroke of 90mm, the capacity had been increased to 441cc, to give a power output of 31.7 bhp at 6,000 rpm. It was with the 441cc Victor GP that Jeff Smith won the World Title for the second year running in 1965 — winning six of the first eleven grands prix by July.

Although that engine was increased still further in capacity to a full 499cc, the world title of 1965 can be construed as the peak reached by a product that had progressed from humble beginnings to celebrated eminence — rather like chorus girl to leading lady, by then sleek and pretty as a picture.

Chapter 17

World Champion

CLAIMING SOMEONE to be the greatest ever at something is very often little more than speculation and individual opinion. As often as not an opinion formed at an impressionable age by one of a new generation, influenced by the acts of current heroes which tend to dim the collective memory of what has gone before. Nonetheless, if facts be studied objectively — without partisan interests of any sort — such judgements can be made. But even then, much depends on the definition of facts. Clearly, in the case of motorcycle events, results must be the major factor. That alone, however, is not enough, for success in a major event carries more weight than that achieved in a minor event. Quality of workmanship too, must count where, in the context of motorcycling, it means method and style. The period of time during which peak form is maintained is yet another factor, indicating a long-term consistent ability.

Taking all aspects into account, Jeffrey Vincent Smith scores virtually maximum points. He won more national and international scrambles and motocross events than any British rider before or since, with a safe and solid style as dependable as the Rock of Gibraltar itself, maintaining his championship skills over a remarkable period of 19 years from 1953 to 1971. When his similar performance in trials is also taken into consideration — he won every major British trial and title, some several times over — his true greatness begins to emerge. Brian Martin claims that Jeff Smith was the most professional and dedicated rider he ever knew.

Right at the beginning of his riding career, at the tender age of 17, Jeff Smith won a gold medal in the International Six Days Trial of 1951 held in Italy. Astride a 500cc Norton on that occasion, it showed that young shoulders can support a wise head.

Although reared in Birmingham, Jeff Smith was born in Colne,

Jeff Smith climbing a Peak District section in the 1953 Bemrose Trophy Trial to gain his first national premier award as a BSA works rider. He won four other nationals and five class cups during the season, to gain his first ACU Trials Drivers' Star. Photo: Ray Biddle.

Lancashire, a fact testified by his accent to this day. Though only three years of age when his parents moved to Birmingham, he was proud to display the Red Rose of Lancashire on his crash helmet throughout his riding career. He came under the influence of motorcycles at a very early age as a result of his father's riding activities. With both father and son bearing the same initials, when the young Jeffrey first entered trials at the age of 16 (his father was still riding a 500T Norton), it was necessary for organizers to distinguish the younger JVS with the added abbreviations Jun. It was years, it seemed, before young Jeff lost this Junior tag.

He had his first bike — a 1929 Triumph — in 1947, at the age of 13, which he was able to use it on private ground in the Barr Beacon area of North Birmingham. Not that he was able to ride it much for petrol was still on ration, but tinkering with it was the next best thing. Nonetheless, he was able to learn the basic skills of riding over rough terrain; indeed, at the age of 15 he won his first trial, a closed-to-club event run by the West Bromwich MCC in a sand quarry at Barr Beacon.

At the age of 16 his father bought him a BSA Bantam, so with a provisional driving licence and 'L' plates he entered open-to-centre trials for the first time. These included Midland Centre Group Trials

On his way to winning the 1954 Victory Cup Trial, an event he won again the following year, Jeff Smith does a tight turn with the works B34. He won four more nationals that year, to win his second successive ACU Star.

A garlanded Jeff Smith after his first Grand Prix victory at the 1954 Dutch Motocross GP. He is flanked by Mr & Mrs Flinterman, the BSA importers for the Netherlands.

Like the British riders before him, Jeff Smith delighted the French crowds at the famous 'Chalk Pit' course at Montreuil, near Paris, where at this event in 1954 he finished second to Rene Baeten (FN) of Belgium.

which usually featured a number of works experts in the entry list. Before graduating to his father's 500T Norton for the 1951 season there was the small question of the Ministry of Transport driving test to be passed, easier said than done. He had failed the test twice before and it dawned on him that the examiners might not be too impressed by his ability to negotiate turns with his front wheel in the air, in an attempt to complete the test circuit in the shortest possible time! However, it proved to be a case of third time lucky.

Graduating to the Norton in 1951 he was soon up amongst the cup winners, securing his very first National trial victory in the Shropshire Traders Cup Trial. This qualified him for the exclusive British Experts Trial of 1951, that year held for the first time in the Peak district of Derbyshire. An event for experts only where the sense of occasion can play havoc with nerves, this young man of 17, riding in his first British Experts against the cream of the country, finished in fourth place, beaten only by winner Tom Ellis (BSA), Hugh Viney (AJS) and Bill Nicholson (BSA). He actually tied with Nicholson with a loss of 17 marks, only to lose to the great Irishman in the special test!

If that remarkable Experts ride went unnoticed by the press, there were those at Bracebridge Street, Aston, who were very much aware of it

Below Left: As the individual winner of the 1955 Motocross des Nations in Denmark, Jeff Smith savours the ovation on the winners' rostrum. With Sweden the overall team winners, there were four BSAs in the first six places.

Above right: Victor of the July 1957 British Motocross Grand Prix at Hawkstone Park, Shropshire, Jeff Smith with his wife Irene. They were married the day before and Jeff is quoted as saying 'some things don't slow you down at all!'.

for their best team rider, Rex Young, had done no better than tenth place, with a loss of 24 marks. They quickly signed Jeff as an official works rider for 1952, notwithstanding the fact that he was already at BSA — having commenced a five-year apprenticeship at Small Heath on 1st January 1951. It was a most unusual case of having a foot in both camps.

Whilst in this instance Norton had beaten BSA to it in spotting new talent, when it came to the ears of Bert Perrigo that at the end of 1952 Norton would be disbanding their trials team, he lost no time in making Jeff an offer for 1953. That was a lucky break with profound consequences. So at 19 years of age, Jeff Smith began his long and glittering association with BSA. In that first season he won the Bemrose Trophy Trial, the Travers, the Red Rose and the Alan Trophy Trial, and 500 Class Cups in the Cotswold Cups, Allan Jefferies, Reliance, the Hoad and the Manville. Not surprisingly, in view of that sequence of success, he won the ACU Trials Drivers' Star for 1953.

His total of premier awards and class cup wins for 1954 was even greater, including for the first time wins in the Victory Cup and Scott Trial classic. Again his points total was enough to secure the ACU Star for the second year running — making it four in a row for BSA. He also won another gold medal in the International Six Days Trial, his second since 1951. His Scott Trial victory was one of his great rides, for he finished no less than 16 minutes ahead of the next fastest and had a conclusive 20 mark margin over John Brittain as the next best on observation.

Although losing the ACU Star in 1955 to Gordon Jackson — who beat him by three marks — during the year he won both the Scottish Six Days and the British Experts. So having won the Scott Trial the year before, by the age of 21 he had scaled the three greatest peaks in the trials world. He had by now taken to scrambling in a big way and by the end of that 1955 season he gained his first ACU Scramble Drivers' Star. A mere three points robbed him of a great ACU Star double in the same season. Already in scramble events he was displaying that masterly neatness which, over the coming years, frequently put him in a class of his own. At the end of the 1954 season, his first in scrambles and motocross, he had finished fourth in the ACU Star contest and third in the European Motocross championship.

Devoting more and more time to scrambles from 1954, he still continued to win major national trials on a regular basis, including his hat-trick of wins in the British Experts — though the third win of 1957 was somewhat compromised by protest and revised results that affected both himself and Gordon Jackson (AJS). He was destined to win the British Experts yet again in 1963, on a C15T, at a time when he was fully

Winner of the 1955, 1957 and 1959 British Motocross Grand Prix, at Hawkstone Park, Jeff Smith is seen being presented with the massive Daily Herald Trophy *by Mrs. Mirabelle Topham, owner of the famous Grand National course at Aintree, circa 1959.*

French motocross events too, can by stymied by atrocious conditions. A mud-plastered Jeff Smith (left) compares notes with a slightly less plastered Brian Stonebridge and his wife Jane at a French course during the 'fifties.

275

committed to scrambles and motocross, and for this reason the win gave him particular pleasure. To beat the dedicated Sammy Miller in his prime was — to use Jeff's own words - 'very satisfying'.

To list the successes achieved by Jeff Smith in national trials during the period 1951-1964 would be tedious and repetitive, winning as he did something like thirty-three premier awards, twenty-three 500 Class Cups; thirteen 250 Class Cups and five 350 Class Cups — not to mention the team awards to which he contributed. Like most riders he excelled more in some events than others, like the Experts, which he won four times. Apart from winning the Scott Trial twice (1954 and 1959) he also made fastest time on five occasions, first in 1954, then for three years in succession in 1958, '59 and 1960, and again in 1962. In addition to the premier awards, he won a 250 class cup three times and a 350 cup in 1961. He won the Victory Cup twice in succession in 1954 and 1955, and later won the 500 Cup in 1958 and the 250 Cup twice in succession in this event in 1959 and '60. Perhaps most remarkable of all was the long sequence of awards gained in the Perce Simon Memorial Trial, in which he gained a hat-trick of wins in 1955, '56 and '57. He won the 500 Cup in 1958 and followed this with two more wins in a row in 1959 and 1960. He followed up with a hat-trick of runner-up awards in 1961, '62 and '63. He won the Northern Experts of 1962, the first BSA rider to do so since Fred Rist's victory in 1946.

If listing all Jeff Smith's trials successes would be tedious, to attempt to do so with his scrambles and motocross victories would be even more so, to the point of often confusing and monotonous repetition, leaving little choice but to feature only his major victories. His main British-event successes during his first full season of 1954 comprised a second place behind Phil Nex in the Senior Race of the Cotswold Scramble and victory in the Experts Grand National, with another in the Lancashire Grand National, the last to be held on the infamous Holcombe Moor course. On the Continent he won the Dutch Motorcross Grand Prix with second places in both the French and Belgian events.

In 1955 — when his future brother-in-law John Draper won the European Motocross title — Jeff Smith really got into his stride in British events with victories at Shrubland Park, in the British Experts Scramble where he won both the Grand National and 500 Race; at Hawkstone Park and a fourth place in the Lancashire Grand National. But most impressive of all was his win in the British Motocross Grand Prix before an emotionally partisan crowd of 35,000 people packing the sandy slopes of Hawkstone Park. Over in Denmark, as a member of the British team, he won the Motocross des Nations. Setting the seal on that highly-successful season was his first ACU Scramble Star. He repeated

A late 'fifties shot of Jeff Smith riding 'BSA 500' with springer rear end. He won about 24 national trial premier awards with the 500cc B34, including the British Experts hat-trick.

that success for 1956 to make it two in a row, and again in 1960, which proved to be the first of a long sequence of six consecutive British title wins. He won the title for the ninth and last time in 1967. To win nine British scramble titles is a remarkable feat and one which later generations have shown no sign of even approaching, let alone equalling.

Although Jeff Smith won the Motocross des Nations in Denmark in 1955, the Swedish team were the overall winners, but when Jeff won the event again in 1956 and 1957 — to make it another hat-trick of wins — 277 the British team were overall victors on both occasions, in Belgium in '56 and on home ground at Brands Hatch in '57.

Stockily build and of medium height, with quizzical light blue eyes, Jeff Smith from then on set course on a relentless pattern of victories all over the United Kingdon and overseas, dazzling and abundant in quantity and style, to the point where they almost ceased to be news. Indeed, it made more news when he failed to win from time to time, for he showed he could lose without rancour, taking comfort from the thought that there was always another race or a new tomorrow. It was this simple philosophy which probably extended his riding career well beyond that of his contemporaries.

To judge the consistency of Jeff Smith's victories, a study of the Experts Grand National results reveals that having won the Experts title at his first attempt in 1954 he won it six times thereafter with wins in '55 and '56 to make a hat-trick. Taking into account the various races at the Experts event, he won no less than 13 during the period 1954-1963. In

Jeff Smith winning the second leg of the 500 Motocross of the 1963 Hants Grand National, hotly chased by Derek Rickman (Metisse) number 73. Mounted on the new 420 Victor for the main events, Jeff also won both 250 races that day.

Yet another individual win for Jeff Smith in the 1965 Motocross des Nations at Hawkstone Park with the 440 Victor. He achieved a hat-trick of individual wins in the international team contests of 1955, 1956 and 1957.

the East Anglian National at Shrubland Park the collective total was even greater, with 14 wins over the same period — including winning the Grand National event four times in succession.

He had five wins in the Lancashire Grand National and won the Senior Race of the Sunbeam Point-to-point in 1956 and 1957. His British Motocross Grand Prix win of 1955 was repeated in 1957, with victory in both legs, a victory he repeated yet again in 1959.

When the 250cc C15S model became available for the 1960 season, it widened further his scope of activity, enabling participation in three separate capacity classes. A good example of this was the two-day televised meeting staged at Hawkstone Park in April 1963 when, with the sole exception of the 250 Race on the Saturday, Jeff won every other race   279

World Champion Jeff Smith with the 440 Victor in the muddy 1965 Cotswold Scramble in which he was placed 2nd in the Senior Race. With four victories over the years, this classic event produced fewer wins for him than most other great classics.

over the two days. These comprised the 500 and Unlimited Races on the Saturday afternoon and on the Sunday, the 250, 350 and 500 events. Apart from the 250 Race he won all with the new lightweight 343cc B40 model, where the opposition included John Burton and John Harris on Gold Stars with Vic Eastwood and Chris Horsfield on the big, powerful Matchless.

So it went on, season after season, frequently winning with a consummate, effortless skill, stimulating lyrical prose from the motorcycle writers of the day. '. . . he (J.V.Smith) was riding so neatly that he appeared to be anything but exciting to watch; Curtis in second place and W.A. Bell (Velocette) third, were stamping on gear pedals, exercising their right arms and using their feet like skis in a bewildered, continuous flurry of movement; but Smith was drawing ahead . . . ' ran one such report on the Cotswold Scramble in *The Motor Cycle*.

At the Inter-Centre Team Scramble at Brill, Buckingham in October 1958, riding for the winning Midland Centre team in absolutely atrocious conditions, Jeff Smith was supremely invincible in a situation where other competitors could not live with him. Having won the team race, he then went out in the 24-Fastest, 6-lap support race, to lap the entire entry, including Brian Martin, who finished second. He then rounded off his masterly display by winning the last 4-lap Invitation Race.

During Jeff Smith's five-year apprenticeship at Small Heath from 1951 to 1955 he spent the first two years in the service department, followed by periods in the mechanical test shop, toolroom, heat treatment, Gold Star engine and machine build and finally, from his point of view the holiest-of-holies, the competitions shop. National Service had been deferred pending completion of the apprenticeship so when the latter came about he was off in khaki to No. 5 Training Battalion, Royal Electrical Mechanical Engineers (REME) at Bordon Camp in Hampshire. Throughout the two seasons of 1956 and '57 he was a serving soldier.

During those two years of National Service he won the British

With purposeful elegance etched in every line, Jeff Smith hurls the 440 Victor round Hawkstone Park in the 1965 British Motocross Grand Prix. Though not winning that year, he won this prestigious event no less than five times, in 1955, 1957, 1959, 1961 and 1964.

Two World Champions battle it out in the Czechoslovakian Motocross Grand Prix of June 1965 with Jeff Smith (1964 500 World Champion) pursued by Joel Robert of Belgium (1964 250 World Champion). The event took place at Sedlcany Coomb, in Central Bohemia.

Experts twice, the Motocross des Nations twice, a gold medal in the International Six Days Trial in Germany in 1956 as a member of the British Vase 'A' team, the ACU Scramble Star for 1956 and was fourth in the Trials Star contest for that year (both Star contests were cancelled for 1957 as a direct result of the Suez crisis and the resulting petrol rationing). He must have been a bit pushed to complete his square bashing.

Having completed his military service by the end of December 1957, he worked in his father's engineering consultancy business, at the same time developing a routine of visiting the works at Small Heath to work on his own machines. It was a mutually convenient short-term arrangement until the decision was made to contest the 250 European Motocross Championship with the new C15S. It was then that he joined the staff of the competitions shop full-time, to assist in the development of this little contender. With the appointment of Brian Martin as competitions manager from 1960, Jeff became his close colleague and confidant in a partnership that was to last throughout the sixties and into the seventies, a period of great accomplishment which ended in absolute calamity.

This was the period where every meeting saw a great battle between Smith on the four-stroke BSA and the flying Dave Bickers of Ipswich on the two-stroke Greeves — and the birth of a great friendship between the two rivals. It was this Bickers/Greeves combination which trumped the BSA's 250 European ambitions in 1960 and '61, before BSA attention was focused on the development of the 343cc B40 and the 500 World Championship. The latter had come into being in 1957, taking over from the more limited European series, with a greatly extended list of

Jeff Smith with the 440 Victor doing battle with the mud and gradients of the famous East Meon course in Hampshire during a TV scramble in December 1966. Jeff had considerable success in winter televised meetings. 283

qualifying rounds including those run by East European bloc countries. With the 500 world series dominated by the Swedes since 1957, when Bill Nilsson won the title (with the one exception of Belgian René Baeton who won the title in 1958) it was akin to the BSA boys entering the lions' den. Sten Lundin, who had won the Swedish National title in 1955 when BSA-mounted, won the world title in 1959. It was a win he repeated two years later, in 1961, by which time he was riding a home-brewed special.

When Sten Lundin won his first world title in 1959, Jeff Smith on the Gold Star had finished in sixth place. For the next three seasons, 1960, '61 and '62, BSA were contesting the 250 European title in which Jeff Smith finished second, third and second respectively. In the absence of Smith, John Burton chased 500 honours in 1961, finishing in sixth place.

Jeff Smith shows-off the BBC TV Scramble Trophy to (right) Arthur Crawford, foreman of the BSA competitions shop and Reg Wilkes, who worked on engine development.

In 1960 Sten Lundin lost the 500 title to his fellow countryman Bill Nilsson, but in 1961 they changed places with Lundin taking the title again, and Nilsson the runner-up. In 1962 the Swedes again took the title but this time it was a newcomer to the ranks of the big-time title chase in the person of Rolf Tibblin, who had previously won the 250 European Championship in 1959. Husqvarna-mounted, Tibblin went on to repeat his 1962 500 title win in 1963, when BSA first re-appeared in the 500 arena with the rather unglamorous, unimposing enlarged 420cc B40. It was Tibblin who was to create the drama of 1964 when Jeff Smith and BSA went on to beat the world.

Although BSA had failed to win the 500 title in 1963, they had good cause to be modestly satisfied. Jeff Smith had finished third, just two points down on runner-up Lundin, with Arthur Lampkin fifth. Riding a Gold Star, John Burton was eighth. With further development planned for the 420cc machine before the start of the 1964 title chase, hopes were high at Small Heath. By then Jeffrey Vincent Smith was 30 years of age and there were those who regarded him as then too old and past his prime for a sport demanding the tough fitness and enthusiasm of younger men. But JV was no ordinary person or rider. By then he had accumulated a wealth of riding craft; he believed in studying every course minutely on foot and planning in advance tactics to be deployed. His combination of ability, experience, intelligence and tactical exploitation was seen over and over again on the television screen when, from a mid-field position on the opening lap, he would annihilate the opposition, one by one, leaving one or two still to pass on the final lap in order to win. He did it so many times it almost looked stage-managed. Jeff Smith always maintained that it did not result from his going quicker; merely a case of sustaining his initial speed throughout whilst those in front wore themselves out and got slower. Only the fittest of riders can overhaul a race leader from a modest start and therein lay one of Jeff Smith's trump cards.

No rider was fitter than he — or tried harder to achieve and maintain fitness. In his own book (written in conjunction with motorcycle journalist Bob Currie) entitled *The Art of Moto-cross*[*], Jeff devotes a great deal of space to the subject of strict physical training, stressing that for many years he had adopted a programme of four-mile runs over Barr Beacon near his home in Birmingham. He had regarded the exercise to be of great benefit until he was introduced to Olympic hurdler Maurice Herriott who won a silver medal at the 1964 Tokyo Olympics and who worked on the BSA production assembly line. He decided Jeff needed a programme of *real* training in readiness for the 1964 world title series. In his book Jeff describes in detail the physical extremes to which he was subjected by Maurice, to the point where he would be literally staggering and amazed at the punishment it was possible to endure and still survive.

He goes on to describe a typical lunch-break training session with Maurice from and back to the great rambling plant at Armoury Road, having set out from the famous test circuit which surrounded the company's sports ground. Sometimes they used the actual track itself,   285

[*] Published by Cassell & Co. Ltd., 1966

Harry Sturgeon (right), BSA managing director from 1964 to 1967 and Brian Martin (centre) BSA competitions manager, have good cause to share smiles of satisfaction with Jeff Smith after his World Title wins of 1964 and 1965.

which included running up and down the 1-in-4 test hill a few times before making their way alongside a meandering stream, across a stretch of parkland then away over the fields (this in the heart of industrial Birmingham!). On occasion they varied the route in order to take in a canal bank and a waste tip or two. They would start work slowly, build up to the really strenuous effort, then tail off, sometimes ending with a walk. That meant a quarter-of-an-hour of running, a similar period of violent exercise and a final quarter-of-an-hour of easing off. They would have covered two miles for starters then, at a steep railway embankment with slopes of something like 45 degrees, they would run up and down the embankment some 20 times before running along the towpath for another mile and returning to the factory to take a shower, a quick cup of tea and sandwich, and getting back to work. It was a kill-or-cure programme which put Jeff in a condition fit enough to face the spring and summer months of 1964 with a confidence which benefited the mental process as well. The world title hunt was on.

The opening round of the 1964 series took place on 12th April in Switzerland, setting the pattern for the rest of the season, with double World Champion Rolf Tibblin winning the first leg and Jeff Smith the second. On aggregate time Tibblin was overall winner with Smith second; 1961 World Champion Sten Lundin was third. The result

286

merited no more than cursory mention in the British motorcycle press. That result became the exact pattern for the next three meetings — in Austria, Denmark and Sweden — with Tibblin winning from Smith and Lundin finishing third. But in France the pattern was broken slightly, with Tibblin still the victor but Lundin pushing Smith into third place.

Then, dramatically, proving that Tibblin was as vulnerable as anyone else, he failed to score in the Italian round on 8th June when Jeff Smith scored his first overall victory in the series, with Olaf Persson second and Bill Nilsson third. That was to be the turning point of the series for two weeks later in the Russian round, Tibblin was in trouble again, retiring in the first leg which Jeff Smith won. In the second leg Tibblin was second to Lundin, with Smith third. This result made Jeff the overall winner — his second victory in a row. In Belgium on 2nd August, the reliable and predictable Smith won both legs after Tibblin had come off in one and retired in the other. Tibblin's points lead had been reduced to four.

When Smith again won both legs in the Luxemburg round one week later — making it four victories in a row — the British motorcycle press began to sit up and take notice. In that round, the ninth in the series, Tibblin had again failed to score, retiring in the first leg and failing to start in the second. The 420 BSA was proving dead reliable, with Jeff Smith applying all the craftsmanship he had acquired during the past ten years. In West Germany on 16th August, the equally consistent and ever-present Sten Lundin scored his first and only victory in the series, with Jeff Smith second and Tiblin third. His points advantage over Smith was now down to a slender two.

In the penultimate round in East Germany two weeks later, the result was dramatic and electrifying, with Tibblin winning the first leg from Smith and the order reversed in the second leg. Aggregate time gave Smith overall victory, with Tibblin second. They were now dead level with 54 points each. The title would be decided in the final round to be run in the blazing Spanish sunshine near San Sebastian.

Despite the one hundred per cent reliability of the 420 BSA, power loss had been experienced due to flexing of the standard 343cc B40 crankcases. Stiffened-up cases had been put in hand but did not become available until mid-season when they were fitted during the July break in the series. There was an immediate improvement in power output which made so much difference during the latter half of the season, both to Smith and the hitherto rock-hard confidence of Tibblin, which then cracked.

For the final and deciding round in Spain on 13th September (unlucky for some) the BSA tactical planning was thorough, with the BSA team electing to get to Spain several days in advance to allow Jeff

Above left: Italian BSA importer Gino Ghezzie (left with cap) displays paternal interest in Jeff Smith at the conclusion of an international event in Italy. In the 1966 Italian Motocross Grand Prix Jeff was second to Paul Friedrichs (360 CZ).

Above right: Another second place for Jeff Smith behind Paul Friedrichs of East Germany, this time in the June 1967 Czechoslovakian Motocross Grand Prix. Smith with Friedrichs on the winner's rostrum, a position which proved to be the final placings in the world series that year.

Smith to become more acclimatized to the heat — known to average about 90 degrees in the shade at that time of the year. Thus for four days they played beach games in the sun, walked and rode round the course to be used on the Sunday, noting every feature and aspect and, most importantly, made several tests with the Spanish fuel, jetting accordingly. By the day of the event, when others were tense and keyed-up, Jeff was relatively relaxed and confidently happy in the belief that to the best of his knowledge, nothing had been left to chance.

In striking contrast, Rolf Tibblin, having travelled a considerable distance from the cooler climate of Sweden, did not arrive until the Saturday evening. On race day, after practice, he was unhappy with the Spanish petrol supplied and sent his mechanic back over the border for some French premium grade fuel, taking with him the tank off the Hedlund in lieu of a petrol can. This jaunt took longer than anticipated and when the first leg of the championship race was due to start, Tibblin was still without his petrol tank. Such a move sounds too ridiculous to be true. The mental anguish and tension this must have created in the mind of Tibblin — World Champion for two years past — must have been such that he was beaten before he even left the line. And so it proved.

With the start of the first leg delayed, Tibblin's mechanic eventually got back with the petrol tank full of French premium grade and the tank was fitted to the bike. Right from the start of that first leg, Smith was off like a rocket, with Tibblin trailing him and visibly unsettled to see his great rival draw ahead lap by lap. Such were his desperate tactics to close the gap that he wrecked his front wheel and was forced to retire. From the viewpoint of the spectators, the event was an anti-climax for the two giants had never come to grips.

Mounted on the 499cc B50 Victor GP, Jeff Smith grapples with the adverse conditions experienced at Farleigh Castle in Wiltshire during the 1968 British Motocross Grand Prix. By 1971 Jeffrey Vincent Smith, MBE, had won a total of 17 titles for BSA.

Jeff Smith won both legs with comfort, followed home by Hubert Scaillet (Metisse) of Belgium — the only Belgian rider to get inside the first three in the whole series — with the dependable Sten Lundin third. Jeffrey Vincent Smith, 30 years of age, was World 500 Motocross Champion. He had brought home to Small Heath their first-ever World Championship of any type; in so doing scaling the peak they had set out to conquer years before. In winning the title Jeff Smith had been the only non-Swedish rider in the first six finishers. Rolf Tibblin in second place was followed by Sten Lundin, Ove Lundell, Bill Nilsson and Olaf Persson, which was indicative of the severe opposition to which Jeff had been subjected. Despite the pre-occupation with the world series, Jeff had still found time to contest the British Championship rounds, winning yet again the ACU Scramble Star for the seventh time.

The world title win stimulated great excitement at the Small Heath factory as it did also in official circles. Before October was out, Jeff Smith had been received by the Lord Mayor of Birmingham, Alderman Frank Price, in the Council House to receive his official congratulations. Jeff was accompanied by his wife Irene (John Draper's sister), Brian Martin and Harry Sturgeon, the new dynamic BSA managing director who expressed refreshing enthusiasm over the Smith success. Eager for the company to profit from it, he soon implemented plans to market a replica model, the larger capacity 441cc Victor being launched at Earls Court in November.

With the bigger capacity Victor engine developing 31.7 bhp at 6,000 rpm without losing an ounce of reliability, Jeff Smith scythed through the grand prix opposition in 1965. By winning six events in the series by July, he ensured retention of his world title for the second year running, to rubber-stamp the peak of his ability reached the year before. At the end of the series he had accumulated 54 points, well clear of the 36 of runner-up Paul Friedrichs (360 CZ) from East Germany. Smith's old protagonist, Rolf Tibblin, was third with 32 points and BSA team mate Vic Eastwood fourth. Sten Lundin was fifth with 27 points.

As in 1964 Jeff Smith again won the British Championship for 1965, making it a British and World Title double two years in succession. He had reached his zenith and from then on there was but one way to go. He won the British title for the ninth and last time in 1967 when he finished runner-up to Paul Friedrichs in the world series. In 1968 he won the 250cc BBC Grandstand Trophy television series but in the 750cc class of the same series he had to give ground to the new, younger generation in the form of John Banks, Vic Eastwood and Keith Hickman. He continued to ride with a fair modicum of success until the dramatic closure of the BSA competitions shop in July 1971.

In a competitive riding career spanning 20 years, Jeff Smith had won everything of note in the world of trials and scrambles. He had given innumerable talks to motorcycle clubs throughout the United Kingdom and conducted lecture tours and demonstrations throughout the world in places as far apart as the USA and New Zealand, where he preached not only BSA but motorcycling with a British flavour. His total contribution to motorcycling was offically recognised and he was honoured with the award of the MBE in the New Year's Honours List of 1970. To this day he remains the only trials and scrambles rider to have been thus officially honoured.

Few would disagree that Jeffrey Smith, MBE, was the greatest scrambles and motocross rider ever produced by the United Kingdom. Fewer still would disagree that he was the most successful in the dynasty of BSA superstars.

Chapter 18

Family Twins

TO A large extent the phenomenal success of the Gold Star transcended all else achieved by other BSA models used in racing and competition including the world-title-winning Victor Grand Prix and success achieved by the 500cc and 650cc twin-cylinder models over the years. It was the penalty of one member of the family rising to illustrious immortality.

The BSA twin-cylinder models, nonetheless, contributed more than a modest share of glory right from the moment Fred Rist stormed British beaches on a 650 A10 Golden Flash with its potential of 140 mph. Over in the USA it was a similar story where, on the Rosamond Salt Lakes in July 1951, Gene Theissen broke national records with a speed of 130.90 mph with an A10 running on petrol and 137.30 mph when using alcohol. On the same occasion Theissen also clocked 123.69 mph with a 500cc Star Twin running on petrol.

Eight months later the 500cc Star Twin was used in the famous 200-Mile Daytona Beach Race for the first time, with 13 such models entered. Ten completed the distance, six of them finishing within the first twenty. Albert Gunter, on one of these models, was actually leading at half-distance before slowing to finish fifth. Gene Theissen made the two fastest laps of the day on a Star Twin in 2 mins 46 secs before breaking his clutch lever and riding the remaining 150 miles without declutching for gear changing. He eventually finished in ninth place.

Two years later, in 1954, Bobby Hill rode a Star Twin to victory in this prestigious American classic with Dick Klamfoth second, on another Star Twin. It was the most important BSA twin-cylinder victory up to that time. It must be admitted, however, that by then overhead camshaft racing models such as the Manx Norton had been outlawed by regulations influenced by the domestic interests of the American Motorcycle Association. Models with overhead-valve operation were limited to a capacity of 500cc and a maximum compression ratio of 8:1.

All machines had to be approved as regular production models of the respective manufacturer. Certain components could be exchanged, provided such parts were also catalogued and sold as standard equipment.

Charlie Salt of Derby rode this A7 twin with its Earles alloy frame, pivoting forks and alloy petrol tank to 18th place in the 1952 Senior TT at 84.46 mph. On the same machine he was 16th in the 1953 Senior TT at 83.51 mph. This picture was taken at a Silverstone meeting circa 1952.

By 1958 British production-machine racers had been eased out completely, leaving the 200-Mile Experts event at Daytona as a Harley Davidson benefit where, for several years, they romped away with victory after victory, virtually unopposed. Not that those mighty 750cc side-valve 'flathead' vee-twin Harleys needed the benefits of handicapping for they had tremendous performance despite a weight of 440 lbs. With enormous inlet valves of $1\frac{7}{8}$ inch diameter and exhaust valves of $1\frac{5}{16}$; large $1\frac{5}{16}$ choke carburettor and a 6:1 compression ratio, they turned out on average 44 to 47 bhp at 6,600 rpm, with a good one even exceeding 50 bhp. Undoubtedly they were the most developed side-valve vee-twins ever, and a great credit to those responsible.

After the Star Twin victory at Daytona in 1954 it was another 12 years before factory-backed BSA twins again contested the 200-Mile Experts Race, though in 1956 Jack Schlaman had finished second in the 100-Mile Amateur Race on a Star Twin. On the home front in the

With front wheel throwing up a bow-wave of water from the saturated and rain-sodden track, Mike Hailwood takes an A65 Lightning to victory in the 1965 Hutchinson 100 Production Machine Race at Silverstone.

Following Mike Hailwood's win in the 1965 Hutchinson 100 Production Machine Race John Cooper, seen here, was in a similar event at Brands Hatch in 1966 on a BSA Spitfire Mk.II Special at 80.12 mph.

United Kingdom the Star Twin had really etched its name in the hall of fame with the historical ACU Certified test of 1952, which culminated in the award of the Maudes Trophy. In the Isle of Man, where the Senior TT was still dominated by the overhead camshaft big single, Charlie Salt* from Derby — sponsored by alloy frame and pivoting front fork specialist Ernie Earles — put in some consistent rides during the early 1950s with an A7 twin. With Earles frame and light alloy pivoting front forks designed and made by Ernie Earles himself, Salt first rode the A7 in the Senior TT of 1951, when he retired on the fourth lap.

In 1952 however, still with the Earles-BSA A7, Charlie had a trouble-free ride in the Senior, to finish 18th at a speed of 84.46 mph and with a fastest lap in 26 mins. 22 secs. Cecil Sandford — who went on to win the 125cc World Title for MV that year — also rode an Earls-BSA A7, retiring on the fourth lap after lapping in 26 mins. 10 secs. Roland Pike, having joined the BSA development department only the month before, also rode his own A7 development model, with a special frame and an alloy engine which was reputed to develop 44 bhp. He toured in to complete his third lap and retired.

Bob Heath racing his A65 Lightning on the Llandow course in Wales during 1967 before he started work at BSA. Later, he raced a 500cc B50 single and a 750cc Rocket Three.

295

---

* Charlie Salt who worked in the BSA experimental department was killed on the last of the 8-lap Golden Jubilee Senior TT of 1957 when riding a 500 Gold Star.

Chris Vincent with his BSA-powered outfit with passenger Derek Bliss sweeping round Parliament Square on the way to their sensational victory in the 1962 Isle of Man Sidecar TT. The 500 Sidecar TT has not been won by a British bike since.

In 1953, when Charlie Salt was the solo BSA A7 rider in the Senior TT, he did even better by finishing 16th at 83.51 mph with a fastest lap in 26 mins. 16 secs. Together with Peter Davey and Eric Houseley he shared in the winning club team prize for the Derby Pathfinder MCC. By 1954, however, with the 500cc Gold Star asserting its authority in the Senior Clubman's TT — that year won by Alistair King with a record lap of 87.02 mph — the A7 lapsed in popularity as a racing power unit. Even the faithful Charlie Salt transferred his allegiance to the Gold Star for the 1954 Senior TT and from then on the A7 twin languished in the shadows cast by that more illustrious member of the BSA family.

Then, dramatically and unexpectedly, a BSA rider found himself on the winners' rostrum after victory in an international TT in the Isle of Man. Chris Vincent had won the 1962 Sidecar TT with his BSA A7 twin-powered outfit. Everybody was taken aback; even the spectators around the course who saw it happen. *The Motor Cycle* race report stated: 'The crowds around the final miles (on the last lap) gaped in astonishment, then recovered their senses to wave and cheer-on the BSA wizard. It was incredible but it was happening. A British rider on a British machine was leading the Sidecar TT — for the first time on the mountain course since 1924.'

Vincent won at 83.57 mph ahead of Otto Kolle, who averaged 82.93 mph with his BMW. During the race he had trailed behind Max Deubel

For a decade or more Chris Vincent with his 650cc BSA-powered outfit was virtually invincible on British circuits such as Brands Hatch, Mallory Park and Cadwell Park.

Chris Vincent relaxing in the paddock with passenger Keith Scott, circa 1963. With seven British Sidecar Championships to his name, Chris Vincent was the undisputed master of British circuits for many years.

and Florian Camathias, both on BMWs, with the former putting in the fastest lap of 90.07 mph. But as always, the winner is he who passes the winning post first. Camathias rammed the bank at Kerromooar whilst Deubel's BMW seized. The Vincent/BSA win produced stunned amazement. If anything, BSA management was more stunned than most. It is relevant to recall that the BSA managing director at the time was Edward Turner, the Triumph apostle who eschewed factory participation in road racing but exploited the publicity of success handed to him on a plate.

It is true that Vincent's Sidecar TT effort had no official factory backing. Had it failed, discreet silence would have been possible. As it

Powered by a 654cc A65 Rocket engine from March 1964, the Vincent outfit broke every unlimited lap record at every British circuit at which it competed, according to the press at that time.

was, delighted management celebrated the victory officially by organizing promptly on the spot a dinner in Douglas during race week, with Chris Vincent the toast of BSA. Working within the BSA factory Vincent did have the advantage of a degree of 'official' support though this varied enormously among those in a position to help — from the wholehearted co-operation and support of Len Crisp, one-time sidecar expert and then foreman of the experimental department — to the downright hostility of others.

Having joined BSA from school, Chris subsequently moved to Nortons where he was employed as a prototype mileage tester, only to

With film star good looks, Chris Vincent was utilized by BSA in a publicity role at an Earls Court Motor Cycle Show circa 1963. Caron Gardner, one of the blonde pilots from the James Bond film Goldfinger *graces the Watsonian Monza sidecar.*

move back to BSA during the latter part of the fifties in a similar role. By then he was into sidecar grasstrack racing and even sidecar speedway racing — as well as solo racing — and in 1958 he won the ACU Sidecar Grasstrack Championship. In 1959 he tried his hand at road racing at a time when British short-circuits were still dominated by camshaft Norton and BMW outfits. That first season with his rather rough-and-ready BSA outfit he did sufficiently well and ruffled enough feathers to finish sixth in the ACU Sidecar Championship.

From then on there was no holding him, and he went on to win the British title in 1961 with a total of 84 points, a massive 30-point margin over runner-up Pip Harris (BMW). Although he lost the title to Bill Boddice (Norton) by a slim margin in 1962, thereafter the British Championship almost became his personal property, when he won it in 1963, '64, '65, '69, 1970 and 1971. For 1966 and 1967 the title went to Owen Greenwood with his 1071cc Mini-engined, three-wheeled car. (It   299

Norman Hanks, passengered by John Glastonbury, on full song with the unfaired Hanks-tuned BSA A65-powered outfit at Thruxton. He won the 1972 British Sidecar Championship.

seems curious that the ACU allowed vehicles with two driven front wheels to compete as 'sidecars'. The FIM banned such vehicles in post-1969 international events.)

There can be no gainsaying that the sixties was the era of Chris Vincent on the British circuits with ultra-reliable BSA twin power units; initially with the 500cc A7 and 650cc A10 then, from 1964, with the 500cc A50 and 654cc A65 engines. *The Motor Cycle* reported that since the A65 Rocket engine was installed in the outfit and first used at the Mallory Park meeting of 22nd March 1964, 'it made rings round the opposition (as usual)'. The comment in brackets is that of the original report, and it went on to say that the Vincent A65 outfit 'had broken the unlimited lap record at every British short circuit at which it had appeared'. Chris Vincent and the BSA were virtually unbeatable. The records prove it.

By then the factory support was official, the engine belonging to the company and bearing an experimental department number. Chris had his own little workshop in which to prepare and work on the outfit. Nonetheless, there were still those who resisted and impeded his work and all bench testing with the Heenan & Froude dynamometer had to be done after normal hours, with Chris often working up to and beyond midnight. He was even known to road test the outfit round the factory test circuit in the dark. The path of the stars is seldom smooth.

With twin GP carburettors and a 10:1 compression ratio, the engine used by Chris employed American cams, special pistons and close-ratio gears, with an energy-transfer alternator feeding twin scramble-type coils encapsulated in resin (as used on the Victor GP model). It was claimed the engine developed 60 bhp at 7,250 rpm. The Vincent BSA success undoubtedly stimulated the trend toward the BSA engine as *the* engine for the job. It was competitive and freely available, and spare parts could be bought at modest cost. Even riders like the veteran Bill Boddice — hitherto loyal to Norton — saw the logic and changed to BSA. He once said, with a great deal of truth, that when a valve dropped-in on a BSA it was a lot less expensive than when it happened with Norton.

The facts prove that the BSA-powered racing outfit became the most popular and successful on British circuits. Chris Vincent alone achieved something like 250 victories with his BSA in event finals alone, not counting heats. It was hardly surprising that others followed his example. Bill Boddice's son Michael, himself serving an apprenticeship at BSA, followed in the racing footsteps of his father by taking up sidecar racing in 1965 at the tender age of 17. He too used a BSA-powered outfit and promptly had his first race victory at the Castle Combe meeting in July. That same year Peter Brown — an Ariel employee who had moved

Roy Hanks, passengered by brother-in-law Gerald Daniel, competing in the 1971 Sidecar TT with his fully-faired BSA outfit. Roy won the two-leg Sidecar TT eleven years later in 1982.

to Small Heath when Selly Oak closed down — took to road racing with a BSA outfit; like Vincent before him, he had graduated from grasstrack racing where he had enjoyed considerable success.

By 1967, the pipe-smoking Peter Brown had become a force to be reckoned with, to the extent of beating Chris Vincent from time to time. In the Race of the Year meeting held at Mallory Park in September 1967 he won heat one then beat Vincent in the final, who had won heat two. In that particular final Terry Vinicombe with the Tom Kirby-sponsored BSA outfit was third and Mick Boddice fifth, with Malcolm 'Mac' Hobson (Cowie-BSA) sixth. It was Tony Wakefield on the BMW in fourth place which prevented a BSA grand slam.

Two of the 'BSA Barrow Boys', Peter Brown (left) and Mick Boddice (right) pushing their BSA outfits along Glencrutchery Road to the starting grid for the 1968 750 Sidecar TT in which Peter finished third. He was second in both 1969 and 1970, his BSA being the highest-placed British outfit.

At the later November Mallory meeting, Peter Brown was again the sidecar victor, with Mick Boddice second and Norman Hanks third, completing another familiar BSA one-two-three. Norman Hanks — one of the famous Hanks family all of whom raced BSA outfits (father Fred and sons Roy and Norman) — also worked for BSA. Thus for several years there was a unique quartet consisting of Chris Vincent, Peter Brown, Mick Boddice and Norman Hanks, all employed by BSA, all racing BSA-powered outfits and dominating British circuits for several years.

Whereas Norman Hanks worked in the competitions department, where Mick Boddice also worked on completion of his apprenticeship, Peter Brown worked in the experimental shop as did Chris Vincent.

They were not alone. In the 1967 Sidecar TT the best placed BSA entry was that of Terry Vinicombe with the Tom Kirby-BSA outfit, who finished sixth in an entry that included Fred, Roy and Norman Hanks, Mick Boddice, Malcolm 'Mac' Hobson and Derek Rumble, all on BSAs. The previous year Terry Vinicombe had finished eighth. But in 1968, the year of the introduction of the 750cc Sidecar TT, Terry Vinicombe — passengered by John Flaxman — was victorious, leading home a trio of BSA outfits that took the first three places. Norman Hanks with Mrs Rose Arnold as passenger was second, with his A65 engine bored-out to 672cc, and Peter Brown, passengered by David Bean, was third. Vinicombe's winning speed was 85.85 mph. Peter Brown went on to finish second in both 750 Sidecar TTs of 1969 and 1970, as the highest placed British outfit, beaten on both occasions only by S.Schauzu's BMW.

Although Peter Brown won the British Championship for 1968, his best season, and was always in contention, Chris Vincent was always the man to beat. When he did everything right and had everything in his favour, nobody could live with him. Sometimes, after a sluggish start, he would electrify the spectators with a meteoric weave through the field as though they were standing still. From time to time he even humbled the sidecar masters from Europe with their world-beating BMWs. One such occasion was during the 1965 Hutchinson '100' meeting at Silverstone when he won the 12-lap Championship race by no less than 45 seconds from F. Scheidegger and Florian Camathias on their BMWs at a speed of 85.85 mph and with a fastest lap at 88.25 mph. On the 10-lap Scratch race it was another Vincent victory with a fastest lap of 93.09 mph.

Like the prolific success of the Gold Star in the fifties, it would make dull and repetitive reading to list all the successes of Chris Vincent and his BSA outfit during the sixties and early part of the seventies; and even more so to include those of his fellow BSA sidecar racers on the British mainland circuits. As few would disagree that Eric Oliver was the greatest ever British sidecar racer, a majority would agree that Chris Vincent was one of the greatest to follow on. He, more than anybody, proved what could be done with BSA 500cc and 650cc twins on the racetracks of Great Britain when such power units were suitably fettled for the job.

Apart from the sidecar boys, there were two other BSA-employed riders who achieved success with the A65 model in production machine racing. One of them was Bob Heath, who worked in the competitions shop and also raced a 350 B40 and a 499 B50 single. He did well with the

An action shot of Peter Brown at Braddan Bridge taken during the 1970 750 Sidecar TT with passenger M.Casey, when they finished second yet again. Peter had won the 1968 British Sidecar Championship.

A65 Lightning at such venues as Darley Moor, in addition to the more popular circuits such as Mallory and Brands Hatch. He later went on to race a 750 Rocket Three in Production events and took part in Coupe d' Endurance long-distance events. The other was Tony Smith, who divided his time between the competitions shop and working for development engineer Clive Bennett. He performed well with a factory A65 production racer, finishing third in the 750 Production Machine TT of 1967 at 89.73 mph (in the 500cc class, sidecar racer Norman Hanks, riding solo for a change, finished fifth at 81.90 mph on an A50). At the Brands Hatch Hutchinson '100' meeting of 1969, Tony Smith was second on a 654cc Spitfire to winner Mick Andrews (750 Norton) in the Production Machine race, putting in a record lap at 86.57 mph. He also did valuable work for the factory testing racers at MIRA.

Probably the most notable success of the A65 Lightning was that accomplished by the great Mike Hailwood when he won the Production Machine Race of the Hutchinson '100' at Silverstone in August 1965. He beat both Phil Read (Triumph) and Percy Tait (Triumph) with a speed of 83.14 mph and a fastest lap at 85.81 mph. Entered by Tom Kirby of Hornchurch, Essex, the Hailwood model was, nonetheless, factory prepared; indeed, Mike elected to use a frame with a steering head angle different to that normally used. No less convincing was the BSA Spitfire victory in the same event of the following year, then staged at Brands Hatch, when John Cooper was the victor at 80.12 mph.

Over the years BSA twins were used for TT travelling marshal duties on several occasions. Here with a 1966 Mk.II Spitfire Special is Jack Harding, who performed such duties for 25 years.

Whilst BSA steadfastly adhered to their long-standing policy of non-involvement in grand prix road racing, increasing interest and support of production-machine racing was manifest. The changing climate can be attributed to Harry Sturgeon, who succeeded Edward Turner in 1964 as BSA motorcycle group managing director. He was a man of dynamic personality who viewed road racing as an aid to sales, quite the reverse of the attitude adopted by Edward Turner. By then, the climate in the United States of America had also changed. The American Motorcycle Association had been affiliated to the FIM, the world governing body of motorcycle sport, and as a result the regulations relative to such events as the prestigious Daytona 200-miler became much less parochial. Limitations on compression ratios had been lifted and racing fairings were allowed, although ohv engines were still limited to 500cc.

Thus for 1966 there was renewed BSA interest and effort for Daytona. Four 500cc A50 models were prepared by the factory, whilst two similar models were prepared in the USA, one by the East Coast division of BSA Incorporated at Nutley, New Jersey, and the other by their counterparts on the West Coast in California. With a compression ratio of 10:1, the power units differed from standard in a number of directions; notably by the use of special Hepworth and Grandage pistons with Dykes pattern top rings and compression and oil control rings in HG22 material. Inlet and exhaust valves were in Nimonic 80 steel and the big-end shells in lead idium. The standard plain metal timing side bearing was replaced with a ball race whilst the oil pump body was made in non-standard cast iron.

Using twin Amal GP carburettors of 13/16 inch bore, maximum bhp proved to be 53.25 at 7,750 rpm with maximum permissible rpm at 8,250. Pulling a top gear of 4.35:1, the best of the factory-prepared models returned a mean speed of 121.6 mph when tested at MIRA. A second one achieved 121.1 mph and a third 119.2 mph, the slowest recording 118.4 mph. The fastest one-way speed (with an easterly wind at 10 mph) was 125.7 mph. Despite the effort put into the job, practice week and the race itself proved a heinous experience for BSA. Initial joy in the 100-Mile Amateur event was dashed when Howard Utsey crashed after leading on one of the American-prepared models. In the main 200-Mile event all six models were forced to retire. Reasons for the failure were many and they provided lessons to be learned and applied in 1967. But it was heart-breaking disaster.

The Daytona exercise of 1968 should have been a case of third time lucky. But it proved to be the now familiar pattern of problems that included carburation, all of which took some sorting out during practice week. During the preceding months, further development had increased power output to 56 bhp at 8,200 rpm. A larger diameter inlet valve was in use in conjunction with an improved inlet port shape. The crankcase housed a self-aligning, drive-side roller bearing within a bronze housing, with a similar roller bearing being used on the timing shaft. A special Lucas racing contact-breaker unit had been fitted and to improve oil flow the cast-iron oil pump housed gears of modified diametric pitch. The heavy steel clutch centre had been replaced by a light alloy component, the power unit being housed in a completely new frame aimed at reducing frontal area and improving handling.

During final testing at MIRA Tony Smith averaged 121 mph over a period of 1¹/₂ hours, with a change down to second gear on every lap. A second model averaged 118 mph over the same period.

1968 was the year in which Cal Rayborn first stormed to victory, once again putting Harley-Davidson up front with a winning speed of 101.29 mph. It was also the year when the Japanese came in from the cold with Bill Lyons winning the 100-Mile Amateur Race on a 450cc Honda at 94.14 mph, ahead of one of the BSA A50 models which did survive, with Ray Hempstead in the saddle.

Cal Rayborn repeated his victory for Harley-Davidson in 1969 — at a slightly slower speed of 100.88 mph — the best placed BSA A50, ridden by Eddie Worth, finishing in 20th place. Having stayed away from Daytona in 1969, BSA returned for 1970 and '71 in grand style, to make amends and redeem the family reputation.

There was no need for that on the home front where Chris Vincent, Peter Brown, Mick Boddice and the Hanks continued their dominating ways on British circuits with their 654cc BSA-powered kneelers. In *The Motor Cycle* of 30th October 1968 Mick Woollett stated that for the past two seasons Chris Vincent's outfit had 'proved to be the best in Britain.' With nine British sidecar road racing championships to its credit within a period of twelve years, it could be claimed that the BSA-powered outfits had been tops for rather longer than that. The twins had done the family quite proud.

Chapter 19

The Final Years

HISTORY INDICATES that the 500cc World Motorcross Championship victories of 1964 and 1965 represent the climax of BSA achievement. In addition to the World and British titles won by Jeff Smith in 1965, Chris Vincent had won the British Sidecar Road Racing title and Scott Ellis had won the solo title in the British Experts Trial. Four titles in one season — a BSA repeat of 1956 — seemed a good omen for the future as 1965 came to a close.

During the winter an even bigger Victor engine had been developed; to be used in a machine of reduced overall weight. The bore and stroke had been increased to 82 mm x 93 mm, to give a cubic capacity of 494cc and an increased power output of 33.4 bhp at 6,000 rpm. In the interests of weight-saving the crankcases were cast in magnesium alloy — though during the course of the season this was abandoned — and a number of other items such as the con-rod, rockers and engine sprocket were made in titanium as were various cycle parts.

But the most radical step of all was the use of titanium for the main frame. When the first completed machine turned the scales at a dramatic 212 lbs, enthusiam was high; only to be dashed as quickly as it had spiralled. Under racing conditions the new frame was found to flex much more than its steel equivalent, which impaired handling and later caused cracking. When the latter occurred, the specialized welding technique needed for repairs could not be carried out 'in the field', so that when a tube fractured it had to be jury-rigged.

Even before the complete machine reached the racing stage complex production problems had to be overcome. As Brian Martin pointed out, 'The entire frame building process was so complex that each frame took days rather than hours to weld-up. The cost was immense. Brian further mused that top management thought spending money would bring results (though credit is due for willingness to increase a budget which,

Above left: The second of the famous Lampkin brothers, Alan (better known as 'Sid') climbs Tyndrum on his way to victory in the 1966 Scottish Six Days, to record the last BSA Scottish win and the last British four-stroke win. With brother Arthur and Scott Ellis he also took the team prize for BSA. Photo: Motor Cycle News.

Above right: An unusual one-legged act by Scott Ellis with a C15T in the 1968 John Douglas Trial complete with 'famous' cap. He continued to use the works C15T (and his cap) after BSA withdrew from national trials at the end of 1967. Photo: Motor Cycle News.

at times in the past, had been regarded as too tight). But the truth was that too little was known about titanium in that application. 'And furthermore' Brian added, 'it was a tactical error to start the grand prix season with an untried product.'

In consequence the BSA dual-spearhead of Jeff Smith and Vic Eastwood — the latter having joined the BSA works line-up from AMC — were forced to revert to normal steel frames before the season was very old. In the first round of the 1966 World series in Switzerland on 17th April, the BSA result bordered on a shambles, with Jeff Smith 309 retiring from the first leg when his carburettor float chamber came adrift, though Vic Eastwood finished a comparatively good fourth. In the second leg Smith's chain came off but he went on to finish eighth after refitting it. Poor Vic Eastwood actually turned-off his petrol tap with his riding boot and when he came to a standstill at the foot of a steep hill, he could not restart the engine.

Scott Ellis at the start of a Colmore Cup Trial with the final version of the 250cc C15T on which he won the 1965 British Experts solo title, the last BSA rider to win this great classic. Photo: Motor Cycle News.

At the next round in Austria it was much the same, with Smith's chain again coming off in the first leg, and a rather poor seventh in the second leg. In Italy it was more like old times, with Jeff Smith second in both legs and second overall to Paul Friedrichs — the latter leading the championship. In Denmark Jeff retired in the first leg when his clutch worked loose on the shaft; but in the second leg there was a ray of sunshine when he won from Rolf Tibblin and Geboers.

In Sweden it was again a mixture of disaster and joy, with Smith retiring in the first leg with slipped ignition timing whilst winning the second leg. Eastwood's chain came off in the first leg and he finished seventh in the second leg.

On 22nd May, Jeff Smith secured his only success of the series on a course near Helsinki in Finland when he finished second to Gunnar Johansson (360 CZ) in the first leg ahead of Paul Friedrichs, before going out to win the second leg and overall victory. In the Russian round he was second to Friedrichs; and in the British round at Farleigh Castle, second overall to Don Rickman (Metisse).

In Holland on 24th July, Jeff Smith was fifth in the first leg before engine trouble put him out of the second leg. That proved to be the end of his 1966 title bid and hopes of retaining the world title for the third year as an injury in a home event kept him out of the remaining three rounds. Riding in his place in the Belgian round on the famous course at Namur — always a difficult one but now made near impossible by overnight rain — Arthur Lampkin scored a notable win by finishing second in both legs, with Vic Eastwood winning the first leg to finish fifth overall after a poor second leg ride.

Paul Friedrichs went on to win the world title for the first time, with ex-champion Rolf Tibblin second and ex-champion Jeff Smith third. A disappointing result no doubt but in view of the trials and tribulations, one which still reflected much credit on Jeff Smith. With Jeff forming the BSA spearhead for the 1967 grand prix season — again backed-up by Vic Eastwood — it was a similar season of ups-and-downs, with more of the latter than to BSA's liking. Nonetheless Jeff Smith finished the season as runner-up in the series to Paul Friedrichs who won the title for the second time with a total of 56 points, well clear of the 35 scored by Smith. With another British Championship win in 1967, it made him number one in the British Isles and number two in the world. Jeff Smith was surely a jewel in the BSA crown. By 1968 however, able and brilliant as he was, Jeff was 34 years of age and well past the considered peak for such a strenuous activity. To introduce new and younger blood to the BSA line-up, who would take over as the spearhead when necessary, Vic Eastwood had been recruited. Then, during the early weeks of 1968 — after finishing second to John Banks in the BBC 750cc Grandstand TV series a difference of opinion with BSA resulted in Vic's contract being terminated. That, in effect, put the tall and good-looking John Banks — the new boy in the works team, into the hot seat. He rose to the occasion like a true champion he became.

By then the Victor engine had undergone further dimensional changes, the bore being increased from 82 to 84 mm and the stroke reduced from 93 to 90mm, to give a bigger capacity of 499cc. This was the ultimate arrangement of what was later to be designated the B50. Those works Victor engines of 1968, with a compression ratio of 10:1, produced 37.2 bhp at 6,000 rpm. Standard Victor cams with 118 degrees of overlap were used, as was a 32mm Amal Concentric carburettor. As had been the case in 1967 the frame was made in Reynolds 531

In 1968 John Banks of Bury St Edmunds finally usurped Jeff Smith as BSA's scramble spearhead by winning the British Championship for the first time. He repeated this win the following year.

manganese-molybdenum steel but now the front forks were of a new type with long, internal springs of variable rate and two-way damping provided by shuttle valves. The fork sliders were in magnesium-alloy with the rear hub also in the same material.

After his splendid start to the season with his win in the BBC TV Grandstand Trophy series (where BSA filled the first four places and Jeff Smith was sixth), John Banks first world series win came at the French Motocross Grand Prix in July when he was second to Roger De Coster (380 CZ) in the first leg and winner of the second leg, ahead of Bengt Aberg (420 Husqvarna). In the Dutch round which quickly

'Big John' Banks had two near-misses in the 500 World Motocross Championships of 1968 and 1969 when he finished runner-up on both occasions, a mere one mark down on the former occasion. In this shot he leads an international event in Poland circa 1968/69.

followed, he won both legs outright. Jeff Smith was third overall. With a second place overall in the Belgian round — behind Aberg and ahead of Friedrichs — John Banks scored enough points to put him in the championship lead.

Another second place overall in Luxemburg was enough for him to keep the title lead, but Friedrichs was only six marks adrift. At the final round in Switzerland, a second place in both legs made Paul Friedrichs the overall winner and a total points score gave him the championship — just one point up on John Banks. Jeff Smith finished jointly in seventh place in with P.Dobty (380 CZ) in the final world placings. A miss is as good as a mile, but with just one mark frustrating a world title, it made that maxim difficult to swallow. However, there was recompense and comfort for the young man from Bury St.Edmunds in winning the

313

BSA: Competition History

British 500 Scramble Championship for the first time (the 'Star' series had been replaced by the new British Championship format in 1966).

After a propitious start to the 1969 season when he beat the Continental opposition of J.Teuwissen and S.Geboers of Belgium, to win the ever-popular Hants Grand National on Good Friday — a form of dress rehearsal for the season — John Banks' experience in 1969 was an almost exact reflection of that of the year before. By the time of the Belgian event in August, he was leading the championship, for he had achieved overall victory in the Czechoslovakian round at Prerov and likewise in the Russian event at Kishinev. Then the rot set in.

In West Germany he was forced out with ignition failure. In the Luxemburg event in August — in which Dave Nicoll secured his first overall victory — John Banks punctured in the second leg after taking third place in the first. He had lost the title lead. In the French round, deep in the countryside of Tarn, just north of Albi, ignition failure again frustrated him. He saw the title slipping from his grasp yet again, In Switzerland he injured his wrist during practice and punctured once again in the race. By then he had slipped to third place in the

Dave Nicholl leads a bunch of riders in the 1969 West German Motocross Grand Prix where he finished 7th overall behind fellow teamster Keith Hickman. Hickman finished 4th overall.

championship. With a fifth overall in the final round in East Germany at Schwerin, his closest contender Friedrichs retiring in the second leg, John improved his position to finish runner-up, yet again, but this time to a new champion; Bengt Aberg (420 Husqvarna) of Sweden.

As in 1968 there was solace for John Banks with a second-in-a-row British Championship title win. So for two years he was British Champion and ranked second in world ratings. Only super riders ever achieve that. He thus became the fourth BSA rider to win the British 500 Star or Championship and the highest placed BSA rider in the world series after Jeff Smith.

During 1968 and '69 Banks had not been the sole BSA contender in the world series for both Keith Hickman and Dave Nicoll had ridden in a way which augured well for the future. Indeed, Keith Hickman had finished in sixth place in the world series of 1969. BSA had good cause to be confident.

Nonetheless, there must have been unease, if only amongst the riders who would know better than most that the big-capacity two-strokes were becoming hard to beat — the CZs, Husqvarnas and Maicos, soon to be followed by the first of the Japanese. It was this more than anything else which shaped future events, for by then the big BSA four-stroke single was a lone cry in the wilderness; a wilderness wherein roamed vicious two-stroke predators.

Viewed in retrospect what happened on the world motocross stage of 1970 and 1971, as it affected BSA, can only by described as a shambles, yet BSA fielded a team of six, top-flight riders, reminiscent of the old Gold Star days, with Jeff Smith, John Banks, Dave Nicoll and Keith Hickman, reinforced by Andy Roberton in 1970, and further still by Vic Allan in 1971. It was a formidable line-up.

The traumas of 1970 began in the very first round of the world series in Switzerland, on 11th April, when John Banks broke his little finger whilst lying fourth in the second leg. Dave Nicoll had already cracked a bone in his right foot during the practice session and had returned with his foot in plaster. Back in action in time for the Dutch round during May, John Banks retired in the first leg when lying eighth and then collided with another rider in the second leg. Keith Hickman retired in both legs and Dave Nicoll was a non-starter. Soon after the Dutch round, John Banks' knee, which had twice been dislocated in the space of five weeks, required an operation for torn ligaments. In June Keith Hickman was injured in Czechoslovakia. Then in August at the difficult Namur course in Belgium, Dave Nicoll collided with a bank in the first leg, whilst Keith Hickman crashed and injured his hand. Both were thus non-starters in the second leg. In Luxemburg, Keith Hickman at least managed a fourth place in the first leg but came off in the second; 315

Dave Nicholl aviates his Victor in the 1968 French Motocross Grand Prix, won by fellow teamster John Banks, with Jeff Smith 3rd. Nicholl's best continental performance was his outright victory in Luxemburg 1969.

likewise Dave Nicoll pranged on the first lap of the first leg, to retire with buckled front forks. At the conclusion of that disastrous season, Keith Hickman was the highest-placed BSA rider in the world series with a modest 14th place. He was also the best BSA rider in the British Championship, in third place. Jeff Smith was third in the 250cc British Championship.

316 There had been few, if any, crumbs of comfort for BSA during that

1970 motocross season; indeed the poor results seemed to mirror the state of the company itself. Nonetheless, plans were made to contest the 1971 world series with the same team of riders, reinforced by the addition of that tough little Scot Vic Allan. If Brian Martin felt at all apprehensive about the future prospects, doubts must have been removed by the results of a televised international motocross meeting staged at Dodington Park, near Bristol, during the damp, dark winter days of February. In the first leg it was a convincing BSA one-two-three, with John Banks leading home Dave Nicoll and Andy Roberton. All three beat the formidable pair from Belgium — Sylvain Geboers and Joel Robert.

In the second leg it was Dave Nicoll's turn to win, with John Banks second, but Nicoll came out the overall victor. A week or two later at a similar ITV World of Sport televised meeting, staged at Beenham Park in Berkshire, the result was a further reassuring confirmation of rosy prospects when the Senior Race and All-Comers Final were dominated

A graphic shot of Dave Nicholl of Royston taken during practice for a British event at Elsworth in 1968. He was the last BSA works rider to compete with the B50 Victor after the BSA competitions department closed down in 1971. Photo: Motor Cycle News.

by the BSA boys and the sleek, stylish Victors. Dave Nicoll won the former, with Vic Allan second, and John Banks third. In the latter, Vic Allan as the winner led home Dave Nicoll, John Banks and Andy Roberton in line astern. A convincing display.

Those tantalizing successes proved to be the sole shafts of sunlight before once again the storm clouds gathered to blot out the memory. The heartbreak began with the Italian Motocross Grand Prix at Cingoli on the 18th April, in which new recruit Vic Allan sustained a severely fractured leg which kept him out of racing for the rest of the year. John Banks managed to finish eighth overall but Keith Hickman was never in the hunt. An unhappy Brian Martin summed up the course as the most dangerous circuit he had ever seen and threatened to take it up with the FIM. Until the British Motocross Grand Prix in July, the only reasonable result obtained by the BSA boys was a third place obtained by John Banks in the Swedish round; the rest produced a mixture of retirements and low placings. And so to Farleigh Castle and the British round where, in front of the home crowd, John Banks was best of the BSA team to finish ninth in the first leg and third in the second, giving him a fifth place overall. Andy Roberton was fifth in the first leg and eighth in the second. With that indifferent result, official BSA participation in scrambles and motocross came to a sad and ignominous end. For that was the week-end when BSA made it known the competition department was to close down. Brian Martin had the sad duty of informing the factory team.

Nonetheless, the existing riders were offered continued use of the works Victors for the remainder of the season with a degree of spares back-up, but at their own expense. Only Dave Nicoll availed himself of the offer. John Banks campaigned the rest of the season with a Husqvarna, once again winning the British 500 Championship. Andy Roberton, who also completed the season on Husqvarna, was third in the Championship.

Dave Nicoll continued with the Victor and, in fact, completed the British season on 12th December with a victorious display of defiance in the World of Sport Televised meeting at Cadwell Park. He claimed outright victory in the World of Sport event. The press report of the meeting in *The Motor Cycle* aptly summed it up by pronouncing that the 'Lanky Dave Nicoll (500 BSA) gave the now-closed BSA competitions department its swan-song with a brilliant victory in Saturday's ITV World of Sport Scramble at Cadwell Park.'

It was indeed a final, victorious gesture of defiance, as had been Andy Roberton's winning performance in the Welsh Two-Days Trial in June, just a week or two before the final closure. With a 500 Victor, he teamed up with Dave Nicoll (504 BSA) and Jeff Smith (250 BSA) to win

Keith Hickman, seen here competing with the B50 Victor in a BBC TV scramble meeting during February 1970, finished 3rd in the British Championships of 1969 and 1970 and was 6th in the World series of 1969. Photo: Motor Cycle News.

the manufacturers' team prize for the factory; a team award destined to be the last of probably hundreds won by BSA since 1910.

Somewhat dramatic perhaps to describe such wins as 'acts of defiance' but truth to tell the big four-stroke single in the world of motocross had been a doomed species for several years past, overwhelmed by the hordes of howling two-strokes with their superior power-to-weight ratio and low centre of gravity. It is true that two years later in 1973 John Banks again won the British 500 Scramble Championship with a Cheney-BSA, but that was to prove the last-ever four-stroke title winner in the British series.

So whilst it was the financial failure of the company which eliminated BSA participation in scrambles and motocross, it is open to conjecture as to what would have transpired had BSA remained in business. The answer surely lies with the history of the mighty Honda company who, like BSA, built their strength on the four-stroke engine. They too, despite their vast engineering resources, had to develop two-stroke horses-for-courses in order to preserve their prestige in the tough world of grand prix motocross and road racing.

319

BSA: Competition History

The irony of the situation is that having relied for many years on trials, scrambles and motocross for product proving and publicity, it was this which fell apart first. BSA had withdrawn official support from sporting trials at the end of the 1967 season, and whilst not saying so openly, clearly they had thrown in the towel having recognized that the traditional British four-stroke trials model was no longer competitive with the new generation of lightweight two-strokes.

The 1968 works 499cc B50 Victor GP — lean, aggressive and functional — weighed 235 lbs with its nickel-plated frame containing engine oil. Fork sliders and wheel hubs were in magnesium alloy and the alloy cylinder barrel had a hard chrome bore. With a Gold Star big-end bearing, it developed 37.2 bhp at 6,000 rpm — and it lost the World MX title by one point.

Production-machine racing however, and the formula derivatives based on production models bestowed with increased works support, mushroomed into a grand finale of resounding success, which reached a peak in 1971 before being torpedoed by the company's demise.

Despite the success of Mike Hailwood, John Cooper, Bob Heath and Tony Smith with production Lightnings and Spitfires in solo form, BSA performance could only be described as modestly successful, in no way comparable with the successes of its sidecar counterpart. Then dramatically in September 1968, to supply the fillip needed, the news broke like a bombshell. The BSA motorcycle group — by then with centralized engineering facilities — was to market for 1969 a three-cylinder 750ccc overhead-valve model under both BSA and Triumph brand names as the Rocket 3 and Trident respectively. The history of this new multi-cylinder model has already been well

Norman Hanks hotly pursued by brother Roy, who always enjoyed a personal feud with no holds barred. The purpose of the identical crash helmet cosmetics was 'to fool the opposition.' Norman's passenger Rose Arnold is now Mrs. Roy Hanks. Picture circa 1971.

Norman Hanks (7) with passenger Rose Arnold leading a quartet of BSA outfits round Devil's Elbow at Mallory Park, with close astern brother Roy (8) and passenger Freddie Holden. Also seen is Mick Boddice (6) with passenger Dennis Roach and Brian Rust (15) with passenger Keith Carter. Picture circa 1971.

documented and rightly attributed as the brainchild of Bert Hopwood and Doug Hele. With both these engineers working within the auspices of the BSA motorcycle division and with both BSA and Triumph variations of the engine unit produced within the BSA plant at Small Heath, BSA family ties existed even if pure BSA pedigree did not.

Within weeks of the sensational announcement, the 750 threes were being 'blooded' on race tracks on the other side of the Atlantic, both in Canada and the USA, where in the former during November Roger Beaumont won a production-machine event with a Trident — to record the model's first-ever race victory. In the Californian Grand Prix Tony

Before Mead & Tomkinson of Hereford raced a 499cc B50 with considerable success, they submitted a 440 Victor to long-distance endurance racing. In this picture Alan Peck speeds round Montjuich Park on the Victor in the 1969 Barcelona 24-hours Race.

Murphy finished fourth on a BSA Rocket 3 after being last away in this event staged at Los Angeles. In the meantime the AMA in the USA had increased the capacity limits for ohv power units based on production machines to 750cc, thus making the new 750 three eligible.

Thus concerted plans were made to contest the 1970 Daytona classic with both Tridents and Rockets as a co-ordinated operation based at Meriden and master-minded by Doug Hele and his team who had developed the model from the outset. The result of their work was published in the motorcycle press in early March 1970 when *The Motor Cycle* dubbed the machines they had been invited to examine as 'The fastest racing motorcycle ever built in Britain.' This was later borne out at Daytona when Gene Romero went through a speed trap on his practice qualifying lap at a staggering 165 mph.

Using a special Rob North frame, the models at 360 lbs were 100 lbs lighter than standard. Rod Quaife five-speed gear clusters were used as were three-into-one megaphone exhaust systems. Ten inch double-sided Fontana front brakes were used together with a nine inch rear disc. With 18 inch diameter wheels, a 3.25 tyre was used on the front and a 3.75 on

Walsall's Bob Heath circulating the Isle of Man in the 1970 750 Production Machine TT in which he finished 5th on the Rocket 3 at 94.09 mph. In 1971 he finished 3rd at 97.08 mph and in the 500-Mile Grand Prix d'Endurance at Thruxton that year he partnered John Barton into second place.

the rear. An hydraulic steering damper, a Screen & Plastic racing fairing and a five-gallon, wedge-shaped, flat-sided petrol tank all enhanced the functional beauty. With Doug Hele claiming 80 bhp at 8,000 rpm, there was good cause for optimism, soon borne out by practice times when the Daytona speed festival got under way.

Most of the Rockets and Tridents prepared were for selected American riders but, additionally, Percy Tait of the Meriden factory was down to ride a Trident and the great Mike Hailwood to ride a Rocket 3. 323

Things went well in practice and it was American Gene Romero on the Trident who put in the fastest qualifying lap at no less than 157.34mph, nearly five miles an hour quicker than Mike Hailwood at 152.90 mph on his BSA Rocket 3. Garry Nixon and Percy Tait, both on Tridents, did 152.83 mph and 150.57 mph respectively, and Jim Rice, on another Rocket 3, did 149.37 mph. Clearly though, the British three-cylinders were not going to have it all their own way: Dick Mann on a Honda 750 four-cylinder qualified at 152.67 mph.

When the race got under way, it was Mike Hailwood who took the early lead; only to retire on the 11th lap with a broken valve. From then on Dick Mann had it all his own way with the Honda to win at 102.69 mph. With Gene Romero and Don Castro second and third respectively on Tridents, the results were rewarding and encouraging.

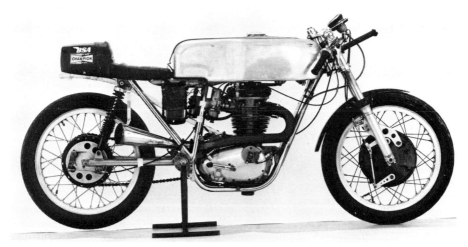

The works B50 road racer used very successfully by Bob Heath during 1971, including a win in the first round of the Shellsport 500 Championship at Mallory Park. It had a claimed output of 45 bhp at 8,000 rpm and a total weight of 240 lbs, giving an excellent power-to-weight ratio. The front brake was a double-sided, twin-leading shoe Fontana.

Two months later in the steamy heat of Alabama, the Rocket 3 registered its first outright win. Dave Aldana won the 200-Mile National AMA Championship at the Talladega International Speedway at 104.59 mph with Jim Rice and Dick Mann, both on Rocket Threes, third and fifth respectively.

On the home front in the 500-Mile Grand Prix d'Endurance at Thruxton in May, Brian Steenson and Pat Mahoney rode a Rocket 3 into third place at 73.20 mph. Then in June in the 750cc class of the Isle of Man Production TT, won by Malcolm Uphill on a Trident at 97.71 mph, Bob Heath rode a Rocket 3 into fifth place at 94.09 mph, and also

After his sensational defeat of World Champion Giacomo Agostini at both Mallory Park and Brands Hatch in the autumn of 1971 with a 750cc BSA Rocket 3, John Cooper went over to California to win the Champion Spark Plug Classic at the Ontario Motor Speedway.

finished fifth on the Rocket 3 in the Hutchinson '100' Production Machine class at Brands Hatch.

With Daytona still the main prize, work began on four new racers for 1971 — two Rocket 3s and two Tridents — and by February details were released, this time the machines being described as having 'the most powerful motorcycle racing engines ever built in Britain'. With power output increased to 82-84 bhp at 8,500 rpm, the statement was true enough.

To reduce frontal area the Rob North frame had been lowered by a full two inches; and the Fontana twin-leading shoe front brakes had been replaced by double Lockheed discs. With the Trident in blue livery and the BSA Rocket 3 in brilliant red, both had been prepared by Doug Hele at Meriden. Mike Hailwood was again down to ride a BSA and Paul Smart a Triumph, the other two, plus some 1970 models, to be ridden by American riders.

On the day of the race the pattern was very similar to that of 1970, when Mike Hailwood took an early lead which he maintained until a valve dropped in at quarter distance. Compatriot Paul Smart on a Trident took over the lead until looking all set for victory with but 12 laps to go, he retired with push rod trouble. This opened up the way for

325

Dick Mann, on another Rocket 3, went on to win at 104.73 mph. Gene Romero, on a Trident, was second, and third on another Rocket 3 was Don Emde, the 20-year-old son of Cliff Emde who had won at Daytona in 1948.

Harley-Davidson were still there and in contention, with Roger Reiman finishing fourth. Significantly, between the Harley-Davidson and two more Tridents in seventh and eighth places were two 350cc Yamahas, in fifth and sixth places. After the bitter set-backs of 1966, '67 and '68, the BSA Daytona victory of 1971 was sweet indeed.

From then on, for the remainder of the 1971 season, the Rocket 3s and Tridents swept all before them on British circuits in the relative classes with their stirring and pulse-tingling exhaust blasting a chorus of victory. Not that success was confined to British circuits for in September Percy Tait and Ray Rickrell rode a Rocket 3 to victory in the 24-Hour Bol d'Or run over the 2.8 mile Bugatti circuit at Le Mans, completing 616 laps at 70.48 mph.

Probably the most profound demonstration of Rocket 3/Trident potency came with the three-meeting Anglo-American Match Race series staged at Brands Hatch, Mallory Park and Oulton Park when the entire British and American teams were mounted on them. With the British team beating the Americans with a score of 183 to 137, Ray Pickrell won three of the legs on a Rocket 3, Paul Smart winning the other three on a Trident. The spectacle of ten 750cc Rocket 3s and Tridents in close combat was a new and exciting experience for British race fans; one not to be forgotten for many a year.

In May the 750 Threes won both the 200-Mile 750 Formula Race and 500-Mile Grand Prix d'Endurance at Thruxton sponsored by *The Motor Cycle* with Ray Pickrell winning the former with a BSA and Paul Smart second on a Triumph. Percy Tait and Dave Croxford shared the winning Trident in the 500-Mile event, with Bob Heath and John Barton bringing home a Rocket 3 into second place.

The pattern was similar in the Isle of Man in June, with Ray Pickrell winning the 750 class of the Production TT on a Trident at 100.07 mph, with Tony Jefferies (Trident) second and Bob Heath third on a Rocket 3 at 97.08 mph. Tony Jefferies then won the Formula 750 TT at 102.85 mph on a Trident from Ray Pickrell who was second on a Rocket 3 at 102.18 mph. At Silverstone in August — the first motorcycle race meeting at the Northamptonshire circuit for six years — Ray Pickrell on a Rocket 3 won the 750 Production Machine Race at 99.34 mph and Paul Smart won the Formula 750 event on a Trident at 103.4 mph with Percy Tait (Trident) second and Ray Pickrell (BSA Rocket 3) third.

A few weeks before, in the USA at Kent, Washington, Dick Mann

The tremendous scrap John Cooper had with Kel Carruthers (Yamaha) at Ontario in 1971 was repeated in 1972 where, in this shot, Carruthers could well be on the back of John Cooper's Rocket 3.

had won the tenth round of the AMA National Championship on a BSA Rocket 3 with Don Emde (BSA Rocket 3) second and Gene Romero (Trident) third.

In September and October with the racing season moving toward its close — and the affairs of the BSA parent company coming to a climax — the BSA Rocket 3 achieved its most dramatic victories. At the much-vaunted 'Race of the Year' meeting at Mallory Park, in front of an almost hysterical crowd, John 'Moon Eyes' Cooper on a red Rocket 3 beat ten-times world champion Giacomo Agostini⋆ on his double ohc three-cylinder grand prix MV with a speed of 91.5 mph, at a time when the sophisticated MV racers from Gallarate dominated the race tracks of Europe. Behind Agostini in third place was Ray Pickrell on another BSA Rocket.

It was a sensational victory for the Derby rider — one he repeated just two weeks later to prove it was no flook. At the Race of the South meeting at Brands Hatch he again pushed Agostini and the MV into second place, in the process beating Mike Hailwood's lap record at 91.03 mph. As had been the case at Mallory, Ray Pickrell on another Rocket 3 was third.

327

⋆ Giacomo Agostini went on to win a total of 15 world titles before retiring.

To underline his superiority and to convince all concerned that his victories on the BSA Rocket 3 over the Italian ace were well deserved, John Cooper went over to the United States where, with a Rocket 3, he won the last big race meeting in the American calendar on the Motor Speedway at Ontario, California. Claimed to be the richest race in the USA, it comprised two legs of 125 miles each.

Third in the first leg, John claimed victory on aggregate after a terrific scrap with Kel Carruthers and his swift 350 Yamaha in the second. He did so by a claimed four inches over the finishing line after losing the lead to the Aussie when he had led for most of the race.

It was fine win for the Derby ace, whose racing season was capped by winning the *Motor Cycle News* Superbike Championship for that year, a crown he retained in 1972.

Another fine action shot of John Cooper aboard the Rocket 3 at Mallory Park in Leicestershire in 1972. It was here the year before that he had thrilled the crowds with his duel with Agostini.

With the indomitable BSA sidecar aces monopolizing the British circuits, it was surely a grand finale for BSA — like an old battleship going down with guns still blazing defiance. The slogan of 'Lead the way on a BSA' was never more meaningful than at that stage when those sleek, BSA-powered outfits destroyed the opposition. At the 1970 Race of the Year meeting at Mallory Park, for example, only G. Boret (700

RGM) managed to get among the BSA armour with a fifth place behind Chris Vincent, Norman Hanks, Brian Rust and Pat Sheriden in that order, with W. Cooper sixth — all on BSA.

At the same meeting the following year the pattern was similar — Vincent first, Roy Hanks second, Mick Boddice third and it was again repeated at the March Mallory meeting, when Norman Hanks was first, brother Roy second, Peter Brown third and Mick Boddice fourth.

At the 'Race of the South' meeting at Brands Hatch in October 1971, where John Cooper humbled Agostini, Chris Vincent led home five BSA outfits with Roy Hanks second, Norman Hanks third, A. Sansum (750 Quaife BSA) fourth and A. Crick (650 Windrick BSA) fifth, Vincent putting in the fastest lap at 82.52 mph. In winning his sixth British Sidecar Championship in 1970, Chris Vincent headed Peter Brown (BSA) second, Norman Hanks (BSA) third, Pat Sheriden (BSA) fourth and Malcolm 'Mac' Hobson (BSA) sixth.

When Chris Vincent won his seventh British Championship on his BSA in 1971, he led home the old brigade of Peter Brown in second place, Norman Hanks third, Roy Hanks fourth and Mick Boddice fifth. A message of superiority could not be more forceful.

If BSA activity in the traditional field of motocross was floundering during the summer months of 1971, that on the race circuits of the British Isles was as successful as never before. And thus it remained until the end of that season. During the previous 61 years, BSA had committed to competition a greater variety of types and capacity sizes than any other manufacturer in the British Isles, if not throughout the world. In so doing they had probably won more trophies and titles than any other British maker; as such they could lay claim to having been the most successful of them all.

Failure and disappointment had not been unknown, but the overall and overwhelming success had been such that all those responsible had good cause to be proud of what had been achieved by their once proud British company.

BSA had surely reaped the lion's share and in so doing carved an honourable place in the history of motorcycles.

Epilogue

THE REASONS behind the collapse of Birmingham Small Arms, many and varied as they were, lie outside the scope of this book. Suffice it to say that by October 1971 the banks had withdrawn credit facilities, BSA share dealings on the Stock Exchange had been suspended and financial consultants Cooper Bros had advised the closure of the BSA plant at Armoury Road.

Nearly 4,000 of the total workforce of 5,400 were made redundant and from then on the programmed production of BSA motorcycles ceased. A quantity of machines, mostly A65 Thunderbolts and Lightnings, and B50 singles, were built and dispatched during 1972, but this was no more than completing work in hand. The parent board of directors was reconstructed and a so-called rescue operation embarked upon, the central plank of which was the objective of basing all future motorcycle production - both BSA and Triumph — at the Triumph Meriden plant. In the event, no BSA motorcycles were ever made at Meriden; nor did there ever exist any firm plans to do so.

By autumn 1971 the manufacture of BSA motorcycles against a forward planned programme of production came to an end. Anything after that was no more than a clearing-up operation — including the production of B50 engine units for Alan Clews and his CCM project. Likewise the plan to build a B50 speedway engine — an activity blessed by works director Alistair Cave and implemented by one-time Gold Star specialist Cyril Halliburn — failed to progress despite the successful performance of a B50-powered speedway bike at Coventry Speedway.

Many people had been employed at 'the BSA' for generations: whole families — mothers and fathers, sisters and brothers — who regarded BSA as their life, rewarding the company with great loyalty and virtually a strike-free record. They were proud of BSA and its products, no matter how humble their own contribution, and to associate themselves with the sporting successes of the company, news of which was conveyed to them every Monday morning over the factory Tannoy system. The great and extensive sporting achievements over the foregoing 60 years had been a prime factor in fermenting and nurturing this proud loyalty — not unlike that experienced by the Japanese manufacturers of today.

The merits — or otherwise — of that last range of updated BSA motorcycles marketed for 1971 have been speculated upon in the columns of the motorcycle press, from time-to-time during the intervening years. One such model to have received a full measure of adverse comment was the 500cc B50 four-stroke single cylinder model which the marketing people of BSA had the temerity to christen the Gold Star (as was likewise done with the B25 250cc model). To the purists such an act was an insult to an illustrious forebear.

Clearly however, those offended by that marketing ploy have not regarded the accomplishments of Mike Tomkinson of Mead & Tomkinson, Hereford, who campaigned and developed a B50 Gold Star in 24-Hour Coupe d'Endurance events to a remarkable extent, achieving a level of success comparable with anything accomplished by its B34 predecessor. An early success with a part-factory sponsored B50 was in the 500cc class of the 500-Mile Grand Prix d'Endurance at Thruxton in May 1971 when Clive Brown and Nigel Rollason (the latter employed in

The Mead & Tomkinson B50 Gold Star covered itself in glory in the 24-Hour Coupe d'Endurance events of the early 'seventies. Taken in the 1973 Barcelona 24-Hour Race, Roger Bowler (who was partnered by Nigel Rollason) cranks over the B50 at Montjuich Park on the way to winning the Production Machine Class in 4th place to become the highest placed British bike.

In June 1975 Phil Gurner broke the 500 Production TT lap record at 95.66 mph with the four-year-old Mead & Tomkinson B50 Gold Star. Here he is seen leading the Isle of Man event on the third lap, before falling at Ramsey Hairpin. It was a last noble act of defiance.

the BSA drawing office) sharing the saddle, finished 8th overall. They completed a total of 201 laps, a mere eleven laps down on the winning Trident of Percy Tait and Dave Crawford.

That same year they went on to win the 500cc class of the 24-Hour race in Barcelona, finishing second overall and actually splitting the two leading 750cc Laverdas. It was almost a repeat performance at the Bol d'Or at Le Mans in France during September where they led the 500cc class until the 23rd hour. Front brake trouble then slowed them down and dropped them to second place in the 500cc class and 8th overall.

At Barcelona again in 1973, in finishing fourth overall, with Nigel Rollason sharing the saddle with Roger Bowler, they won the Production Machine class and had the highest placed British bike (the two works John Player Norton Commandos had retired during the night). The machine enjoyed another 500cc class win at Barcelona in 1974, Nigel Rollason on this occasion sharing the saddle with Frenchman Bernard Berger.

Without doubt one of the most remarkable results obtained was seventh place overall in the 24-Hour Coupe d'Endurance at Spa, Belgium in 1973. Lapping consistently at over 100 mph, with Clive Brown sharing the saddle with Phil Gurner, the model averaged 50 miles per gallon. *This with a naked, unfaired motorcycle!*

Receiving a degree of help from the BSA competitions department, all the development work had been carried out by Mike Tomkinson himself in his private workshop, devising and making modifications which enhanced both performance and reliability.

332   Twenty-four hours endurance racing is the most demanding form

of motorcycle racing and one guaranteed to reveal any flaw or weakness. It is a case of the survival of the fittest, with only the fittest surviving. In this context the Mead & Tomkinson BSA B50 Gold Star achieved a record of success in such events that has no parallel, unequalled by any other British ohv four-stroke single. Its finest hour, short-lived though it was, came rather ironically in the Isle of Man in 1975 — just 54 years after that humiliating BSA débâcle in the 1921 Senior TT.

A Mead & Tomkinson B50, ridden by Clive Brown, had taken third place in the 500 Production TT of 1973 and again in 1974 with Phil Gurner in the saddle. But it was in that event of 1975 that Phil Gurner, again aboard the Mead & Tomkinson B50, created the sensation of the race, at a time when Japanese machines were dominating, by coming through in the lead at the end of the second lap. With *The Motor Cycle* report describing Phil Gurner as riding the incredibly quick Mead & Tomkinson BSA B50, the paper went on to describe events thus: 'There was sensation as Gurner roared past the Grandstand to start his third circuit ahead of the two Suzukis and Bill Smith's Honda. But the dream of a British 500 win was shortlived when Phil dropped the bike at Ramsey Hairpin.'

Although Phil Gurner continued in the race wasting a great deal of time at the pits, going on to finish 12th at 87.37 mph, he had, during the course of the race put in the fastest lap and broken the 500 Production TT lap record at 95.66 mph. Four days later he was tragically killed in the Senior TT.

Today, Mike Tomkinson points out with obvious pride and relish that Gurner's record lap speed was well in excess of anything ever achieved by the vaunted B34 Gold Star round the Mountain Course of the Isle of Man. 'The B50 engine was vastly underrated' Mike Tomkinson added with a challenging tone. But he did agree there was need to allow for the time lapse when comparing the performance of both models.

But there can be no denying that the performance of the four-year-old Mead & Tomkinson B50 Gold Star had been a remarkable and fitting climax to all that had gone before.

It was rather like the old stager taking his last, sad curtain call.

Appendix

1929
British Experts Solo, Bert Perrigo

1931
British Experts Solo, Bert Perrigo

1932
British Experts Sidecar, Harold Flook

1933
British Experts Sidecar, Harold Flook
British Experts Solo, Fred Povey

1934
British Experts Sidecar, Harold Flook
British Experts Solo, Fred Povey

1935
British Experts Sidecar, Harold Flook

1936
British Experts Sidecar, Harold Flook

1946
British Experts Sidecar, Harold Tozer

1947
British Experts Sidecar, Harold Tozer

1948
British Experts Sidecar, Harold Tozer

1950
British Experts Solo, Bill Nicholson
British Experts Sidecar, Harold Tozer
ACU Sidecar Trials Drivers' Star, Harold Tozer

1951
British Experts Solo, Tom Ellis
ACU Solo Trials Drivers' Star, Bill Nicholson
ACU Sidecar Trials Drivers' Star, Harold Tozer (tied with
A.J. Humphries)

1952
British Experts Sidecar, Harold Tozer
ACU Solo Trials Star, Bill Nicholson
ACU 500 Scramble Star, John Avery

1953
ACU Solo Trials Star, Jeff Smith

1954
British Experts Solo, Bill Nicholson
British Experts Sidecar, Frank Darrieulat
ACU Solo Trials Star, Jeff Smith

1955
European Motocross Championship, John Draper
ACU 500 Scramble Star, Jeff Smith
British Experts Solo, Jeff Smith

1956
British Experts Solo, Jeff Smith
British Experts Sidecar, Frank Darrieulat
ACU Sidecar Trials Drivers' Star Frank Darrieulat
ACU 500 Scramble Star, Jeff Smith

1957
British Experts Solo, Jeff Smith

1958
ACU Sidecar Trials Drivers' Star, Frank Darrieulat

1959
ACU 500 Scramble Star, Arthur Lampkin

1960
ACU 500 Scramble Star, Jeff Smith
British Experts Sidecar, Bill Slocombe

1961
ACU 500 Scramble Star, Jeff Smith
ACU 250 Scramble Star, Arthur Lampkin
British Road Racing Sidecar Championship, Chris Vincent

1962
ACU 500 Scramble Star, Jeff Smith

1963
ACU 500 Scramble Star, Jeff Smith
British Experts Solo, Jeff Smith
British Road Racing Sidecar Championship, Chris Vincent

1964
World 500 Motocross Championship, Jeff Smith
ACU 500 Scramble Star, Jeff Smith
British Road Racing Sidecar Championship, Chris Vincent

BSA: Competition history

1965
World 500 Motocross Championship, Jeff Smith
ACU 500 Scramble Star, Jeff Smith
British Experts Solo, Scott Ellis
British Road Racing Sidecar Championship, Chris Vincent

1967
British 500 Scramble Championship, Jeff Smith

1968
British 500 Scramble Championship, John Banks
British Road Racing Sidecar Championship, Peter Brown

1969
British 500 Scramble Championship, John Banks
British Road Racing Sidecar Championship, Chris Vincent

1970
British Road Racing Sidecar Championship, Chris Vincent

1971
British Road Racing Sidecar Championship, Chris Vincent
British Experts Sidecar, Ray Round
British Sidecar Trials Championship, Ray Round

1972
British Road Racing Sidecar Championship, Norman Hanks
British Experts Sidecar, Ray Round
British Sidecar Trials Championhip, Ray Round

SUMMARY
World titles 2 : European titles 1 :
British Titles 60 : Total 63

Index

A

Aberg, Bengt 312, 313, 315
Acheson, QMS Joe 60
ACU-Certified Tests
  1938/39: 33
  1939
  1952: 83, 234, 295
ACU Grasstrack
  Championships
  1958: 299
ACU Scramble Drivers' Star
  1951: 141
  1952: 141, 150, 152
  1953: 152, 161, 166,
  215/16
  1954: 141, 154, 166, 173,
  274
  1955: 141, 164, 170, 175,
  277, 283
  1956: 141, 164, 170, 175,
  277, 283
  1957 Not held
  1958: 141, 227, 240
  1959: 141, 227
  1960: 177, 240, 277
  1961: 178, 265, 277
  1962: 178, 267, 277
  1963: 267, 277
  1964: 267, 277, 290
  1965: 179, 267, 277, 290
ACU Six Days Trial
  1913: 14
  1919/20: 19
ACU Trials Drivers' Star
  (Sidecar)
  1950: 102, 110
  1951: 102, 111
  1956: 190
  1959: 193
  1960: 193
  1971/72: 195
ACU Trials Drivers' Star
  (Solo)
  1950: 86/87, 116
  1951: 81, 87, 88, 124, 142,
  180

  1952: 88, 142, 180
  1953/54: 180, 240, 274
  1955: 274
  1956: 240, 282
  1959: 126
Adcock, Eric 204
Agostini, Giacomo 327, 329
AJS Club Scramble, Victoria
  1953: 209
Alan Trophy Trial
  1946 73, 103
Alan Trophy Trial
  1949: 202
  1951: 182
  1953: 274
  1954: 193
Aldana, Dave 324
Allan Jefferies Trophy Trial
  1949: 202
  1953: 274
  1965: 207, 259
  1966: 193
  1967: 209
Allan, Vic 315, 317, 318
Allen, F 187
Alves, Jim 68, 73, 81, 83, 85,
  86, 87, 88, 89, 91, 99, 116,
  117, 118
AMA Championships
  Laconia 1963: 138/39
  Alabama 1970: 324
  Washington 1971: 326/27
American/UK Match Races
  1971: 326
Amott, Jack 20, 21, 29, 44,
  48, 64, 94, 96, 98, 106,
  131, 132, 151, 200
Andrews, Mick 304
Anning, Miriam (Mrs) 29
Applebee, 'Pa' 14
Archer, Les 64, 125, 145, 168
Ards MCC 79, 80
Argent, H 141
Armstrong, Roger 138
Army Motorcycle Association
  238
Arnold, Rose (Mrs) 303
Arnotte, E 187

Ashenden, B 210
Ashworth, Jack 29, 40, 46,
  106
Australian Scramble
  Championships
  1954: 210
  1958: 39, 211
  1960: 139
  1963: 139, 211
Australian TT
  1956: 140
  1957: 210
Austrian Alpine Trial
  1955: 184
  1966: 310
Avery, Harold 152
Avery, John 117, 141, 142,
  150-153, 157, 158, 200,
  214
Axhelm, Walter 137

B

Baeten, Rene 127, 284
Banks, John 229, 290, 311,
  312-315, 317, 318, 319
Bantam Racing Club 211
Barcelona 24-Hour Race
  1971/73/74: 332
Barker, T 204
Barrett, D.H. 207
Barton, John 326
BBC Grandstand Series
  1968: 229, 290, 311
Beamish, Graham 117, 157,
  158
Bean, David 303
Beaumont, Roger 322
Beenham Park TV Scramble
  1971: 317
Beggars Roost Trial
  1946: 103
  1950: 94
  1952: 202
  1953: 216
  1955-58: 191
  1960: 193

Index

Belgium Coup d'Endurance
 1973: 332
Belgium Motocross GP
 1953: 149
 1955: 125, 276
 1956: 168
 1958: 126
 1964: 287
 1966: 311
 1968: 229
 1969: 314
 1970: 315
Bell. Artie 48, 50, 73, 78, 79
Bell, W.A. 280
Bemrose Trophy Trial
 1946: 73, 103
 1948: 83
 1949: 116
 1950: 94
 1951: 182
 1953: 238, 274
 1956: 205/6
 1960: 191
 1961: 261
 1963: 240
 1965: 226
 1966: 261
Bennett, Clive 304
Bennett, Lt Col C.V. 58
Beranek, E 203
Berger, Bernard 332
Bessant, Eddie 48, 64, 145
Bickers, Dave 126, 264, 283
Bickerton, Dave 172
Birmingham Motor Cycle
 Club 53, 143
Bird, Bertie 20
Blackwell, Jack 44, 46, 48,
 50, 65, 91, 94
Boddice, Bill 299, 301
Boddice, Michael 301, 302,
 303, 307, 329
Bol d'Or 24-Hour Race
 1971: 326, 332
Booker, Jack 21
Boret, G 328
Bottomley, Jack 220
Bowler, Roger 332
Bowers, Michael 207, 208
Bowling, G 211
Boynton, John 50
Bradley, Peter 36
Brands Hatch meeting
 1971: 327, 329
Bray, Jim 172, 175
Brealey, Noel 94
Breese, Maurice 14
Breffitt, Ted 93
Brewster, P 25
Briggs, Harold 17
Briggs, Mollie (Mrs) 48
Brittain, John 118, 120, 121,

122, 240, 274
Brittain, Vic 21, 50, 212
British Experts Trial
 1929-31: 20, 35
 1933-34: 23
 1932-36: 22
 1938: 55
 1939: 60
 1929-39: 106
 1946: 48, 73, 74, 103, 104
 1947: 98
 1950: 87, 113, 116, 142
 1951: 142, 183, 273
 1952: 111
 1953: 122
 1954: 93, 190
 1955: 122, 274
 1954-57: 142, 249, 274,
 281
 1960: 193
 1963: 207, 226, 255, 274
 1965-66: 258, 259
 1969: 195
 1971-72: 195
British Motocross GP
 1952: 154, 161
 1953: 149, 161, 163
 1954: 154
 1955: 125, 276
 1956: 231, 241
 1957: 279
 1958: 241, 252
 1959: 279
 1963: 228
 1966: 311
 1971: 318
British Road Racing
 Championship (Sidecar)
 1959/61/62/63/64/65/66/
 67/70/71: 299
 1968: 303
 1970-71: 329
British 250 Scramble
 Championship
 1970: 316
British 500 Scramble
 Championship
 1967: 277, 290, 311
 1968: 313/14
 1969: 315
 1970: 316
 1971: 318
 1973: 319
Brooklands race track
 13, 14, 25
Brown, Clive 331, 332, 33
Brown, Kenny 138
Brown, Peter 301, 303, 307,
 329
Bryen, Ken 141
BSA MODELS:
 1911 3¹/₂hp sv 9, 12

250cc 'Round Tank' sv 10
1924 ohv 350, 10
770cc sv vee-twin 10
986 sv vee-twin 10
1926 493cc 'Sloper' 10
1932 350cc/500cc Blue
Star 10, 25, 37
1937 500cc Empire Star
10, 25
1938 250cc Empire Star
21
1938 M23 500cc Silver
Star 10
1938 B25 350cc 55, 235
1938 M24 500cc Gold
Star 10, 26
1939, 250cc B21 64, 150,
200
1939/40 500 sv M20 42,
56, 57, 128
1940 B29 350cc Silver
Sports 128
1940/41 B30 350cc (WD)
78, 128
1945 350cc B31 131
1946 350cc B32 44, 50
1947 500cc B34 62
1948 500cc A7 twin
(trials) 81
1949 123cc D1 Bantam
89, 198
1949 350/500 Gold Star
129, 131
1949 500cc B34 68
1949 650cc A10 twin 62
1950/54 500cc A7 Star
Twin 136, 181, 234
1952/53 250cc MC1 175
1955/56 140cc D3 Bantam
122, 203, 204, 292
1956 250cc Gold Star 175
1956 174cc D7 Bantam 207
1958 250cc C15 249
1959 250cc C15T/C15S
207, 226, 240, 252
1961 343cc B40 193, 253,
260, 261
1963 420cc Victor 266
1964 A50/A65 Twins 300
1965 441cc Victor GP
261, 268, 290
1965 A65 Lightning 304
1965 A65 Rocket 300
1966 A65 Spitfire 304
1966 BSA-Triumph
hybrid 264
1966 494cc Victor GP 308
1967 175cc D10 Bantam
207
1968 499cc Victor GP 311
1969/70/71 750cc Rocket
3 304, 320

338

1971 B25/B50 Gold Stars
331
Buck, George 187
Burton, John 142, 172, 177,
178, 227, 266, 267, 280,
284, 285
Burton 'Squib' 177
Burton-on-Trent MCC 215
Butler, Frank 13

C

Cadwell Park TV Scramble
1971: 318
Caldecut, L.B. 209
Californian Grand Prix
1968: 318
Cambrian Trial
1947: 110
1949: 86, 116
Camathias, Florian 298, 303
Cameron, Don 210
Canadian Production
Machine Race 1968, 322
Carey, R 13, 14
Carruthers, Kel 328
Castro, Don 324
Catalina Grand Prix
1951/1956: 137
Cave, Alistair 330
Chambers, Jackie 14
Chapman, D.G. 141
Checklin, Bernard 193
Cheshire Centre
Championship 1947: 98
Cheshire, Fred 151
Cheshire Grand National
1955: 174
Cheshire, Terry 164, 172,
173-175, 217, 222
Chidgey, Bob 94
Child, Alf 99
Clayton, Dick 149
Clayton Trophy Trial
1946: 73, 103
1947: 98
1951: 182
1956: 215
1962: 259
1963: 207
Clegg, Cliff 53, 203
Clews, Alan 330
Cleveland Sporting Trial
1951: 214
Clubman's TT
1951: 123, 191
1952: 220
1954: 132, 296
1955: 132, 140
1956: 132

1947-56: 143
1949-56: 132
1955: 132, 140
Codd, Bernard 132, 141
Collett, Kim 104
Collier, Harry 13
Colmore Cup Trial
1926: 19
1928: 20
1937: 40
1939: 29, 106
1946: 46, 48, 50, 53, 61,
76, 102
1947: 76, 81, 95, 102, 109
1948: 82
1949: 200
1950: 110
1952: 125, 234
1954: 125
1955: 125
1961: 127, 259, 261
1962: 261
1969: 195
1964/65/67: 258
Cooper, C 203
Cooper, John 304, 320, 327,
328, 329
Cooper, W 329
Cotswold Cups Trial
1938: 22, 96
1939: 29, 56
1946: 53, 73, 103
1948: 83
1950: 116, 163
1952: 202
1953: 125, 238, 274
1959: 252
1961/62: 261
1964: 127
1967: 207
Cotswold Scramble
1946: 64, 73, 74, 203, 204
1947: 65, 76, 204
1948: 65, 85, 115, 147,
204
1949: 86, 99, 147, 204
1950: 89, 149, 150, 203
1951: 122/23
1952: 152
1953: 125, 151, 217
1954: 151, 153, 154, 163,
276
1957: 175
1960: 177
1962: 127
1963: 229
1946-1960: 141
Cottle, Marjorie 22, 29
Couper, M 25
Coventry & Warwickshire
MC 150
Cox, Marcel 86, 117

Cranmore, Phil 19, 20
Crawford, Arthur 52, 99
Crick, A 329
Crisp, Len 298
Crooks, Eddie 140, 218
Croxford, Dave 326, 332
Crozier, P 210
Cumberland Grand National
1954: 173
1958-59: 142
1958-60: 227
Currie, Bert 253
Currie, Bob 285
Curtis, Dave
126,141,155,161,164,172,
173,174,175,177,178,280
Czechoslovakian
Motocross GP
1969: 314
1970: 315

D

Dalby, Sgt. J.T. 29, 54
Dance, George 212
Daniell, Harold 27, 48
Danish Motocross GP
1964: 287
1966: 310
Darrieulat, Frank 189-191,
193, 195
Dartmoor Scramble
1953: 158
Davey, Peter 296
Davies, Tom 105/6
Davis, Tony 207, 258, 260,
261
Davison, Geoff 212
Daytona Beach Race
1948: 326
1949: 100, 136
1950: 100
1952: 292
1953: 136
1954: 100, 136, 292, 293
1956: 100, 137, 293
1957: 138
1966-1969: 306/307
1970-71: 307, 322, 325
Debenham, Nancy & Betty
20
De Coster, Roger 312
Derby Pathfinders MCC 296
Duebel, Max 296
Dick Farquharson Trial
1965, 258
D.K. Mansell Sidecar Trial
1947-51: 50
1952: 190
1947-51: 111
Dobty, P 313

Index

Docker, Sir Bernard 230
Dodington Park Scramble
 1971: 317
Dow, Captain Eddy 132, 133,
 140, 187, 218
Doyle, A.C. 'Paddy' 29, 54,
 56, 57, 58, 60, 61
Draper, Harold 114
Draper, John 83,86,89,
 91,99,113-127,142,145,
 149,158,164,180,183,187,
 199,204,205,214,217,220,
 222,233,234,253,255,276
Duke, Geoff 96-99, 180
Dussek, E.A. 25
Dutch Motocross GP.
 1954: 276
 1955: 125
 1958: 126
 1966: 311
 1968: 312/13
 1970: 315

E

Eacott, E.P. 141
Earles, Ernie 295
East German Motocross GP
 1964: 267, 287
 1969: 315
Eastwood, Vic 229, 280, 290,
 309, 310, 311
Edge, Colin 109
Edwards, Harry 19
Ellis, Scott 258, 261, 263, 308
Ellis, Tom 89,142,149,158,
 180,181-189,217,218,253,273
Emde, Don & Cliff 326, 327
Emmett, K 210
England, Bert 147
European Motocross
 Championship
 1952: 150
 1954: 274
 1955: 125
European 250 Motocross
 Championship
 1959: 284
 1960/61/62:
 264,265,283,284
 1960-61: 126
Evans, Don 117, 170
Evans, Roy, 26
Everett, George 137
Experts Grand National
 Scramble
 1949: 170
 1950: 89,149,150,163
 1951: 123, 151
 1952: 89, 151, 152
 1953: 125, 154

1954: 151,163,276,278
1955: 164, 204, 278
1956: 141, 164, 204, 278
1957: 153, 175, 204
1960: 178
1954-64: 278
1949-1960: 141
1961-1962: 178
1964: 179

F

Fenn, Archie 14
Fernihough, Eric 147
FIM
Finnish Motocross GP
 1966: 311
Fisher, George 122, 202
Fithian, Ted 50, 234
Flaxman, John 303
Flinterman, J 70, 188
Flook, Harold 22,27,102,
 103,104,106,109,110
Foster, Bob 48, 53, 114, 212
French Grand Prix
 1913: 14
French Motocross GP
 1950: 149
 1952: 152
 1954: 276
 1956: 168
 1958: 126
 1964: 287
 1968: 312
 1969: 314
Friedrichs, Paul 290,310,
 311,313,315
Frith, Freddie 27
Frost, S 187

G

Gaymer, Bert 147
Geboers, Sylvain 310, 314,
 317
Gibon, John 100
Gibson, John 137
Giles, John 178, 249
Gill, Edmund 48, 50
Gillam, Cpl. R 29, 54
Gloucestershire Grand
 National
 1953: 217
 1961: 228
Godfrey, Tony 141
Gold Star Owners Club 144
Golland, A 128, 129, 135
Greensmith Memorial Trial
 1951: 151
 1961: 259

Gunter, Albert 292
Gunther, A1 138
Gurner, Phil 332, 333

H

Hadley, Fred 209
Hailwood, Mike 304, 320,
 323, 324, 325
Hall, Basil 86,94,99,116,
 117,145-150,157,
 159,161,162,170,177
Hall, Jim 25
Halliburn, Cyril 132, 151,
 330
Hallman, Torsten 264
Handley, Walter 25
Hanks, Fred, Norman, Roy
 302, 303, 304, 307, 329
Hardwicke, Dennis 158, 159,
 168, 204, 222, 230, 231
Hargreaves, Bernard 220
Harris, B 204
Harris, John 212, 229, 266,
 280
Harris, May (Mrs) 50
Harris, 'Pip' 299
Haywood, Bill 103
Heath, Bob 303, 320, 324,
 326
Heath, Joe 46
Heath, Len 21, 55
Hele, Doug 322, 323, 325
Hempstead, Ray 307
Herriott, Maurice 285
Hewitt, Phil 48,50,52,74,
 76,89,94,99
Hickman, Keith 172,179,229,
 290,315,316,318
Hill, Bobby 292
Hill, Terry 48,74,78,115,
 180,181,186,217
Hill, W.J. 141
Hobson, Malcolm 'Mac' 302,
 303, 329
Holden, Cliff 48
Holden, Ken 13, 14
Holdsworth, George 21
Holmes, Alan 135
Hopwood, Bert 322
Horn, C 202
Horsefield, Chris 280
Houghton, John 204
Houseley, Eric 296
Host Trial, Sweden
 1957: 240
Howard, Bill 48
Howe, G.P. 14
Hughes, D.J. 203
Hughes, Mrs P 203
Humphries, Arthur 102, 110,

Humphries, Jack 20
Huse, G 140
Hoad Trophy Trial
   1953: 238, 274
   1959: 193
   1960: 155
   1961: 193
   1962: 261
   1963: 260
Hurst Cup Trial
   1947: 64
   1948: 66, 83
   1949: 86, 116
   1950: 116, 118
   1951: 87
   1955: 125
   1963: 259
Hutchinson 100 Road Race
   1965: 303, 304
   1966-1969: 304
   1970: 325

I

Ilkley Grand National
   1946: 96
Inter-Centre Team Scramble
   1958: 281
International Six Days Trial
   1932: 33, 36
   1937: 40, 46, 106
   1938: 29, 54, 106
   1939: 54, 58, 67, 106
   1948: 67, 92, 184
   1949: 68,92,99,111,
   133/34,149,157,184,203
   1950: 68,93,111,149,181,
   203,217
   1951: 123,133,149,185,
   203,217,234,269
   1952: 71,81,188,217,241
   1953: 188, 218, 241
   1954: 188,203,218,241,
   274
   1955: 188, 242
   1956: 175, 242, 283
   1957-58: 242
   1961-62: 229, 260
   1963: 229, 260, 261
   1964: 260, 261
   1965: 261-63
   1966: 229, 264
Irish End-to-End Trial
   1914: 14
Irish Experts Trial
   1955-57: 240
   1958: 252
Isle of Man Grand National
   1947: 80
   1952: 175
   1955: 174

Isle of Man TT Races
   1910/13/14: 13, 14
   1921: 16, 17
   1926: 20, 95
   1928: 20
   1951-52: 209, 295
   1953-54: 296
   1962: 296
   1966/67/68/69/70: 303,
   304, 324
   1971: 326
   1973/74/75: 333
Italian Motocross GP
   1950: 86, 89
   1953: 155
   1958: 126
   1964: 287
   1966: 310
   1971: 318

J

Jackson, Gordon 88, 122,
   240, 274
Jackson, R 202
James, Ken 141
Jansen, Nick 86
Jarman, Niel 172
Jarman, Paul 164, 172, 175
Jefferies, Allan 21, 40, 74
Jefferies, Tony 326
Johansson, Gunnar 311
John Douglas Trial
   1946: 73, 103
   1947: 98
   1948: 83
   1950: 87, 116
   1954: 125
   1958: 249
   1962: 261
   1964: 193
Jones, C 14
Jones, G 202
Jones, Stan 211

K

Kelly, A.C. 193
Kemp, H.R. 118
Kershaw, Bert 212
Kickham Trophy Trial
   1946: 46, 102
   1948: 66, 82, 99, 115
   1951: 87
   1952: 99, 202, 214
   1954: 214
   1966: 207
Kidstone Scramble
   1953: 217

1954: 175
1955: 173/74
1962: 229
King, Alistair 132, 296
Kirby, Tom 302, 304
Klamfoth, Dick 136, 137, 292
Knijnenburg, P 70, 188
Knutt Trophy Trial
   1958: 292
   1969: 195
Kolle, Otto 296

L

Lamborelle Trial
   1953: 93
   1956: 240
   1965: 258
   1968: 195
Lampkin, Alan 212,226,
   229,258,261,264
Lampkin, Arthur 118,121,
   122,126,141,176,177,178,
   212,222-229,253,258,261,
   264,265,266,267,285,311
Lampkin, Martin 229, 261
Lancashire Grand National
   1946: 53, 73
   1947: 65, 76, 98, 146
   1948: 83, 116, 147
   1950: 116, 150, 163
   1951: 163, 214
   1952: 152, 214
   1953: 214
   1954: 276
   1955: 142, 276
   1956: 168, 241
   1957: 171, 227, 241
   1958: 176, 241
   1950: 116, 150, 163
   1959: 175
   1961: 178, 229
   1956-62: 142
Langston, Dave 255, 258
Langston, Ron 102, 141
Lawrence, R 141
Leamington Victory MCC
   252
Lee, A 211
Lee, Andy 126, 172, 175
Leek, James 31, 41, 42
Leloup, Victor 150
Leonard, Joe 138
Lewis, John 261
Lewis, R.M. 14
Lincolnshire Grand National
   1954: 177
   1961: 127
Lines, Harold 117, 145, 149
Lister Trial
   1937: 40

Index

Lloyd, Iver 141
Lloyd, John 20
Lomas, Bill 204
Lord, Cyril & Muriel 20
Lundell, Ove 290
Lundin, Sten
  125,127,178,267,
  284,285,286,287,290
Luxemburg Motocross GP
  1955: 125, 155
  1958: 127
  1964: 287
  1968: 313
  1969: 314
  1970: 315
Lyons, Bill 307
Lyons, Ernie 78, 79, 80

M

Mahoney, Pat 324
Mallory Park Meeting
  1964: 300
  1967: 302
  1970: 328
  1971: 327, 329
Mann, Dick 139, 324, 326
Mansell, Dennis 103, 104,
  106, 110
Manufacturers Union (MCA)
  20
Manville Trial
  1948: 150
  1950: 89
  1953: 274
  1955: 205
Marsh, Bill 104
Martin, Bill 204
Martin, Brian 48,71,89,126,
  142,172,174,205,207,208,
  212,222,230-248,249,264,
  265,266,269,281,282,290,
  308,317,318
Martin, Michael 207
Mathews, Bill 136
Manx Grand Prix
  1946: 50
  1947: 128, 129
  1955: 135
Manx Three-Day Trial
  1965: 226
Maudes Trophy
  1938-39: 33
  1952: 72, 236, 295
Mayes, Freddie 266
Maylott, F.A. 14
Mead, J 27
Mein, Charlie 98
Merret, Arthur 50
Meunier, M 86
Middlesbrough & Stockton

MCC 80
Midland Centre Group Trial
  (6th)
  1958: 252
Miles, Ron 210/11
Millburn, W.H. 99
Miller, Sammy 122, 206, 207,
  208, 261, 276
Minert, Charles 137
Mingels, Auguste 86, 117,
  150
MIRA 131, 304, 306, 307
Miryless, Tom 89
MCC Three-Day Trial
  1913: 14
MCN Superbike
  Championship
  1971-72: 328
Mitcham Vase Trial
  1955: 205
  1958: 191, 252
  1959: 255
  1963: 193
Mitchell Memorial Trial
  1945: 44
  1946: 53, 73, 103
  1948: 83, 115
  1949: 150
  1951: 123, 182, 214
  1952: 184
  1962: 261
  1967: 209
Morewood, Colin 208
Motocross des Nations
  1947: 65, 86, 116
  1950: 116, 149, 150, 157
  1951/52: 150
  1952: 152, 162
  1954: 168
  1955: 276, 277
  1956/57: 170, 277, 278,
  282
  1962: 265
  1965: 179
Mountford, Peter 193
Murphy, K 140
Murphy, Tony 322
McCandless, Cromie & Rex
  78, 79, 80
McCredie, Jock 27
McDermott, Tommy 99, 136,
  137
McGregor, Bob 22
McLean, George 17, 31, 34

N

Nash, Harry 191, 192
Newcastle Grand National
  1954-55: 173, 174
Nex, Phil 142, 153-157, 158,

168, 173
Nicholas, Jody 138
Nicholson, Bill 48,50,54,
  64,65,73-93,94,98,99,
  100,109,110,113,114,115,
  116,117,124,129,142,145,
  146,147,149,157,180,183,
  199,204,212,222,236,238,
  273
Nicholson, Nick 136, 137
Nicoll, Dave 314, 315, 316,
  317, 318
Nilsson, Bill 125, 127, 168,
  284, 287, 290
Nixon, Garry 324
North v South Scramble
  1949: 100
  1966: 179
Northern Experts Trial
  1946: 53, 74
  1950: 213
  1951: 214
  1955: 204
  1962: 276
  1963: 226

O

Ogden, Ted 76
Oliver, Eric 303
Oliver, J.S. 193
Oliver's Mount,
  Scarborough 61
Ontario Motor Speedway
  (USA)
  1971: 328

P

Page, Val 25
Parker, Jack 20
Parsons, W.G. 'Nipper' 94
Partridge, A.C. 74, 104
Patland Cup Trial
  1942: 78
  1946: 73
  1955: 184
Peacock, Bill 111
Pendine Sands
  1949: 64
Peplow, Roy 249
Perce Simon Trial
  1947: 110
  1950: 87
  1951: 88
  1957: 249
  1955/56/57: 276
  1958: 276
  1959: 255, 276
  1960: 276

1961/62/63: 260, 276
1966: 258
Perks, Fred. C 29, 48, 104
Perrey, Harry 17, 18, 19, 33
Perrigo. A.E. 'Bert' 19,20,
21,28,29,31-43,44,45,
46,48,50,54,60,80,83,96,
97,98,105,111,113,147,
158,180,181,199,203,213,
230,234,236,274
Persson, Olaf 287, 290
Pickering, George 200, 202,
203
Pickrell, Ray 326, 327
Pike, Roland 175, 295
Plowright, Jack 204
Porter, R 202
Pound, Trevor 140
Povey, Brian 252, 260
Povey, Fred 20,21,23,27,
48,50,87,94,113
Powell, Derek 141
Price, Alderman Frank (later
Sir) 290
Pulman Arthur 193

Q

Quincey, Maurice 209

R

Ratcliffe, Artie 87, 118, 249
Ratcliffe, Derek 118
Ray, Bob 65,68,73,74,
80,89,90,118
Rayborn, Cal 307
Read, Phil 304
Red Marley Hill Climb
1961: 266
Red Rose Trial
1946: 103
1949: 200
1951: 88
1953: 274
1963: 207
Reiman, Roger 326
Reliance Trial
1946: 53, 103
1949: 202, 212
1952: 193
1953: 274
REME 8th Batt 238
REME 5th Trn Batt 281
Renfrew, Gordon 140
Rice, Jim 324
Richards, K 211
Rich Child Corporation 99
Rickman, Derek 164, 170-172
Rickman, Don 126,164,

170-172,177,178,266,311
Righten, J.F. 141
Riley, Mike 22, 46
Rist, Fred 29,48,53-72,74,
76,86,91,94,99,116,145,
149,150,180,187,199,200,
212,222,234,276,292
Robert, Joel 317
Roberton, Andy 315, 317,
318
Roest, J 70, 188
Rogers, Charlie 21,68
Rogers, Sir Hallewell 12
Rollason, Nigel 331,332
Romero, Gene 323, 324, 326,
327
Rose, Bill 104
Rose, Peter 131
Rosenburg, M 241, 242
Round, Ray & Derek 195
Rowland, Dave 207, 208,
209, 258
Rowley, George
21,36,37,50,212,234,235
Royal Signals & M/C Display
Team 96, 97
Royal Tank Corps 29, 53, 54,
56, 58
Roydhouse, Peter 193
Rumble, Derek 303
Rumble, Ken 140, 209, 210
Rusk Memorial Trial
1946: 80
Russian Motocross GP
1964: 287
1966: 311
1969: 314
Rust, Brian 329
Rutherford, F.A. 141
Ryall, Peter 155, 156

S

St Cucufa Trial
1957: 240
St Davids Trial
1950: 87
1951: 182
1954: 93
1956: 184
1959: 191. 252
1961: 261
1967: 207
St John, J.J. 22, 46
Salt, Charlie 295
Sam Seston Sidecar Trial
1968, 195
Sandford, Cecil 295
Sandiford, Jim 258, 259, 261
Sansum, A 329
Savage, George 17, 33, 181

Scaillett, Hubert 290
Scott, Jerry 172, 179
Scottish Six Days Trial
1913: 14
1919-22: 18
1930: 19
1932: 22
1934: 22, 105
1935/36: 22
1937: 22, 40, 106
1938/39: 29
1947: 89, 109, 183
1948: 89,110,115,180,183
1949:66,90,113,116,150
1950: 118, 180
1951: 118, 142
1952: 118, 184
1953: 122, 215, 238
1954: 91, 99, 122
1955: 122, 143, 274
1956: 122, 224
1957: 118
1958: 193
1959: 122, 252/53
1960: 122, 126, 192
1961: 259
1963: 226, 258
1964: 261
1965: 226, 261
1966: 226, 258
1967: 207, 261
Scottish Speed
Championships 63
Scott Trial
1938: 55
1946: 65,74,80,96,180
1947: 65, 98, 180
1948: 83, 115
1949: 86
1949-52: 83
1947-60: 143
1950: 87, 116
1951-52: 88
1954-59: 276
1956: 93
1958-60: 276
1959: 257
1960: 215
1961: 226, 261, 276
1962: 276
1963-65: 226
1959-66: 258
Scovell, Ray 58,64,65,74,154
Schauzu, S 303
Scheidegger, F 303
Schlaman, Jack 138, 293
Sealey, Len 19
Sedgley, Ken 207
Seston, Sam 191, 192
Sheriden, Pat 329
Shropshire Traders Cup
Trial

Index

1951: 273
1955: 93
Shrubland Park Scramble
  1949: 86,99,147,150
  1950/51: 89,149,150,
  204,214
  1954: 125, 151
  1955: 164, 277
  1956: 164, 168
  1958: 172, 191
  1961: 266
  1954-1964: 279
  1962: 178
Shutt, Arthur 141, 204
Silverstone Meeting
  1971: 326
Slade, Miss Ruby 48
Slinn, Pat 261, 263, 264
Slinn, Reg 48
Slocombe, Bill 191, 193
Smart, Paul 325, 326
Small, Ernie 193
Smith, Gilbert 98
Smith, Irene (Mrs) 290
Smith, Jeff 91,118,119,
  120,122,125,126,142,
  155,158,164,168,172,
  173,175,177,178,184,
  191,207,212,218,222,
  225,226,227,229,240,
  247,249,253,255,257,
  258,261,264,265,266,
  267,268,269-291,308,
  309,313,315,316,318
Smith, Tony 304, 307, 320
Solihull Half-Crown Trial
  1966: 207
Southern Centre Scramble
  Championships
  1953/54: 155
Southern Experts Scramble
  1948: 116
Southern Experts Trial
  1946: 73, 103
  1951: 88, 111
  1953: 125, 217
  1958: 240, 252
  1959: 256/57
  1960: 261
Southern Scott Scramble
  1963: 179
Southern Trial
  1935: 105
  1946: 95, 103
  1948: 83
  1950: 87
  1951: 151, 214
  1952: 111
  1956: 240
  1961: 193
  1963: 193
  1968: 195

Spanish Motocross GP
  1964: 287-290
Spokes, Reg 29, 46
Statham, George 131
Steenson, Brian 324
Stocker, Jack 64, 68, 157, 190
Stonebridge, Brian 117,123,
  142,154,157,159,161-165,
  168,173,175,204
Stronge, T.J.B. 181
Stroud MC 203
Stroud Team Trial
  1945: 44
Sturgeon, Harry 290, 305
SUNBAC 46, 50
Sunbeam Point-to-Point
  1947: 64, 76
  1948: 85, 147
  1949: 86, 116, 147
  1950: 116, 157, 162
  1952: 152
  1953: 163, 127
  1954: 149
  1955: 163, 175
  1956: 168, 279
  1957: 175, 279
  1958: 125, 172
  1959: 126
  1955-59: 164
  1947-60: 141
Swedish Motocross GP
  1947: 65
  1951: 149
  1952: 152
  1953: 155
  1955: 125
  1964: 287
  1966: 310
  1971: 318
Swiss Motocross GP
  1953: 149
  1954: 155
  1958: 126
  1964: 286
  1966: 309
  1968: 313
  1969: 314
  1970: 315

T

Taft, Paul 172, 175-176, 204
Taft, Peter 126, 164, 172,
  175-176
Tait, Percy
  141,304,323,324,326,332
Tanner, Geoff 135
Taylor, Harold 102, 104, 110,
  117
Taylor, Len 104
Teuwissen, J 314

Thiesen, Eugene 137, 292
Thruxton 9-hour Race
  1955: 140
  1956: 141
Thruxton 500-Mile Race
  1970: 324
  1971: 326, 331
Thruxton 200-Mile 750
  Formula
  1971: 326
Tibblin, Rolf
  267,284,286,287,289,290,
  310,311
Tiffen Jun, Bill 21, 91
Todd, George 209
Tomkinson, Mike
  331,332,333
Tozer, Harold 28,29,40,
  48,94,102-112,118,180,
  189,195
Travers Trophy Trial
  1939: 56
  1946: 53, 103
  1948: 83
  1949: 202
  1951: 204
  1953: 274
  1963: 261
  1965: 259
Turner, Edward 298, 305,
  306
Turner, G.H. 141
Turvey, Fred 19
Tye, David 89,158,164,
  168,173,175,187,212-222

U

Ulster Grand Prix
  1938: 26
Ulster MCC 79
Uphill, Malcolm 324
Utsey, Howard 306
Uzzell, Howard 20, 34

V

Veer, H 93
Venables, Ralph 145, 155
Vic Brittain Trial
  1954: 240
  1956: 205
  1958: 191, 240, 249
  1960: 240
  1961: 260
  1969: 195
Victorian Scramble
  Championships
  1953: 210
Victorian TT

1953: 209
Victoria Two-Day Race
 Meeting
 1954: 210
Victory Cup Trial
 1926: 34
 1937: 40, 105
 1939: 29
 1946: 53, 95, 103
 1948: 66, 83
 1949: 86
 1951: 87, 214
 1952: 202, 234
 1953: 125
 1954-55: 274, 276
 1956: 240
 1946-56: 143, 249
 1958: 276
 1959-60: 207, 252, 276
 1960: 126, 191
 1962: 258
 1963: 261
 1965: 193, 258
 1967: 207, 258, 261
Vincent, Chris 298,300,301,
 302,307,308,329
Viney, Hugh 68,82,83,85,
 87,89,90,91,122,273
Viney, R.T. 46
Vinicombe, Terry 302, 303

W

Wagger, R.W. 187, 203
Wakefield, Tony 302
Walker, Bill 48
Walker, Graham 37
Wallach, Miss Theresa 48
Walsh, Eric 209
Ward, Geoff 89,117,123,
 141,145,154,157,159,161,
 163,164,165-170,173,175
Warner, Dave 189

Watson, B 210
Watson, E
Waycott, Stuart 106
Welsh Speed Championships
 1948: 62
Welsh Trophy Trial
 1957: 207
 1964: 207
 1965: 193
Welsh Two-Day Trial
 1971: 318
West Bromwich MCC 271
West, Charlie 140
West, Jock 26
West of England Trial
 1946: 73, 95, 103
 1948: 83, 115
 1950: 87
 1951: 151
 1952: 111, 238
 1962: 261
 1965: 193
 1966: 229
 1967: 258
West German Motocross GP
 1964: 287
 1969: 314
West London Trophy Trial
 1938: 56
Wheeler, Tom 175
Wheat, C.H. 137
Whittle, Fred 29, 110
Whitworth, Dave 27
Wilkes, Jack 102, 106, 111
Wilkes, Reg 200
Wilkins, Frank 110,111,190
Williams, Harvey 209
Williams, Jack
 21,40,53,74,114,123,212
Winters, Robert 137
Wise, Roger 204
Wolfindale, Don 209
Wood, H.O. 13
Wood, Jackie (IOM) 135

Wood, Jackie 54,56,57,58,60
Wood, J.L. 29
Woodhouse, Jack 14
Woods, Stanley 27, 48, 50
Woods, W.J. 14
Wollett, Mick 307
Worcestershire Grand
 National
 1952: 238
World 500 Motocross
 Championship
 1957: 283/84
 1958: 126, 284
 1959: 284
 1960: 254
 1961: 178, 267, 284
 1962: 267, 284
 1963: 228, 267, 284, 285
 1964: 229, 267
 1965: 179, 268, 290
 1966: 309
 1967: 290, 311
 1968: 312
 1969: 314
 1970-71: 315, 317
Worth, Eddie 307
Wright, Alec 193
Wye Valley Traders Cup
 Trial
 1937: 40
 1949: 200
 1950: 116
 1952: 202
 1957: 240, 249
 1963: 261

Y

Yorkshire Grand National
 1955: 174
Young, Dan 14
Young, Rex 74,87,88,98,
 116,180,274